Organization Development for Facility Managers

Organization Development for Facility Managers

Leading Your Team to Success

Stormy Friday

AMACOM

American Management Association

New York • Atlanta • Brussels • Buenos Aires • Chicago • London • Mexico City
San Francisco • Shanghai • Tokyo • Toronto • Washington, D.C.

This publication is designed to provide accurate and authoritative information in regard to the subject matter covered. It is sold with the understanding that the publisher is not engaged in rendering legal, accounting, or other professional service. If legal advice or other expert assistance is required, the services of a competent professional person should be sought.

Library of Congress Cataloging-in-Publication Data

Friday, Stormy
    Organization development for facility managers : leading your team to success / Stormy Friday.
        p.   cm.
    ISBN 0-8144-0630-0
    1. Organizational change.   2. Facility management.   I. Title.

HD58.8 .F764 2003
658. 4'02—dc21   2002153915

Printing number

10 9 8 7 6 5 4 3 2 1

To my family:

Margaret and Durant Friday
Kit Bradley
Nicole and Kerry Bradley
Alex and Chris Bradley

CONTENTS

PREFACE

What Do OD and DNA Have to Do with FM?

If you picked up this book thinking it is a work on substance abuse and overdosing in the workplace, you need to read it even more than I thought you might. This book has nothing to do with drugs and facility management! Fascination with two seemingly unrelated subjects—the design and function of organizations and the study of the basic building blocks of human life, or the genetic makeup of individuals—is my inspiration for the book's title and content. The word *seemingly* is used on purpose because the two topics have a lot more in common than I originally suspected. To better understand the synergy between the two subjects, though, you need more detail and background.

When clients ask me what it takes to develop a top-performing facility management (FM) department, my answer is always the same. There are two things these departments all have. First, all high-performance FM departments have characteristics that serve as building blocks for the organization's growth and development. Second, successful FM departments have staffs who know how to review the characteristics and dynamics of organizations on a regular basis, then apply the right strategies for strengthening and improving them. In other words, top-notch FM departments know how to assess the "health" of their organizations, by examining how the people and processes are functioning, and determine the most appropriate prescription or formula to make them better.

The design and function of organizations are organization development, or OD. The genetic makeup of human beings, or their individual building blocks, is DNA. Just as we are able to determine the makeup of human beings by tracing or mapping personal DNA, we can identify what makes FM departments effective by tracing or mapping organization DNA.

The mapping process to trace FM department DNA involves a variety of diagnostic tests. Running these organization diagnostic tests is similar to what forensic scientists and criminologists do when they use DNA to solve crimes: They take DNA found at crime scenes, analyze and trace it to specific individuals, and then use it to link these individuals to the crime. Similarly, professionals in high-performance FM departments perform routine diagnostic tests on their organizations to isolate the root cause of problem areas and trace the source of strengths. Then they figure out how to correct problem areas, or build on organizational strengths. To successfully diagnose and apply OD strategies, FM professionals must have highly specialized skills.

Knowing more about their department's makeup and the building blocks of success better enables FM professionals to influence the way the department behaves and functions. Thus, OD in FM involves the use of fine-tuned diagnostic skills to understand and influence organization DNA. Analyzing an FM department and implementing strategies for improvement is similar to the way forensic scientists and criminologists use specialized skills to trace and analyze personal DNA.

Why Write About OD in FM?

One reason to write this book is to set the record straight about the uniqueness of FM departments. Facility practitioners often describe the problems they encounter within their departments as specific to FM. This description implies that tested approaches to analyzing and solving organizational problems aren't applicable to the FM environment. Granted, the practice of FM has some peculiar quirks, but the OD issues my consulting firm, The Friday Group, encounters in FM departments are typical of those we experience in departments far removed from FM. Identifying and addressing the issues associated with the design and function of organizations require skills that are consistent across organization types. Because organizational issues often are more difficult to trace and resolve than technical ones, FM professionals must be able to apply sophisticated diagnostic tools and techniques associated with OD to their own FM departments.

Another reason for writing this book is to respond to a question FM professionals ask all the time: "Can't you just give us your FM organization model so we can use it to pattern our own FM department?" Believe me, if I had one, this book would be short and to the point. Unfortunately, there is no cookie-cutter approach to achieving an effective FM organization, whether creating one from scratch or reengineering an existing one. The Friday Group has yet to identify a model organization scheme that works for all FM departments or any documented research to indicate a universal model even exists. I'll go out on a limb and state we haven't found a model that works 100 percent of the time within a specific industry or market segment such as manufacturing and education or service and high-tech industries. Even with our extensive consulting experience, The Friday Group hasn't observed or heard of a single model for FM organizations that can be applied consistently to a particular market segment. We do not believe one organization model can be used for all FM departments in a single market segment, let alone across the board for all of them. Without the ability to apply a universal model, I believe the need to understand and develop an evaluative approach to OD is even more critical for FM professionals.

There is one final reason for this tome on OD. Three years ago I was asked to teach a course on OD for the Michigan State University, Virtual University Graduate Program in Facility Management. I was delighted with the opportunity to participate in a groundbreaking Internet program and enthusiastically began developing course materials. As I began my research, however, I soon discovered that other than my colleague Dave Cotts's work, the consulting experience of my firm, and some International Facility Management Association (IFMA) publications, there was little written on FM organizations. Dave's book, *The Facility Management Handbook,* is the best and most comprehensive, particularly on two important OD building blocks—leadership and organization structure. He and I frequently talk about FM organizations and I value his opinion highly. I reference and incorporate his ideas at various stages of our discussion in this book, particularly in the chapters on leadership and organization structure.

The latest work on FM organizations, the 2001 IFMA Foundation report, *Designing the Facility Management Organization*, has data on FM organizational practices. I refer to this research often, for I found some excellent data on FM organizations that reinforces the underlying premise of this book. The findings in the foundation report came from responses to questionnaires IFMA received from 905 IFMA members in the United States and Canada, in addition to some focus group information. While I find the foundation publication to be quite good, it is a profile of what exists within FM organizations and isn't intended to be a how-to guide on developing an FM department with healthy, thriving DNA.

My own years of consulting to FM departments and this absence of solid how-to documentation on FM organization design and development convinced me to devote an entire book to OD topics. It is my strong belief that when FM practitioners, and especially FM managers, have the ability to use OD tools and techniques, they can better position their departments to achieve their mission and serve as organizational role models within their companies.

Please do not consider my work to be the most comprehensive source of information on the total subject of OD. There are many experts on the subject who are far more knowledgeable than I am, and also more prolific writers. What I present in this book are seven characteristics, or links—leadership, individuals, groups, culture, visioning and strategic planning, structure, and future—The Friday Group has found to be the most significant building blocks for designing and developing organizations with strong DNA. For each of these seven DNA links, there is a specific set of OD skills that are applicable to FM, so practitioners can do OD the right way. I hope you will find the subject matter so appealing that you want to explore other OD writers on your own. My ultimate goal is to enable FM practitioners to build effective FM departments that achieve a high level of performance.

What Does It Take to Write a Book Like This?

After finishing this book, I now know why I called my firm The Friday Group. Just as I found in my consulting practice, producing a book like this would not have been possible without a huge support group. Developing a book of this nature highlights just how much there is to learn about OD. The group served to prop me up emotionally, as well as to help with the physical aspects of creating the book.

It would be impossible to adequately describe the depth of my gratitude for the assistance provided by this group. They stuck with me on days when I didn't think I could put pen to paper and encouraged me to create a valuable tool for our profession. Acknowledging them is but a small token of my heartfelt thanks. Public acknowledgments always are tricky, though, for fear of omitting someone who labored long and hard. Please don't be offended if I inadvertently forgot to mention your name here, for I truly am indebted to all of you.

Laura McMarlin—An associate with The Friday Group for many years and now an independent consultant for us, Laura has been involved with the book since its conception. She lived with the material for a long time, having researched topics, reconfigured material from our Internet course, listened to me moan and groan about my lack of progress, and produced the final manuscript for the publisher. Laura probably knows more about the book than I do, and without her encouragement and technical help, I never would have gotten this far.

Paola Then—As a new associate with the firm, Paola fell into the book's development toward the end of the process. She provided much needed clean-up work on sources, permission granting, bibliography refinement, and text editing. She also refined existing graphs and developed many new ones. Paola provided invaluable assistance to make sure the final i's were dotted and t's crossed. She also cheered me to the finish line.

Margaret Moore—Margaret was a research associate with The Friday Group and helped with some of the research.

Natalie P. Green—A leading management consultant in her own right, Natalie helped create a logical order and framework for presenting the key OD concepts. She also worked diligently to edit and refine the wonderful company vignettes you find in each chapter. Like the shoemaker's children who need new shoes, management consultants usually need a consultant of their own, and Natalie was mine.

Kit Bradley—My husband deserves a lot of credit for putting up with me throughout the process. At least twice a day for a long time, he heard me talk about the issues and challenges associated with the book. Always my trusted confidant and sounding board, it was his job to tell me "quitters don't finish" over and over again.

Margaret and Durant Friday—My parents have been my allies for over fifty years, and they also listened to author trials and tribulations each night. Supportive of everything I do, they were there for me when I just needed a friendly ear. Our phone conversations will be at least 20 minutes shorter each night from now on!

Dave Cotts—My writing and conceptual soul mate on FM, Dave is an FM practitioner and expert par excellence. With each conversation Dave inspires me to make educational contributions to our profession. Thanks, Dave, for pushing me along. Not only is Dave an esteemed colleague, but a most valued friend.

Students in my three Organization Development courses at Michigan State University, Virtual University Graduate Program in Facility Management—You served as guinea pigs for much of the material in the book and provided valuable insight into how to improve it. I believe several of you may write your own treatise on FM organizations some day.

Organization development theorists and researchers—I have enjoyed studying all of you since my undergraduate days. Even as an unsuspecting student, I knew you were on to something when you wrote about organizations, and I have followed a lot of your teachings throughout the years.

My vignette writers, Doug Aldrich, Rusty Hodapp, Johns Hopkins Applied Physics Laboratory Facilities Management Staff, Bob Kraiss, Mert Livingstone, Phil Roberts, and Ed Wimer—These folks devoted tremendous time and effort to writing stories about their FM departments. Their vignettes appear in each chapter and make the book believable. While their bios appear after each vignette, you need to know that these practitioners are some of the finest I have ever encountered. They have successful FM departments formed with the DNA links discussed in the book.

Alex Bradley—My two-and-a-half-year-old grandson is the source of inspiration for much of what I do these days. His constant "What is this?" and "What does this do?" reinforce my belief that we can never be too old to grow and learn. I encourage all FM practitioners to share his hunger for information and his zest for exploring new concepts.

INTRODUCTION

What Will You Learn from This Book?

The role of facility management (FM) professionals is to deliver FM services in support of the mission and goals of the company or institution in a quality, cost-effective manner while also adding value to the overall enterprise. Facility managers have the added responsibility of determining how to lead, manage, structure, and staff the department to deliver these services. Regardless of whether you are a facility manager or staff within an FM department, the more you know about the department's makeup, or DNA, and are able to diagnose its problems, issues, and occasional ailments, as well as understand its strengths, the more effective you will be in suggesting and implementing strategies to change and improve the way the department functions.

Your ability to evaluate an FM department means you are knowledgeable and skilled in organization development (OD). The purpose of this book is to give you a foundation in OD, but more importantly to help you develop the specific set of skills you need to perform these assessments. Even if you know something about OD and have acquired OD skills, this book should give you greater confidence to apply the tools and techniques associated with OD within your own department.

Who Should Read This Book?

The book is intended for all who are practitioners of FM. At times I address FM professionals as a generic group, and at times I talk specifically to those who manage FM departments or subunits within departments. It really doesn't matter which audience is highlighted, as the concepts presented apply to every individual working inside an FM department. It isn't enough for FM managers alone to have these skills. In order for a whole department to be effective, everyone in the department must understand the dynamics of organizations and have the ability to influence and change these dynamics. All staffs within the department have a responsibility to make a positive contribution to the organization's development.

Will You Be Confused by the Terms That Are Used?

If you don't read this section, you might be confused at times. To write a book of this length, the word *organization* is used about a zillion times. Even I got confused after I penned the term *organization* to mean the FM entity consisting of staff and managers as well as "organization" in the context of OD and the skills involved. I finally settled on the term *FM department* when I am talking about specific FM entities and *organization* when I am referring to organizations in a general sense or OD constructs. The use of FM department is the best I could come up with, even though I know that not every FM entity is a department. Please use your imagination and good sense when you see this term. FM department could be an FM group, an FM unit, an FM section, an FM division, or whatever your particular corporate nomenclature is to describe the "entity."

Most of the time I use the words *company* and *corporate* to represent both public and private sector organizations. Sometimes, though, when I am trying to make a difficult point, I differentiate the two by calling the private sector organization the *company* and a public sector one an *institution*. Again, I am sure you will be able to figure out the difference.

The term *business unit* is used in several chapters when I refer to subunits of companies or institutions other than an FM department. In most instances, the term is used to describe an organizational entity that is a customer of the FM department.

While not always considered the best writing form, I have a tendency to switch back and forth from "you" to "we." Since I truly believe all of us are in this FM thing together, I like to use the collective "we." As one giant FM team striving to make our profession better, "we" exemplifies the spirit of collaboration I am trying to convey throughout this book. At times, I also use "we" after I have talked about my firm, The Friday Group. You will be able to decipher when this reference means my firm.

Finally, I apologize to anyone who is offended by my use of the term *his* instead of his and/or her throughout the book. I realized I wasn't going to like a book that had him/her or his/her within the text. Using both terms tends to be distracting and seems to dilute the content. I certainly don't intend any gender bias; I just wanted to cut down on the number of words that don't add content value to the book.

How Do You Navigate Through This Book?

You don't need much of a road map to navigate through the book. Like the book I coauthored with Dave Cotts, *Quality Facility Management: A Marketing and Customer Service Perspective,* this one is pretty straightforward and easy to follow. There are bulleted and numbered items in the text to highlight important points and charts and graphs to illustrate points.

The book has seven chapters organized around links mentioned in the Preface—leadership, individuals, groups, culture, visioning and strategic planning, structure, and future—that I have labeled *DNA links.* Within these DNA links, skills that FM practitioners need to apply in order to diagnose FM departments and develop effective development strategies are delineated. Also contained in each chapter are tools and techniques The Friday Group has applied with our clients or heard about from other FM departments that have proved to be successful to OD. Figure I-1 is a summary of the DNA links and the set of skills that accompany them.

Are Any Real FM Department Examples Provided?

At the end of each chapter is a vignette about an FM department that illustrates the DNA link discussed, plus practical OD learning

Figure I-1. Summary of DNA links and skills set.

CHAPTER	DNA LINK	COMPONENTS OF OD SKILL SET
Chapter 1: Organization Development (OD) and How We Apply It to Facility Management	Leadership	❏ Management and leadership relationship ❏ Situational assessment ❏ Leadership style assessment ❏ Follower readiness ❏ Climate for leadership
Chapter 2: Understanding and Influencing Individual Behavior in FM Organizations	Individuals	❏ Self-awareness ❏ Awareness of others ❏ Individual assessment of needs ❏ Self-motivation ❏ Expectations of individuals ❏ Rewards and incentives ❏ Climate for motivation
Chapter 3: Understanding and Influencing Group Behavior in FM Organizations	Groups	❏ Group dynamics and development ❏ Group process ❏ Group motivation ❏ Appropriateness of teams ❏ Self-directed teams ❏ Rewards and incentives ❏ Climate for motivation
Chapter 4: The Importance of Culture to FM Organizations	Culture	❏ Corporate culture influence ❏ Values and norms ❏ Culture maladies ❏ Culture change ❏ Cultural integration
Chapter 5: The Role of Strategic Planning and the FM Organization	Visioning and Strategic Planning	❏ Added value to enterprise ❏ Intelligence gathering ❏ Action planning ❏ Institutionalized process ❏ Continuous process
Chapter 6: Designing the FM Organization Structure	Structure	❏ Design and structure relationship ❏ Business drivers ❏ Function and structure ❏ Position in enterprise hierarchy ❏ Customer-driven designs ❏ Outsourcing influences ❏ Staff skills mix ❏ Benchmarking structures ❏ Strategic alignment

		❏ Structure and customer commitments
		❏ Flexibility and reinvention
Chapter 7: Linking FM Organizations to the Future of Facility Management	Future	❏ Technology assessment ❏ Nontraditional role identification ❏ Global influences ❏ Cultural workplace integrator ❏ Due diligence participation ❏ Knowledge gap assessment ❏ Corporate role model ❏ Continuous learning

points. These vignettes, written by living, breathing FM professionals, are about actual FM departments. They are the best way to demonstrate what FM practitioners accomplish when they have a firm grasp of the concepts and principles of OD. Figure I-2 is a summary of the vignettes by chapter and the learning points associated with each.

Figure I-2. Summary of vignettes and learning points.

COMPANY	CHAPTER AND DNA LINK	LEARNING POINTS
Dow Corning	Chapter 1: Organization Development (OD) and How We Apply It to Facility Management. DNA Link: Leadership	❏ Leadership role to integrate FM with technical customer needs ❏ Leadership role in setting standards, determining metrics, making sourcing decisions, and piloting improvements ❏ Leadership role to balance cost, timing, and quality ❏ Organizational leadership role as player in corporate governance
Adaptec	Chapter 2: Understanding and Influencing Individual Behavior in FM Organizations. DNA Link: Individuals	❏ Creation of entrepreneurial environment to motivate individuals ❏ Individuals are best marketing agent for FM organization

(continues)

Figure I-2. (Continued.)

COMPANY	CHAPTER AND DNA LINK	LEARNING POINTS
		❑ Empowerment of individuals to make smart decisions with customers
Applied Physics Lab	Chapter 3: Understanding and Influencing Group Behavior in FM Organizations DNA Link: Groups	❑ Team-oriented approach to service delivery ❑ Use of self-directed teams to perform construction and operations functions ❑ Sharing of unique skills across organization lines ❑ Customer focus orientation created need for single-point-of-contact role for Operations Center team for work reception and dispatch
Hertfordshire County Council UK	Chapter 4: The Importance of Culture to FM Organizations DNA Link: Culture	❑ FM service team structure culture mirrors corporate culture ❑ Culture centered around people as most valuable asset to create center of excellence ❑ Partnership approach with outsource provider ❑ Strategic service link to corporate business plans
Metavante	Chapter 5: The Role of Strategic Planning and the FM Organization DNA Link: Visioning and Strategic Planning	❑ Goals mapped to business objectives ❑ Acceptance of goals by management team as realistic, doable, and measurable ❑ Assignment of lead management responsibility for goals and objectives ❑ Institutionalization of planning process as annual activity ❑ Regularly scheduled plan versus actual progress sessions as component of planning process

DFW Airport	Chapter 6: Designing the FM Organization Structure DNA Link: Structure	❏ Customer focus drives service delivery structure ❏ Flexible structure designed to adapt to changing requirements ❏ Matrix management approach of horizontally integrated functions ❏ Performance tied to achievement of business results
Pharmacia	Chapter 7: Linking FM Organizations to the Future of Facility Management DNA Link: Future	❏ Merger integration of FM functions achieved through process action team ❏ Creation of new corporate culture key to integration strategy ❏ New vision and strategy tied to performance management ❏ Integrated organization model for major sites structured around linked and matrixed functional teams ❏ IT strategy maximizes technology tools to deliver business plan and track performance

CHAPTER ONE

Organization Development (OD) and How We Apply It to Facility Management (FM)

DNA Link: Leadership

What Is OD?

It was a struggle to find the best way to introduce facility professionals to the subject of organization development since it has complex concepts that are difficult to get your arms around at first. Enough information has to be presented in the first few pages to serve as a foundation for the rest of the book without making the topic so weighty and theoretical that you get bored and lose interest before leaving the first chapter.

In order for the content to have ultimate utility for facility management (FM) practitioners, I decided to risk losing you in the first chapter by talking about the genesis of organization development (OD) and then connecting it to the first FM department DNA link—leadership. Once there is an understanding of what we mean by OD and how it came into practice, it is easier to see that its application can reap tremendous benefits for FM departments. These first few pages are critical so don't skip them or you will have difficulty tracking the rest of our discussion on OD.

The first order of business is to provide a working definition of *organization development*. Having researched what others have written, I borrowed a definition that seems to capture accurately the essence of what we are discussing. We use the following definition of OD:

> Organization development (OD) is a powerful set of concepts and techniques for improving organizational effectiveness and individual well-being.[1]

This definition appeals to me for many reasons. First, it uses the word *powerful* to describe the concepts and techniques. Organization development is one of the most powerful tools available to facility professionals to meet the challenges of today's FM environment. Second, the definition incorporates two elements that are necessary for OD to succeed: the organization and the individual. Without regard for the well-being of individuals, an organization cannot be effective. Conversely, although individuals within an organization are important, if they don't have collective goals and objectives, there is no cohesive organization.

Finally, the use of the term *set* is attractive because it implies there is more than one concept and multiple techniques that must be applied in order for OD to work. These concepts and techniques are very much the reality of OD—hence the use of DNA *links*—in that any one concept or technique by itself will not result in the desired outcome for the organization. The ability to use OD concepts and techniques by applying them in a systematic and strategic fashion is what makes them really powerful management tools.

Building on the preceding definition, it also seems that OD can be viewed as the totality of human and social interaction within an organization. Because it involves people and the way they interact with one another, OD is action-oriented rather than passive. I find this basic underpinning of OD to be especially appealing for the practice of FM, since the bulk of what facility professionals do is dynamic rather than static. Since we are in the service business, we are doers. While at first blush you might think that OD is a theoretical construct, in actuality it is all about doing and implementing.

Still another way of looking at OD is to view it as a process of planned system change that attempts to make organizations (viewed as social-technical systems) better able to attain both short- and long-term objectives.[2] Notice that this statement doesn't stipulate that OD makes organizations better, but specifically makes them "better able" to support their goals. Stressing the planning and process aspects of OD is significant because without both, it is almost impossible to effect constructive organizational change. Strategic planning is such a vital DNA link in OD that I devote Chapter 5 to visioning and strategic planning. In order to keep an organization alive and vibrant, the organization needs to be infused with change on a regular basis, but the change has to be well orchestrated in order for it not to be disruptive to the well-being of individuals nor the group as a whole. This is one of the reasons FM practitioners need to understand and manage OD.

Perhaps an even simpler way of looking at OD is to view it as an organizational improvement strategy, one that is planned and executed by the individuals responsible for managing the organization as well as those who are in staff roles. Successful OD requires leadership not only by executives who are in charge of the organization but also by those in other positions.

One thing to keep in mind as we explore OD is that the analytical skills presented have a solid history of success, which is why I chose to trace the evolution of OD in the first chapter. Reading about how others have used OD even before it became a recognized practice helps us appreciate how valuable OD can be to FM. In other words, OD is not a management fad or trend. It is a compendium of concepts and techniques with a proven track record. OD is not going to go out of style in a few years, so the analytical capabilities described in this book will serve as a solid framework for your future management endeavors. I concur with, and have added my own thoughts to, what authors French, Bell, and Zawacki[3] have characterized as the reasons why we want to understand and practice OD:

❐ Organization development efforts can improve individual performance, create better morale, and increase organizational profitability. There is ample documentation to support the belief that chronic organizational problems can be cured by OD techniques.

☐ The use of OD is on the rise. The approach and methods of OD are applied throughout a wide range of organization types and industries. In manufacturing and service companies, high-tech industries, educational and health care organizations, and public and private sector institutions, successful OD programs have been instituted.

☐ It is now a recognized fact that the most important assets of organizations are its human assets—those individuals who perform the work. Organization development finds ways to protect, enhance, and mobilize human assets.

☐ Organization development is a critical management tool. Those who have watched, used, and studied OD over the years believe that it is as important to the successful manager as financial skill, technical knowledge, and customer-service orientation. When OD capability is coupled with other generic management tools, a manager is armed with forceful weapons.

After working in the field of OD for many years, it became my mission to share this valuable information with my fellow FM practitioners. As you read on, you will see how OD equips you to face the future in FM.

How Did the Concept of OD Develop?

The origins of OD are deeply rooted in the behavioral sciences. Those who have studied or had exposure to psychology, sociology, or human resources management may be familiar with the individuals who contributed to its development. There is tremendous documentation on OD supplied by both theorists and practitioners, and this chapter is not intended to be an exhaustive review of the entire spectrum of thinking on OD. Encapsulated in this chapter are the highlights of OD evolution, which demonstrate how it has been applied in the laboratory of real-world organizations.

Organization theory, or an emphasis on the formal management of organizations, was not considered much before 1900, as most of society's infrastructure was based on models from the military, the Catholic Church, and European governments. These entities served as the basic models for organizations, yet little, if any, thought was given to what made these organization models effective or ineffective. It wasn't until the Industrial Revolution in the late nineteenth century that any real thinking about organizations took place. With the Industrial Revolution, a factory-based economy emerged, creating the need to structure the way work was performed, as well as the need to determine ways in which the work could move faster and more accurately.

Although the term *organization development* was not yet in use, many OD historians credit Frederick Taylor, early in the twentieth century, with some of the most significant work in the field. Taylor, a foreman at Bethlehem Steel Works in Bethlehem, Pennsylvania, helped craft organization management into a true field of study. Taylor made observations and wrote about what he considered to be "industrial efficiency." He was convinced that management in general was a science, and he felt strongly that there were distinctly different roles and responsibilities for both managers and staff. He stressed the importance of developing clear definitions of these roles and responsibilities.

In his work, Taylor talked about organizations as if they were machines that could be created and developed by using manufacturing principles. Once specific tasks and functions were identified and assigned, the basic organizational framework would work in any environment. He coined the term *scientific management* to describe his views about organizations and management.[4] Taylor also began to make specific recommendations for the creation of organization structures and management functions/activities within manufacturing environments. Engineers among us should be familiar with Taylor and no doubt will remember the concept of "time and motion" studies. Because Taylor was focused almost exclusively on manufacturing, he drew a direct correlation between a task performed by workers on an assembly line and the level of productivity they were able to sustain. We can thank Taylor for the notion that if one studied the time and motion of workers and made adjustments, productivity could be increased.

At this stage we still are talking primarily about organizations absent any regard for individuals within these organizations and how they contribute to the organizational success or effectiveness.

As we move along in the progression of OD, it is important to talk about the work of French manager Henry Fayol, who is credited with the development of the classical movement in OD. It was in 1916 that Fayol, whose works were not even translated into English until the end of the 1940s, developed our basic structure for organizations and managers. Fayol's work laid the foundation for the functions of a manager that are still used in contemporary management education and training programs to teach individuals how to manage. Fayol believed there are 4 basic features of any organization:[5]

1. *Specialization*—Workers within organizations should be arranged by logical groupings such as place of work, product, expertise, or functional areas. As an example, General Motors groups its workers by specific make of car into a single division.

2. *Unity of Command*—A member of an organization has only one direct supervisor and does not receive direction from another organization unit's supervisor.

3. *Chain of Command*—The organization structure is formal and begins with the individual who is the chief executive and extends down the organization to the least-skilled employee. The chain of command concept also specified the reporting relationships in the total organization. We talk more about chain of command when we address organization configurations in Chapter 6.

4. *Coordination of Activities*—Managers within organizations use specific tools to ensure communication among the different groups. These tools may vary from the most formal written directives in the form of policies and procedures to informal policies that are "understood" within the organization through use and practice.

Fayol further refined these features into five basic managerial functions. These functions have become the classic management functions within most organizations. Fayol is credited with establishing the five managerial functions of *planning, organizing, coordinating, commanding,* and *controlling.*[6]

Our next player in the evolution of OD, German sociologist Max Weber, is a particular favorite of mine. Weber is the individual who first started calling organizations *bureaucracies,* a term most of us know as one of the most common descriptors for particular types of organizations. To Weber's way of thinking, a bureaucracy is crafted by the need for order, system, rationality, uniformity, and consistency within organizations. When those five characteristics are applied to an organization in a systematic fashion, there is equitable treatment for all within the organization. He believed that the creation of a bureaucracy using those characteristics eliminates any opportunity for favoritism or special treatment within the organization's setting that might diminish the capability of the organization to perform.

The essence of Weber's bureaucracy includes the following:[7]

❑ Responsibility fields derived from the competency and expertise of the individual

❑ The use of specific rules and regulations that are articulated for the benefit of employees as tools in the management process

❑ The use of training in the area of job requirements

❑ The use of rules in a consistent and complete manner

As mentioned earlier in this chapter, the engineers among us can relate well to the progression of OD thus far. Early thinkers about organizations were applying precision, discipline, consistency, and structure to organizations, all concepts that are compatible with engineering doctrine. None of these early thinkers— Taylor, Fayol, and Weber—placed any meaning or importance on the *people* within the organization in terms of how they behaved, how they communicated, whether or not they were dysfunctional within an organizational setting, how they were motivated to do work, or whether or not they could be inspired to perform at varying levels. For these OD pioneers, the impact of a human resources factor was not a consideration.

While there was other OD activity throughout the early 1940s, the emergence of laboratory training as an OD technique was the next major OD breakthrough. This breakthrough came about during a workshop held in the summer of 1946 at the State Teachers College in New Britain, Connecticut. A fellow named Kurt Lewin, head of the Research Center for Group Dynamics at MIT, was involved in the workshop. Lewin already was known as a researcher, theorist, and practitioner in interpersonal, group, inter-group, and community relationships.[8] He was well respected, having coined the phrase "group dynamics" in 1939.

The workshop was later dubbed a "T-Group" (with the "T" for training) because its group process included the use of a group leader, group members, and an observer who made notes but didn't interact with the group. This group process has evolved into one of the most widely respected learning experience formats for management exercises. It is interesting to note that during this 1946 break-through session, flip charts were used for the first time as a means of recording data and information. Today, who can imagine conducting an FM organization or strategy session without using flip charts or the technology equivalent, the whiteboard? The laboratory training and learning technique is a direct outgrowth of Kurt Lewin's research. His work led to the concept of *group dynamics,* for it was Lewin who found that individual behavior is influenced in part by group interaction and behavior while, at the same time, adding its own influence. He is a major player in the OD field and his work greatly influences our discussion of individuals and teams in Chapters 2 and 3.

In the practice of FM, we have come to rely heavily on the use of survey research and feedback, especially in the area of measuring customer satisfaction with service delivery. As someone who has written and lectured extensively on the importance of surveys and feedback as a research tool, I would be remiss if I didn't give special attention to one particular figure in our walk-through of OD history. Rensis Likert became the Director of the Institute for Social Research at the University of Michigan after he served as the Director of the Division of Program Surveys at the Federal Bureau of Agricultural Economics during World War II. Likert is well known for his work in action research, most notably survey research. His doctoral dissertation, "A Technique for the Measurement of Attitudes," ultimately led to the five-point Likert scale commonly used in survey instruments to measure attitude.[9] This one-dimensional scaling methodology judges favorability of a concept rather than belief. Likert also is remembered for his work within the public sector and for conducting extensive research on leadership motivation, productivity, and morale. His association with the Detroit Edison Company led to the development of the survey feedback method and support for the idea that group discussion regarding results of employee attitudes and behaviors surveyed is a valuable tool, allowing organizations to plan improvements together as a team. Likert often is quoted with regard to his concepts of highly effective work groups that we talk about in Chapter 3.

Authors French and Bell attribute coinage of the actual term *organization development*[10] to Robert Blake, Herbert Shepard, and Jane Mouton, all contemporaries of another luminary in OD, Douglas McGregor, whom we focus on shortly. While McGregor was working with Union Carbide in the late 1950s, the other three were conducting organizational experiments at Exxon (then called Esso Standard Oil). They discovered a need for support and involvement of upper management and a requirement to tie efforts back to people's jobs. They used behavioral feedback and team development to resolve intergroup conflict, acknowledging the complexity of an ongoing organization and the need for its various groups to collaborate. French and Bell suggest the likelihood that the trio of OD practitioners at Esso, who used the term *development groups* in their work, drove the concept of OD by combining their early terminology with the emerging insights of their time.

Another term we often use in OD work with FM organizations is *team building*. Robert Tannenbaum, an industrial relations specialist, along with Paul Buchanan and Herb Shepard of the above-mentioned Esso project, conducted team-building sessions with individuals at the U.S. Naval Ordinance Test Station in China Lake, California. Tannenbaum used what he termed *vertically structured groups* dealing with "personal topics (departmental sociometrics, interpersonal relationships, communication and self-analysis) and with organizational topics (deadlines, duties and responsibilities, policies and procedures and interorganizational-group relations)."[11] These sessions stressed the human side of an organization and the impact of certain issues on the health and well-being of individuals and groups. As we discuss in Chapter 3, team building is an essential OD skill for FM practitioners to understand and use.

Still another prominent figure in our OD discussion is a fellow named Chris Argyris who made contributions to theory and practical research on laboratory training, OD, and organizational learning. He focused on the social and ego needs of people in groups and worked to channel individual psychological energy to meet both the individual's and the organization's needs. Argyris, a pro-

lific writer and trainer, also is well known for incorporating intervention strategies with top executives of companies such as IBM,
Exxon, and other large corporations.

Perhaps of all the luminaries in the field of OD, the individual
who is most recognized, remembered, and quoted is MIT profes-
sor-turned-consultant Douglas McGregor. In the early 1950s at
an Advisory Committee meeting of the MIT School of Industrial
Management, Alfred P. Sloan raised a now-famous question. Alfred Sloan, you might remember, was the president and CEO of
General Motors and creator of the Sloan Foundation. In 1952, he
established the MIT School of Industrial Management, which later
bore his name. The question Mr. Sloan raised was whether or not
"successful managers are born or made."[12] This question led to a
Sloan Foundation grant to McGregor and a colleague to conduct a
study that eventually spawned a new movement well known to OD
specialists. To find an answer to Sloan's question, McGregor em-
barked on a project that gave him notoriety as the father of Theory
X and Theory Y.

The result of McGregor's study is his book *The Human Side
of Enterprise,* published in 1960, in which he discusses his perspective on organizations. McGregor's writings and teachings have
been the inspiration for many contemporary management gurus
who have worked hard to dispel or support his premise. The book
describes McGregor's belief that much of the literature of his time
and the managerial practice within organizations was based on assumptions that he labeled Theory X, which I have summarized
below:[13]

❑ The average human being has an inherent dislike of work and
   will avoid it.
❑ Because of this inherent dislike, most people must be coerced,
   controlled, directed, and threatened with punishment to get
   them to put forth sufficient effort to achieve an organization's
   goals.
❑ The average human being wants to be directed, wants to avoid
   responsibility, has relatively little ambition, and wants security
   above all.

Given his assumptions, McGregor felt that there was only one
logical motivational tool that could be used with employees, and

this he labeled as the carrot-and-stick approach. McGregor did not stop with his Theory X, however. He also proposed a Theory Y as a counter to Theory X, which is comprised of the following assumptions, which I have also summarized:[14]

❐ The expenditure of physical and mental effort in work is as natural as play or rest.

❐ External control and the threat of punishment are not the only means for bringing about effort toward objectives of the organization.

❐ Commitment to objectives is a function of the rewards associated with their achievement.

❐ The average human being learns, under proper conditions, not only to accept but to seek responsibility.

❐ The capacity to exercise a relatively high degree of imagination, ingenuity, and creativity in the solving of organization problems is widely, not narrowly, distributed in the population.

❐ Under the conditions of modern industrial life, the intellectual potentialities of the average human being are only partially utilized.

We need to dwell on the Theory X and Theory Y assumptions because they represent a crossroads in OD thinking. Contained in the work of Douglas McGregor and some of his contemporaries is a new recognition of some inherent worker attributes. From McGregor's writings, a positive belief in human beings emerged. This belief in the positive side of human nature has had long-lasting applicability for the management of organizations, even in today's changing management environment. Of all the words I could provide to you from OD experts, I think those of Douglas McGregor are the most enduring.

> The assumptions of Theory Y point up the fact that the limits on human collaboration in the organizational setting are not limits of human nature but of management's ingenuity in resources. Theory X offers management an easy rationalization for ineffective organizational performance: It is due to the

> nature of the human resources with which we must work. Theory Y, on the other hand, places the problems squarely in the lap of management. If employees are lazy, indifferent, unwilling to take responsibility, intransigent, uncreative, uncooperative, Theory Y implies that the causes lie in management's methods of organization and control.[15]

McGregor firmly believed that managers had to accept responsibility for the way in which their organizations performed, thus implying that managers also would be influential in the performance of the people in the organization.

We have reviewed a respectable amount of OD history in a relatively few number of pages. While some of you might commit to memory the various OD experts and their contributions to the field, it is useful to have a handy reference guide to use as a cheat sheet. Figure 1-1 provides a summary of the contributions made by the OD players we have discussed thus far.

Is There Any New Thinking on OD?

At this stage you might be wondering if anything is being done in the OD field that is more current. The answer is both yes and no. French, Bell, and Zawacki feel strongly that "the context for applying OD approaches has changed to an increasingly *turbulent* environment."[16] By turbulent they mean an environment filled with "hazards" that were not as prevalent in the early years of OD. French and his colleagues feel that professionals are working in an organizational environment that is filled with mergers, acquisitions, downsizing, rightsizing, reengineering, consolidation, and privatizing. These changes in the organizational environment have created new and challenging opportunities for the application of traditional OD concepts and techniques. Those of us in the FM world are well aware of how difficult these changes make the workplace.

French, Bell, and Zawacki term the current OD efforts *second-generation.*[17] Given the climate within which these second-generation OD initiatives are being implemented, there is a growing trend toward mixing the best attributes of both the scientific and behav-

Figure 1-1. OD key players.

KEY PLAYERS IN EVOLUTION OF
ORGANIZATION DEVELOPMENT

PLAYER	TIME FRAME	CONTRIBUTION
People in Organizations Not Considered Important		
Frederick Taylor	1910s	**Scientific Management**—Viewed management as a science. Felt industrial efficiency is achieved once task and functions are defined. Adjusting worker time and motion enhances productivity.
Henry Fayol	1910s	**Classical Movement**—Structure for organizations and managers. Established five classic managerial functions: Planning, Organizing, Coordinating, Commanding, and Controlling.
Max Weber	1920s	**Bureaucracy**—Need for order, system, rationality, uniformity, and consistency in organizations. Belief that bureaucracies eliminate favoritism.
People in Organizations Considered Important		
Kurt Lewin	1940s	**Group Dynamics**—Individual behavior influenced by group interaction and behavior while adding own influence. T-Group consisting of leader, members, and observer.
Rensis Likert	1940s	**Survey Research**—Five-point Likert scale to measure attitude.
Robert Blake, Herbert Shephard, Jane Mouton	1950s	**Organization Development**—Coined term by using feedback and team development to resolve intergroup conflict. Tied OD efforts to people's jobs.
Robert Tannenbaum	1950s	**Team Building**—Vertically structured groups to deal with personal and organizational issues. Stressed human side of organizations.
Chris Argyris	1950s	**Intervention Strategies**—Focused on social and ego needs of people in groups; energy toward both individual and needs. Team building with senior executives.
Douglas McGregor	1960s	**Theory X and Theory Y**—Carrot-and-stick approach to motivation, versus management responsibility to motivate.

ioral approaches. The results of this integration have led to an OD *systems theory* in which an organization is compared to a living organism that processes inputs into outputs and has a series of environmental factors that have bearing on the input/output relationship.

Yet another second-generation OD concept is one called *situational analysis* in which it is incumbent on those who are embarking on OD to take a diagnostic or analytical approach to a situation or series of events and then look at the type of organizational behavior and structure that is responsive to that situation. This situational-analysis approach is similar to our earlier analogy of the diagnostic tests forensic scientists and criminologists perform when they use DNA to solve crimes. In situational analysis, it is critical to have the right skills to be able to analyze certain aspects of organizations such as leadership, individual and group behavior, corporate culture, visioning and strategic planning, structure, and the future as key to any type of organizational transformation we are seeking. These are the DNA links around which this book has been structured.

It is within the framework of traditional OD concepts, augmented by the teachings from the second-generation OD experience, that we move into the application of OD to our FM realm.

How Do OD Concepts of Management and Leadership Impact an FM Organization?

The first OD concepts and related skills we need to discuss in detail are those of management and leadership. Before we discuss individual and group behavior and their impact on creating organization structures, we need to spend time on the concepts of *leadership* and *management* and their pivotal role in organizational effectiveness. In an increasingly more turbulent business environment, both the leadership and management of FM organizations serve as two distinct, yet complementary, concepts to guide FM practitioners. Understanding the synergies as well as the distinctions between the two, and learning how to apply them in a complementary fashion, constitute part of the diagnostic skills set we have discussed thus far.

When I defined OD at the beginning of this chapter, I mentioned that OD consists of a *set* of concepts and techniques. Those concepts and techniques have to be applied as a whole for effective OD to exist. Management and leadership are a perfect example of this in that they are a matched set. Management and leadership have a hand-in-glove relationship, and facility professionals have to understand the functions and characteristics of each in order to make them work in tandem.

Management

The definition of management I like to use comes from John P. Kotter in his *Harvard Business Review* article on "What Leaders Really Do." Kotter indicates that management is "coping with complexity" and the fact that without good management "complex enterprises tend to become chaotic."[18] Introducing good management brings "order and consistency" to the enterprise.

To expand on this further, management consists of working with and through individuals and groups to accomplish goals of the organization. Although there are many versions of what constitutes managerial work, through years of OD consulting and reading what experts have said about the role of a manager, I still subscribe to a list of managerial responsibilities (with some adaptation and language updating on my part) I first discovered in the early 1980s and have used consistently since then.[19] This list incorporates the five characteristics we learned previously that Fayol considered to be associated with management.

An effective manager:

Sets goals

Plans

Does not schedule others' work

Anticipates problems

Plans the staffing of supervisory positions

Knows all relevant functional areas

Delegates training

Finds new resources

Represents the organization

Requires information from company executives

Spends time with peers in other departments

Makes contacts and establishes a network outside the organization

Mediates and negotiates at organizational levels

Has ceremonial duties such as speeches, presentations, civic activities, etc.

Management, in theory, is about structuring functions and requires some discrete skills such as planning, organizing, and budgeting. It places a strong emphasis on rationality, directing, and control in a positive, rather than negative, way. Managerial effectiveness is determined by how well you implement each of your stated functions or responsibilities.

Leadership

Leadership is a broader concept than management. It is the process of *influencing* the activities of an individual or a group in their efforts toward achieving a goal, often in a given situation. According to John Kotter, leadership is "about coping with change"[20] and often, in the more typical enterprise environment, about stimulating or initiating change. As a complement to management, leadership requires one to be proactive instead of reactive, shaping ideas instead of responding to them, as a manager does. Leaders look at long-standing problems and develop fresh approaches to solving them. There are many managers who are not effective in a leadership role, just as there are excellent leaders who do not possess strong management skills. If we compartmentalize a manager's role, we could say that all good managers need to work on good leadership skills. Today's facility managers must set the tone and develop a leadership style if they want to become good leaders.

Another important component of leadership is that it is a *relational* concept. Two components have to exist in order for leadership to work: the leader(s) and those who are led, or the influencer and those who can be influenced. In other words, without an individual or group of individuals to follow, there can be no leader. The study of leadership in the context of OD involves the relationship of interpersonal behavior between the influencer and those who can be influenced. The real challenge for facility managers is achieving a balance between strong management and strong leadership.

For some, the concept of leadership takes on almost mystical proportions. When asked about the traits of a successful leader, people often talk about wizardlike qualities that place an individual in another realm. Alfred Sloan raised the question of whether leaders are "made or born," which has sparked ongoing debate. Some OD theorists truly believe only certain people possess leadership characteristics and are therefore "born leaders." They view leadership as a quality coming from within an individual. If this is true, leadership characteristics are intrinsic and are found only in natural leaders.

Other schools of thought discuss the fact that leaders often emerge as they develop in certain types of circumstances. They have the ability to perform the situational analysis that we talked about earlier. These OD theorists believe a person can acquire or learn the character traits that permit a leader to be "made." It seems that this school of thought applies well to FM, for we have witnessed some very competent managers who, when they discovered they weren't leading their FM organizations, turned their attention toward developing leadership skills, resulting in very positive outcomes.

Leaders often find themselves in an environment in which they are faced with several variables. These variables include the leader's followers, superiors, associates, the organization itself, job demands, and other situational variables. A really good manager knows that in order for a leader to function appropriately, the manager must create an organizational environment allowing all of these variables to interact in a successful manner.

We spend significant time in Chapter 2 discussing how a leader motivates followers by involving them directly in the process to achieve the organization's vision. Giving employees challenging opportunities in which to contribute their ideas to improve an organization, for example, permits leaders not only to get results but also to develop leadership for the future of the organization. Effective leaders have the ability to look at a problem from a distance, see the whole picture, identify the problem, and then outline the important questions needed to solve the problem.

Leadership Styles

Leadership style is defined as the consistent behavioral patterns leaders use when they are working with and through other people as perceived by those people.[21] There is a myriad of leadership style theories because experts have long attempted to explain why and how certain individuals rise above others in order to influence them. While that in and of itself is a fascinating topic, we focus only on the four major theories of leadership style.

Trait Leadership   One leadership style theory, called the *trait* theory, identifies specific personal characteristics that seem to be exemplified in most leaders. The trait theory stipulates that leaders create their own leadership style over time from experience, education, and training. These traits and skills seem to account for the difference between leaders who are and aren't effective. Some researchers have captured what they consider to be the dominant traits and skills of a leader, which I have adapted below.[22]

A leader's traits:

Adaptable to situations

Aware and alert to the social environment

Both ambitious and achievement-oriented

Assertive

Decisive

Cooperative

Dependable

Dominant (having a desire to influence others)

Energetic

Persistent (not giving up readily)

Self-confident

Tolerant of stress

Able to assume responsibility

A leader's skills:

Clever (meaning nimble of mind, rather than cunning)

Able to conceptualize

Creative

Diplomatic and tactful

Able to speak fluently

Knowledgeable about group tasking

Organized from an administrative standpoint

Persuasive

Social

This list doesn't seem to be complete, however, as there are several missing critical skills. In the current business environment, I would add and highlight entrepreneurial, customer service, and marketing skills to this list as critical success factors for a leader.

Many early theorists took issue with the concept of traits and skills and felt that using these benchmarks had little practical application for the modern manager. In the 1950s, new research supported a clear correlation between tasks and relationships and demonstrated that the behavior of leaders was key to effective leadership. A flurry of studies identified patterns of behavior that were popular for a time, but as the complexity of organizational situations changed so, too, did the thinking surrounding behavior.

Current thinking suggests there is no single pattern of behavior that works in all cases for leaders, which also supports our efforts to develop diagnostic skills for facility managers allowing them to assess the most appropriate course of action at a particular time. Thus, great leaders *can be made*, fashioned from, perhaps, managers who enjoy the right combination of traits, develop certain critical skills, have the right professional pressures and responsibilities, and a set of willing followers!

Situational Leadership   Paralleling our earlier discussion about situational analysis is situational leadership. Situational leadership is the ability to assess the most appropriate course of action for a particular time. The theory purports that effective leadership often results from the fit between a leader's style and the readiness of his followers. If an individual understands situational leadership, the individual can adjust his style according to the characteristics of the situation.

In its purest form, this theory of leadership also explains, in part, why some individuals may be able to provide leadership in one type of situation although not having exhibited these same characteristics in another setting. As an example, we often hear about individuals who make daring rescue attempts, lead others out of dangerous situations, and make strategic decisions to win major battles even though they have never exhibited leadership traits in other environments. In our work with FM departments, we have seen situational leaders rise to the occasion when they become the natural leader of a team project or problem-solving exercise, never having shown leadership characteristics before.

Charismatic Leadership   Yet another type of leadership style is that of the charismatic leader. A charismatic leader is one who uses charisma to inspire his followers. Throughout the twentieth century, there have been charismatic leaders such as John F. Kennedy, Gandhi, Winston Churchill, Theodore Roosevelt, and Franklin Roosevelt. This type of leader uses self-confidence, dominance, moral conviction, and charisma to inspire others to follow him.[23] A charismatic leader motivates followers to improve themselves in such ways as raising their consciousness about the importance of certain outcomes, showing the value of concentrating on the benefits that the work team can generate rather than on personal interests, and raising the workers' need levels so that they value challenges, responsibility, and growth.

Superleader   Our final type of leadership style is the superleader, who is similar to the charismatic leader but goes one step further. Superleaders help their followers discover, use, and maximize abilities by turning them into self-leaders, whereby subordinates take responsibility for motivating and directing their own personal behaviors.[24] It is this leadership style that most intrigues me and would seem to have the best payoff because it involves influencing the creation of an organization filled with motivated, fulfilled, and proactive partners. Facility managers should emulate the superleader in order to achieve ultimate OD.

Although leadership styles sometimes conflict with the followers' styles and therefore need to be altered, it should be noted that it is very difficult to change a leadership style. Other than situational leaders who may not know that they have leadership skills, the more traditional leaders develop their skills over time and through experience.

We do know there is a difference between being a successful leader and being an effective one, and when styles fail to match the situation appropriately, this difference becomes readily apparent. On the one hand, a *successful* leader is one who achieves a positive outcome resulting from the endeavors or achievements of individuals or groups. An *effective* leader, on the other hand, can determine that the outcome will produce the intended or expected result. Ideally, a leader wants to achieve both at the same time.

How Do We Become FM Leaders?

Over the years, I have found the topic of leadership in FM to be both fascinating and revealing: fascinating in the sense that FM leadership traits and styles can be ascertained, assessed, and then developed; and revealing in the fact that often FM managers overlook the impact of their leadership style on the total performance of their organizations. All too often we marshal our training and development efforts for FM professionals around specific management functions and tools and forget about the need to focus on developing leadership capabilities.

By now you should realize that leadership is a powerful and necessary component of your OD diagnostic skills set in order to be effective within your own FM department. What you may not know, however, is that becoming a leader means you also acquire the ability to conceptualize how the FM department fits into the larger whole—the corporate entity—in addition to the ability to visualize the potential of the department as its own entity. The truly effective FM leader can energize his followers to realize the FM organization potential while at the same time contributing value to the overall corporate goals. To become an effective leader, there are a number of specific activities that need to be undertaken.

Discover Your Leadership Capabilities and Style

In his book *The Facility Management Handbook* (2nd edition), my friend and colleague Dave Cotts writes extensively and thought provokingly on the subject of leadership in FM. Among the significant points he makes, and the one I find particularly poignant, is the fact that most individuals who are in FM due to their backgrounds, education, and nature do not easily fit the "profile" for effective leadership. I think this is an important "take-away" from his writings because it underscores the need to develop competent organization diagnosticians.

For those of you who are actual facility *managers*, I urge you to do a bit of self-analysis to determine what your leadership strengths and challenges are and how you will go about improving yourself. To be perfectly blunt, facility managers cannot ignore the mandate to provide effective leadership if they want to create an effective organization. If you concur with this perspective, it also means that you have agreed, at least in part, with the leadership theory I mentioned in the last section. This theory argues for leaders to *develop* skills and abilities, rather than just being born with them. In order to be effective, facility managers should adopt this approach and broaden their view of management.

It also appears that facility managers should review the ways in which they influence their staff to achieve the organization's goals. It is not enough to manage an FM organization; you also must be able to lead it. Simply stated, this means you must understand how critical it is for your followers to share in your vision for the organization and your passion for its mission, as well as embrace the service strategies required to obtain your organization's objectives. The ultimate FM leader needs to create this framework for his staff.

So much has been written about the mechanisms used to assess individual leadership styles and traits that we could spend the rest of the book on this subject alone, and I'm not certain I could do justice to all the nuances of leadership style analysis. What makes sense here is to talk about one of the more common assessment tools you need to know something about. Our discussion may pique your interest to explore the subject further on your own.

One of the foremost approaches to leadership style assessment is the Managerial Grid developed by Robert Blake and Jane Mouton, who we know from our earlier discussion are considered to be the originators of the term *organization development*. In the Managerial Grid, five different types of leadership center on a leader's concern for production (task orientation) and people (interpersonal relationships) that are situated in four quadrants used to determine leadership proclivities. The leadership styles associated with the grid include:

- ❏ *Impoverished leadership,* in which the emphasis on exertion of minimum effort to get required work done is appropriate to sustain membership in the organization.

- ❏ *Country club leadership,* in which the emphasis is on thoughtful attention to the needs of people for satisfying relationships that leads to an organization with a comfortable, friendly atmosphere.

- ❏ *Task leadership,* in which efficiency in operations results from arranging conditions of work in such a way that human elements interfere to a minimum degree.

- ❏ *Middle-of-the-road leadership,* in which adequate organizational performance is possible through balancing the necessity to get work out while maintaining morale of people at a satisfactory level.

- ❏ *Team leadership,* in which work accomplished through committed people and a sense of interdependence through a "common stake" in the organization's purpose leads to relationships of trust and respect.[25]

Those who support and use the Managerial Grid model tend to believe that, in order to be successful, a manager should identify a leadership style and adopt it consistently.

At the other end of the spectrum are OD experts who take issue with the "one-style-fits-all" approach to leadership. The analogy I use with my students is to think about leadership styles in the same way women's clothing designers and manufacturers think. Through their extensive market research, clothing designers and manufacturers know most women do not have the good fortune to be the "perfect" size. Because of this discrepancy in size, they often have trouble buying the same size for both the top and bottom parts of an outfit. Again, through market research, clothing designers learned that most women want to be able to mix and match both parts. To meet customer needs, designers and manufacturers invented separates, or coordinates, so women can tailor outfits to suit their individual requirements. Selecting a leadership style is pretty much the same thing.

Facility managers need to be wary of trying to force fit a leadership style that isn't suited for them, the situation, or the group. In the FM business environment, we should "try on" different approaches, see how they work for us personally and for our organizations, and determine when and where these approaches are most appropriate. Although leaders need to be consistent so their followers know what to expect, it also is important for them to determine when a particular leadership style is most effective. Determining which approach to use within FM departments is dependent on certain variables such as the level of maturity of the staff, how well they are performing under the current leadership, and how well they are achieving the results established for the organization. A facility manager must have the desire to become the type of leader who has the ability to diagnose his own leadership dynamic, as well as the ability to piece together the puzzle of applying the appropriate leadership style to a given situation.

If you are wondering where to start in assessing your personal leadership characteristics before you become immersed in more leadership theories, consider how you would evaluate yourself against the following statements. If you can answer yes to all of these statements, you already have pretty well-developed leadership capabilities.

- ❐ I make a habit of assessing the enterprise vision and mission and communicate changes to my staff.

- ❐ I regularly communicate my vision for our FM department to my staff.

- ❐ Our entire FM department has developed organization values statements.

- ❐ Our entire FM staff is involved in strategic planning for the department.

- ❐ I regularly make time to listen to my staff and value their input.

❏ I am open to making changes within the department.

❏ I am considered by my staff to be available and accessible.

❏ I encourage my staff to come forward with their suggestions and recommendations for improving our service delivery.

❏ I provide general guidance to my work groups with respect to goals and objectives and allow them to determine the best methods for accomplishing them.

❏ I convey to my work groups and teams what is expected from them.

❏ I provide feedback to my staff on their performance on a regular basis.

❏ I provide incentives both to individuals and peer groups to be creative and innovative.

❏ I have delegated decision making to individuals at all levels within the department.

❏ I encourage all my staff to be proactive in representing the department as marketers.

❏ I regularly promote my department to all levels within the company.

❏ I inspire my staff to be entrepreneurial in their thinking, particularly with respect to thinking outside the box.

Create an Organizational Climate for Leadership

Another element of leadership for facility managers is that of creating an organizational climate to foster leadership development among staff. This leadership element means we have to create a culture within the FM organization to promote the emergence of potential leaders both formally and informally. We explore the subject of culture extensively in Chapter 4. Too often I see facility managers who are reluctant to create an organizational environment in which risk-taking, delegation of decision-making authority, creativity and innovation in service delivery, and strategic thinking outside the box are held in high esteem. Usually this is an indication of insecurity on the part of the facility manager who is afraid this type of organization will diminish the facility manager's role. When this occurs, facility managers are trapped in the managerial mode rather than stepping out into a leadership role. A strong leader recognizes that having quick, bright, and smart followers will only enhance the leader's ability to achieve goals and, ultimately, enhance the leader's stature in the eyes of others who will judge the leader's effectiveness.

We also must consider that the FM department, which really means the staff, has a style and set of expectations about the organization's behavior that develop over time and through tradition. The "face" of the FM department or the corporate image becomes institutionalized over time through the infusion of values, customs, and norms. The FM leader is the one who has tremendous impact on how the organization is perceived both internally and externally. To illustrate the point, think of how intertwined a leader such as Jack Welch has been to General Electric (GE). Although Welch is retired, his presence will continue to be felt throughout every facet of the enterprise. For many OD experts, Jack Welch is the epitome of leadership—respected both by colleagues and competitors outside the company and by his followers within GE.

Explore the Potential for Staff Leadership and Create Staff Leadership Opportunities

If you remember our discussion about the superleader theory earlier in this chapter, you will recall that the overarching attribute of the superleader is the ability to assist followers (staff) to identify, employ, and utilize their abilities. In other words, to be a superleader we must be able to diagnose the potential leadership talent within our organization and cultivate it by providing opportunities for leadership capabilities to surface and develop. Facility managers in particular must guide and motivate employees to reach their full potential, knowing that some staff will rise to the ranks of leadership if given the opportunity. Our next two chapters outline methodologies to achieve superleader status with individuals and groups. This aspect of leadership is a more contemporary, proactive version of Robert Tannenbaum's team-building concept described earlier.

In our work environment, the more traditional approach to team building, which favors development of staff to function within given parameters of an organization, gives way to a transformational approach to staff development. This approach highlights the ability of leaders to energize followers or subordinates so they understand the need for constant organization revitalization. Team building in a progressive business environment highlights the ability of leaders to inspire their workers to regenerate the organization on a continuous basis. In FM terms, facility managers have to engender in their staff the desire for continuous improvement, serving not only the individual but also the department as a whole.

Why Is OD Important to the Practice of FM?

We have learned a lot about managing facilities over the past 20 years and our industry has been generous with publications, textbooks, educational courses, workshops, and seminars on almost every facet of FM except OD. As stated in the Preface, with the exception of *The Facility Management Handbook* written by Dave Cotts and the IFMA Foundation Report, it was difficult to find any books or practitioner training manuals on how to organize, structure, staff, and maintain a facilities organization.

We know that all organizations are comprised of *people*, which means that by their very nature they are fluid and dynamic entities. Particularly in the turbulent business environment described by French and his colleagues, organizations are in a perpetual state of movement as they respond to the addition or deletion of missions and functions, market and corporate-driven mandates for reorganization and downsizing, outsourcing initiatives, and the basic ebb and flow of personnel and personalities who enter and leave the organization.

FM departments are no exception. Even with sophisticated technological tools, such as work order and performance management, and automated building systems designed to make service delivery faster and more cost-effective, the vast majority of services are provided by *people*, either in the facility department or through external service providers. Individuals who currently are in or have a desire to be in leadership positions within facility departments must have finely tuned skills in order to stimulate others to accomplish the goals and objectives established for them.

This is how OD comes into play for facility managers. Understanding the dynamics of OD arms the facility manager with robust tools to perform critical FM functions such as structuring, staffing, leading, managing, and maintaining an FM department. OD provides the tools a facility manager needs to be able to anticipate change in the organization, plan for the dynamics accompanying that change, and act accordingly. There is a catch, however. Unlike many of our more technical FM skills, OD does not consist of a 10-step program that will work in every situation. Unfortunately, there is no magic formula associated with OD to guarantee an effective, successful facilities department, but there are some specific skills to guide you in making the right decisions.

The beauty of OD skills and the reason they are so relevant to the FM environment is they give you the capability to know when and how to apply the right techniques based on your knowledge of people and what makes them tick within different organization settings and corporate environments. Understanding OD principles alone is not sufficient; facility managers have to know how and when to apply them.

This book provides a context for practicing OD as well as concrete OD diagnostic skills to assess the impact of corporate culture and appropriate leadership style on an FM department, motivate individuals and use teams, lead strategic planning efforts, and select the most appropriate organization structure to deliver customer-oriented services. If you can do all of the things we discuss here and in the next six chapters, you will have the right DNA for a winning FM department.

■DNA Link: Leadership

Company: Dow Corning Corporation (manufacturing research)

Background

Dow Corning Corporation (DC) has traditionally been a technology-driven company. As a 50:50 joint venture of The Dow Chemical Company and Corning Incorporated, it was formed (with a handshake) in 1943 to make unique products called silicones for military aircraft. Almost disappearing after World War II, the company rebounded through an outpouring of products from its laboratories. Silicone materials rapidly made contributions to markets such as construction, transportation, medical, aerospace, electrical, electronic, and personal care. DC is approaching $3 billion in sales, with 60 percent outside North America. About 7 percent of sales are invested annually in science and technology (S&T), and its 1,300 technical people are in 13 sites around the world. The genesis of these multiple lab locations occurred in 1947 with DC's first facilities in Midland, Michigan.

The early labs were typical of the industry in those days: benches, fume hoods, glassware, storage shelves, and instruments. Safety practices were emerging, as lab activities led to "interesting" situations (fires, explosions, spills, and gas releases). There were pilot plants with larger equipment for scale-up and early production. A senior leader supervised each lab area, but there was little coordination regarding facility needs and solutions. Administrators oversaw purchasing, safety, repairs, and clerical staffs. Periodically, teams were formed to design new facilities throughout the 1950s and 1960s. Projects were managed by DC's engineers for the burgeoning S&T population. In 1975, the first architect-designed lab building at a new corporate site was completed. Support was modest but relatively satisfactory for the times.

Their Story

In 1985, Doug Aldrich, a 20-year veteran with chemical engineering and management experience, was assigned to evaluate a $6 million lab renovation project. Professing no background and not knowing the difference between net and gross spaces, he accepted. Reporting 6 months later, he recommended killing the project and building a new facility instead. Challenged to put his money where his mouth was, he accepted the new assignment. At the time, DC's space planning and real estate were managed centrally with 99 percent emphasis on offices since most of the facilities built or leased were this type. Their skills were in interior design, real estate, office moves, and administrative operations. Manufacturing plants managed their chemical processes, offices, and quality assurance labs. Facility management in DC was highly sophisticated regarding its offices, but labs were just there, waiting for an FM revolution.

Aldrich reported into the S&T function from the outset as requested by the S&T vice president. While most facility managers were part of engineering or maintenance throughout the 1980s, in the following decade many were shifted to human resources (HR) and finance. The innovation was to have Aldrich deliver a project with the expectation that he would then operate it. (This was traditional for project managers of new chemical plants.) Thus, the introduction of FM into DC's labs was primarily through the learning curve of one individual. Learning during the design, engineering, and construction phases was facilitated through networking (International Facility Management Association's R&D Council), seminars, and personal contacts. These exchanges supported the development of a skill and knowledge base in DC about what laboratory FM could be when its labs "grew up."

During the period 1985–1990, DC's concepts about lab operation, standardization, tactical planning, building missions, and FM philosophy evolved. Not only was the new lab an experimental opportunity, but successes could be applied to other facilities. Completion of the project brought an operational phase, with lessons learned that were rich but sobering. Optimizing the new infrastructure molded, and was molded by, the lab work of 200 people (growing to 300), with changing DC needs and culture. At the same time, other domestic labs were rolled into the fold for consistent budgeting, operations, and philosophies. The complementary lab concept—using space capabilities in multiple buildings rather than duplicating them within buildings—was a tactical asset and a strategic opportunity. This learning-by-doing evolution continued during 1990–1994.

The next innovative step occurred when Aldrich reviewed the status, mission, and outlook of DC's international labs. In Europe, his report integrated lab capabilities as a response to country business plans, which resulted in two new lab facilities, three closed labs, and one renovation. The same approach was used to modify an initial Brazilian lab addition into a stand-alone strategic application facility for South America. A lab was completed in Germany, as were modest expansions in the United States. New facilities brought together multifunctional teams, and FM staffing was integrated into each of the manufacturing sites where the labs were located. Science and technology managers and DC site staffs combined to implement new philosophies, but with built-in needs for business relevance and country culture. This synergy with supply chains and commercial teams promoted collaboration in the 1990s.

From this step change forward, the global evolution started, as Aldrich's planning and implementation processes were put into further practice with new facilities in Belgium, the United States, and China. A formal strategic planning process, implemented with hard copy and electronic tools, focused on living documentation readily accessible to space planning, engineering, telecommunications, and maintenance teams. The supply-demand model meshed building capabilities and missions with business goals to develop a 10-year global facility plan that was reviewed semiannually by executives. Techniques for prototyping lab and workplace environments, team/collaboration spaces, and new design layouts pushed the envelope of how well-integrated lab facilities could support a spectrum of work processes. Evaluation of FM efficiencies versus user effectiveness began identifying how labs could be leveraged so their internal clients could better meet external customer needs.

Organization

The functional alignment of the mid-1980s in DC was an organization of VPs for S&T, marketing, manufacturing, and administration, whose people supported the businesses that existed as profit centers. A decade later, 50 percent of the functional people reported to the businesses, while the rest were still "solid-line" to the function. This trend continued until only technology platforms and Aldrich reported to S&T. While there was a comfort factor with owning the labs, it was the integration of the physical workplace with the lab people and equipment that needed to be seamless, aligned, and proactive. (Real estate and space planning continued in administration, and plant facilities remained in the supply chain asset base.) The labs' strategic planning, execution, and operation were deemed to be critical in supporting businesses that globally spanned industries and technologies. The lab costs (15 percent of the global S&T budget) were still evaluated and traded off with the annual budgets that directly supported lab people.

An important part of the organizational alignment of DC's labs with S&T has been the continuity, focus, and integration of lab facilities with their technical clients. Despite 15 years of management and VP changes, there has been FM constancy. This constancy has built a knowledge base, consistency in philosophies and practices (with continuous improvements), and executive confidence. The focus—while initially on design, engineering, and operation of labs and technical support spaces—has migrated into other areas: offices, conference rooms, and soft spaces. These other areas include people planning, technical programs, and budget targets, as S&T responded to business direction. Even with these changes, lab buildings have been in a neutral corner charged to meet *all* needs.

Service Providers

The reduction of FM staffing has been a key aspect of these organizational shifts. Fewer resources deliver more services by brokering service providers internally and externally. Facilitation, influence, and clout rather than head count earmark facility managers in the new provider thinking.

Three phases defined the growth of the service provider. Services were decided on, approved, charged, and changed for lab users and their facilities. In the first 5 to 8 years, everything was ordered and paid for by individual cost centers. This strategy evolved so that more goods and services were centrally provided or coordinated by facility managers as part of streamlining to stimulate lab work and eliminate red tape. In the following years, FM took a stronger role by setting standards, determining metrics, making sourcing decisions, and piloting other improvements. The third phase introduced an FM entrepreneurial philosophy that said, "Anyone who can provide what buildings or lab people need, with speed, cost, and quality (not two out of three!), may get our business!" This philosophy resulted in the elimination of one internal engineering group because of time and cost inefficiencies. FM independence to deliver lab services by internal, external, and combination providers was a major productivity gain.

A governing rule is to keep core competencies inside, routine services outside, and to evaluate other FM activities to determine whether or not they should be outsourced. Mail, copying, food service, custodial service, and groundskeeping are generally nonbusiness critical (routine), so are good candidates for outsourcing. Supplies, gases, lab coats, materials handling, packaging/assembly, safety, and other support activities are also good outsourcing possibilities. Depending on the size, scope, skills, speed, and cost of the activity, some other services that might be outsourced to one or some combination of providers include:

Design/engineering
Security

Maintenance

Lab automation

Operations of building

Telecommunications

Utilities

Environmental Health and Safety (EHS)

Test or analytical needs

Consider both cost and level of service required before eliminating or outsourcing services. And think hard before outsourcing any core competency.

There are 4 core competencies that are invaluable for labs to acquire and nurture:

1. *Process Management*—Strategic planning and alignment of lab facilities (goods/services and infrastructure) must exist to support business goals and fulfill their strategic intent. This includes balancing facility supply with user demands in many dimensions, understanding new workplace concepts and behaviors, and defining solutions that keep the lab buildings ahead of the curve.

2. *Capabilities*—The ability to decide as well as perform or manage design/engineering/construction projects at a variety of scope levels. This ability includes proficient use of tools to access information and people to ensure decision making has the optimum balance of the triangular balancing of cost, timing, and function (quality).

3. *Lab Knowledge and Experience*—Understanding of these workplaces in their totality: integration, user leverage, global consistency, local differences, real and virtual, technological changes, and customer satisfaction.

4. *Linkages*—Focus on both internal and external connections through networking and facilitation. Linkages place lab facility managers in the communications and decision-making crossroads of their organizations.

Best Practices

There are 4 current DC practices that Aldrich believes will be proved over time:

1. *Standardization (different from "standards")*—Labs are organic entities that must be molded to corporate and user demands. Working within philosophies, cultures, physical/ regulatory environments, and budgets, the rigid standards have given way to "Let me understand the business needs and user wants and I'll figure out how to do it!" There needs to be some consistency for global labs; the framework of standardization is an excellent lubricant to make diverse activities and complex spaces fit together successfully.

2. *Experimentation*—The willingness to prototype different designs for the workplace keeps facility managers on the leading edge for what users might require in the near or far future. The theory versus practice of radical concepts or implementation of new ideas can be smoother and more successful. Even occasional failures give information that is useful to creating an environment of change, particularly vital in the arenas of innovation and technology. Being known as a learning organization isn't a bad reputation for an FM team.

3. *Collaboration*—Spending time internally with groups (users, providers, stakeholders, associates, and uninvolved parties) means constantly having the net out for what's going on and what's coming in. Dialogue helps the "Dr. No" approach shift to "Let's make a deal!" and brings many second invitations for involvement. The external connections keep you abreast of megatrends that will impact your company or profession. They also stimulate new ideas, practices, and techniques that solve problems or offer opportunities.

4. *Leadership*—The best "supportship" comes from the best leadership. Leading an FM organization is not the same as managing it; there are fewer leaders than able managers.

Cultivating the former is how your business will find you to be a critical, rather than disposable, asset. Understanding business plans and interpreting their physical implications, preparing options within appropriate frameworks, and delivering the resource questions and answers are signs of strong leadership.

The next FM revolution may be governance, the oversight of facilities that are truly mission-critical to ensure they have strategic reliability. In 2001, DC established a new organization comprised of two units to support its key businesses: a service enterprise unit (to sell skills and services internally and externally) and a governance unit (key parts of HR, finance, legal, communications, and laboratory FM). The clear signal is that governance FM transcends service provision, operations, and planning with a long-term view of hard (cost, capital, and timing) and soft (culture, behaviors, change management) performance elements and impact. This newly emerging revolution will need to be sampled and tested before being absorbed, but it portends an FM role that is breaking new ground.

Learning Points

❏ Leadership role to integrate FM with technical customer needs

❏ Leadership role in setting standards, determining metrics, making sourcing decisions, and piloting improvements

❏ Leadership role to balance cost, timing, and quality

❏ Organizational leadership role as player in corporate governance

---

About the Author

Doug Aldrich, CFM, is the global manager for Dow Corning's laboratories and served as chairman of the International Facility Management Association (IFMA) in 1999–2000. His 20-year career in chemical engineering was superseded by 15 years in FM. His magazine covers, articles, and talks have given him visibility and notoriety about why labs are mission-critical and how strategic facility managers can make a difference. He has both a bachelor's and master of science degrees in chemical engineering from South Dakota School of Mines and Technology and received an honorary doctorate in human letters from his alma mater.

Endnotes

1. Wendell L. French, Cecil H. Bell, Jr., and Robert A. Zawacki, *Organization Development and Transformation: Managing Effective Change*, 5th ed. (Boston: Irwin McGraw-Hill, 2000), p. vii.
2. Ibid., p. 3.
3. Ibid., p. viii.
4. F. W. Taylor, *The Principles of Scientific Management* (New York: Harper and Brothers, 1911), pp. 36–37.
5. Judith R. Gordon, *Organizational Behavior: A Diagnostic Approach*, 6th ed. (Englewood Cliffs, NJ: Prentice Hall, 1999), p. 16.
6. Henry Mintzberg, *The Nature of Managerial Work* (New York: Harper & Row, 1973), p. 9.
7. French, Bell, and Zawacki, op. cit., p. 17.
8. Ibid., p. 32.
9. Ibid., p. 28.
10. Ibid., p. 28.
11. Ibid., p. 22.
12. Douglas McGregor, *The Human Side of Enterprise* (New York: McGraw-Hill, 1960), pp. v–vii.
13. Ibid., pp. 33–34.
14. Ibid., pp. 47–48.
15. Ibid., p. 48.
16. French, Bell, and Zawacki, op. cit., p. 28.
17. Ibid., p. 36.
18. John P. Kotter, "What Leaders Really Do," in *Harvard Busi-*

     ness Review on Leadership (Boston: Harvard Business School Press, 1998), p. 39.

19. Madelyn Burley-Allen, *Managing Assertively: How To Improve Your People Skills* (New York: John Wiley & Sons, 1983), p. 5.
20. Kotter, op. cit., p. 40.
21. Paul Hersey and Kenneth H. Blanchard, *Management of Organizational Behavior: Utilizing Human Resources*, 3rd ed. (Englewood Cliffs, NJ: Prentice Hall, 1977), p. 135.
22. Judith R. Gordon, *Organizational Behavior: A Diagnostic Approach*, 5th ed. (Englewood Cliffs, NJ: Prentice Hall, 1996), p. 311.
23. Ibid., p. 332.
24. Ibid., p. 335.
25. Hersey and Blanchard, op. cit., p. 100.

CHAPTER TWO

Understanding and Influencing Individual Behavior in FM Organizations

DNA Link: Individuals

Why Do We Need to Understand Individuals?

John D. Rockefeller once said, "I will pay more for the ability to deal with people than any other ability under the sun."[1] Considering the business acumen of this winning entrepreneur, his statement underscores a deeply held belief that managers with extraordinary human resources skills can make significant contributions to the bottom line and overall success of any company. Rockefeller's quote sums up the value of human resources skills for FM professionals.

We learned in Chapter 1 that without human beings, we wouldn't have organizations. While it is important for all members of FM departments to know what makes human beings tick, it is especially important for those who are in management positions.

Without human resources, you don't even have an FM department. The ability to manage those resources and understand and evaluate how and why individuals within your department behave in a certain way and what you can do to have a positive impact on their behavior gives you an edge on the competition. This chapter concentrates on how individuals think, what motivates them, and how to apply that information within your own FM department.

Two definitions guide this chapter's discussion. First, our working definition of human resources skills:

> Human resources skills consist of understanding and influencing the behavioral patterns of individuals within organizations.[2]

Second, our working definition of organizational behavior:

> Organizational behavior is the actions and attitudes of individuals who support the mission and function of an organization.[3]

Why Focus on Individuals First?

There is an order to the progression of discussion about behavior. In this chapter we concentrate on individual behavior in organizations, and in the next chapter we look at how individuals behave in groups and teams. Individuals and groups exhibit both similarities and differences in behavioral patterns, which is why we need to understand both of them. First you must be able to assess what lies behind your own behavior as an individual before you can gain a broader understanding of other people's behavior. Once you know more about yourself, you can appropriately and effectively influence the behavior of your colleagues.

What Constitutes Behavior?

The work of Paul Hersey and Kenneth H. Blanchard, leading authorities and pioneers in the study of management and organizational behavior, provides us with core information about behavior. Kenneth Blanchard is renowned for his book *The One Minute Manager* that won international acclaim as one of the most widely read management books ever written. Paul Hersey is known for his Situational Leadership Model, which gained prominence when it first appeared in a series of articles in the 1960s. His model is the basis for the theory of situational leadership we talked about in Chapter 1.

The first collaboration between the two was the 1969 book, *Management of Organizational Behavior: Utilizing Human Resources*, which, through five subsequent editions, has become a classic text for managers throughout the world. The book is based on a study of managers within organizations and establishes the fact that managers need to have 3 specific areas of expertise related to the behavior of individuals.[4]

1. *Past Behavior Understanding*—Managers need to have a firm understanding of an individual's past behavior in order to learn what is characteristic of that individual. The manager's focus is on trying to discern what produces a particular behavioral pattern.

2. *Future Behavior Predicting*—After determining what is characteristic behavior for an individual, managers often can predict how that individual will behave in the future.

3. *Directing, Controlling, and Influencing Behavior*—It is not enough for managers to be able to understand past behavior and predict how staff will act in the future; managers must be able to channel behavioral characteristics toward actions that have positive impact on the goals and objectives of an organization. In this way, managers are able to influence the ability of individuals to be more productive within the organization. In essence, this is the skill Rockefeller referred to as the "ability to deal with people."

Some additional principles add meaning to why individuals behave in somewhat predictable ways:

❐ *Behavior* is almost always *goal-oriented*, although often the individual does not have a conscious knowledge of what the specific goal is.

❐ *Goals* typically are *outside* of an individual in that they often can be described as something an individual hopes for, as in a *reward* or *incentive*.

❐ *Rewards* are based on an individual's *need* at a particular time.

❐ *Goal achievement* is attained through an *activity* or series of activities and it is important to understand why an individual engages in one activity versus another.

❐ *Drivers* that impact the behavioral patterns of individuals either consciously or subconsciously are called *motivators*.

To summarize, the behavior of individuals generally is motivated by some desire to attain a goal because achieving that goal is expected to result in the hoped-for reward or incentive. Many behaviorists have spent considerable time trying to understand the power of subconscious motivation in order to answer the basic question, "Why did an individual do that?" Within an FM department, staffs who are able to understand what motivates them and their colleagues, and managers, in particular, who figure out what motivates individuals and groups become human resources professionals skilled with the ability to influence individual outcomes.

What Is the Hierarchy of Needs Theory?

Remember, the behavior of individuals is driven by a particular need at a particular time. An American psychologist and prominent OD figure, Abraham Maslow, pioneered research about needs and developed a theory about how individuals prioritize their satisfaction of those needs. He described his theory, Maslow's Hierarchy of Needs, in his 1954 book *Motivation and Personality*.

Maslow felt there are five specific needs common to all individuals: physiological, safety, social, esteem, and self-actualization.[5] His theory purports a hierarchical sequence to these needs, which starts with the physiological need and ends with the self-actualization need. The well-known graphic portrayal of the Hierarchy of Needs Theory in Figure 2-1 shows physiological needs as the foundation of the hierarchy and self-actualization as the pinnacle.[6] This depiction provides an easy reference for remembering the hierarchical structure.

Figure 2-1. Maslow's Hierarchy of Needs Theory.

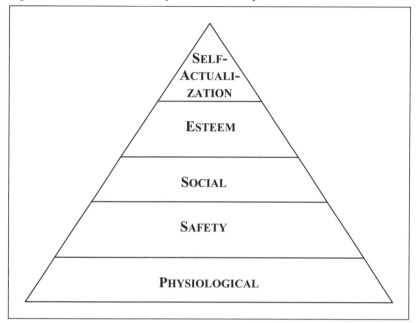

Physiological Needs

Maslow felt physiological needs are the strongest in terms of serving as the foundation of the needs pyramid. These needs must be satisfied or they remain the predominant need. He defined physiological needs as those that are most basic in terms of what every human being needs to sustain himself and his family. Items such as food, water, shelter, and clothing are physiological needs. The classic example of physiological need is being stranded on a desert island without food, water, shelter, or clothing. Stranded individuals have to struggle to meet the basic requirements for survival. These are primal needs, and an individual's energies are dedicated to satisfying these core survival needs until they are fulfilled.

We tend to think of our highly sophisticated societies as having these basic needs met on a consistent basis. In fact, we tend to take basic needs for granted. But when a natural disaster such as a hurricane, typhoon, or earthquake occurs, these basic needs often are stripped away and individuals struggle for their basic survival. Other dramatic examples of having to satisfy physiological needs include wars and terrorist attacks. In the aftermath of these disasters, victims may find themselves without the means to satisfy their primal needs for food, clothing, and shelter.

In FM work environments, The Friday Group sometimes hears physiological needs expressed a different way. FM staffs say they feel their employment is strictly the means to an end—a paycheck. These individuals tell us the only reason they come to work is to make certain their physiological needs can be met. For some of these folks, a paycheck truly might be the motive behind coming to work every day, particularly if their basic physiological needs still are of primary concern. Often, though, there is hidden meaning behind the paycheck statement. If physiological needs are no longer of paramount importance, then saying employment is merely a means to an end may be an excuse. These individuals may have other needs further up on the hierarchical pyramid that are not being satisfied so they fall back on the most basic need as the rationale for coming to work.

Safety Needs

Maslow describes the next category of need as that of safety, or security. This need has been articulated as an individual's basic ability to be free of physical harm or danger, as well as the ability to maintain physiological needs. Individuals need to feel secure in their knowledge that they can preserve themselves both now and in the future.

We have several examples from our FM environment to illustrate the safety-need category. Our first example follows the events of September 11, 2001, when terrorists hijacked planes that crashed into the World Trade Center in New York City and the Pentagon in Washington, D.C. The plane crashes destroyed the World Trade Center towers and a large portion of the Pentagon building, resulting in thousands of deaths. One residual from those attacks is extreme anxiety in and around our workplaces. Throughout the world, employees have a heightened need for safety within the workplace environment, which places tremendous pressure on FM departments to help satisfy that need.

Not only do employees fear for their physical well-being, they also have an intensified concern about the potential for subtle forms of attack such as biological terrorism, which also could penetrate the work environment. Before the events of September 11, 2001, the safety needs of individuals within the workplace largely were focused on potentials for domestic violence and assault in parking lots and garages. After the terrorism attacks, both the threat of bioterrorism and new physical attacks on facilities have given the safety need in the workplace a higher priority on the needs hierarchy.

Starting in the 1990s, the FM environment witnessed a new type of safety need associated with the impact of outsourcing. Employees of FM departments feel that their safety need is threatened as the trend for FM outsourcing and downsizing grows within corporations and the public sector. They are concerned that their job security is being threatened by outsourcing used as a means of reducing the size and cost of FM departments. When wholesale outsourcing was popular in the 1990s, FM staffs became particularly aware of their employment safety need. In recent years, though, FM employees seem to be better educated about the positive outcomes associated with outsourcing, which helps to mitigate the negative aspects. While still skeptical about outsourcing, FM employees are beginning to view it as a potential tool rather than just a threat. The impact of outsourcing on FM departments is discussed further in Chapter 6.

Social Needs

Once individuals feel comfortable that they have satisfied both their physiological and safety needs, they move on to the social, or affiliation, need category. People want and need to belong to groups whether defined as an organization, work group, team, or social/fraternal affiliation. More on how the social need can be met within a work group or team is covered in Chapter 3.

There are many individuals whose only outlet for satisfying their social need is the workplace, which can be disruptive and create problems for colleagues and managers. This situation is because individuals with a heightened sense of social need in the workplace often fail to focus on activities that contribute to organizational goals and objectives. Instead, they spend most of their time engaged in social activities. Some individuals within FM departments spend the majority of their time organizing the sports teams, volunteering to manage the Christmas party, or orchestrating after-work social activities. These individuals may be attempting to fulfill too much of their social need at work. For them, the office serves as the only, or most important, vehicle through which their social needs are met.

Other individuals within FM departments are better able to balance their social needs between work and external activities. These are the people who always support and participate in work-related events but don't let the social aspects of the workplace take precedence over the work. A manager can count on them to direct or organize an event yet feel confident they won't let the event consume all their work time or jeopardize job performance.

Esteem Needs

In the Maslow scheme of needs, recognition and self-esteem are the next factors in the hierarchy. Individuals want more than just belonging; they also want to feel important, have self-esteem, and be able to influence others or be powerful. The esteem factor plays a key role in how individuals behave within the group setting, explored in Chapter 3, Understanding and Influencing Group Behavior in FM Organizations.

Within our FM context, an employee who consistently demonstrates an ability to lead a group and have group members admire, respect, and produce for the individual is a positive manifestation of the esteem need. Conversely, an FM employee who repeatedly has difficulty with customers, acts out in staff meetings, or disrupts a project work group may be seeking attention, but in a way that is destructive to the overall organization.

Self-Actualization

The pinnacle of Maslow's hierarchy is an individual's need to reach full potential. In other words, people want to become what they know in their heart of hearts they have the potential to become. Individuals want to excel. When the other needs are not as dominant or have been satisfied, individuals can focus on self-actualization.

Self-actualization within an FM department takes many forms. Perhaps individuals want to achieve a very senior management position in another company or become a facility manager, vice president of corporate real estate, or other corporate executive in their current company. Maybe self-actualization takes a less visible form of fulfillment such as the desire to be known as having superior customer service skills, the ability to make presentations to large groups of people, or mastery of some technical skill. Often when colleagues and managers know that individuals are striving to satisfy their self-actualization need, they can stimulate them to be their most productive by combining personal self-actualization goals with those of the department. I talk more about the synchronization of these goals later in the chapter.

Is the Needs Hierarchy Always the Same?

FM employees, like those within all organizations, go through different stages in their personal and professional lives and may find they also have differing levels of need at various times. Personal and professional tragedies, fulfillments, and challenges may place an individual at a lower or higher need status in any of the five categories as their situation changes. In reality, most individuals are never truly in one pure state of need. Typically, we never completely satisfy one need before we move on to the next such that we function in an environment in which all our needs are never totally satisfied. Most of us reach a certain level of satisfaction in one category and then move on. We come back from time to time to a lower or higher need depending on our personal and professional situations. The goal for most of us is to be able to satisfy our baseline of needs in each category.

How Do You Apply Maslow's Theory of Needs to FM?

As a staff member in an FM department, familiarity with Maslow's theory helps you understand your own pattern of behavior and the behavior of your colleagues. For facility managers, Maslow's hierarchy arms you with a tool to assess the needs of your staff at any given point in time and evaluate how those needs are manifested in the behavioral patterns affecting your department. Once you determine what compels individuals within your department to behave in certain ways, you can craft a course of action designed either to build on existing behavioral patterns that are having a positive impact on the department or focus on strategies to alter them in order to achieve maximum organizational effectiveness and efficiency.

What Is the Connection Between Management Practices and Individual Need?

Douglas McGregor's theories regarding the ability of workers to be motivated by managers and those of Maslow about satisfying individual needs come together in the research and writing of Chris Argyris. Argyris has been a major contributor to the field of OD for over 50 years and continues to explore new approaches for organization growth and development.

One of Argyris's earliest works from 1957 focuses on the relationship between the individual and the organization.[7] His Immaturity-Maturity Theory states that individuals develop through seven basic stages from infancy to adulthood and often organizations are responsible for preventing individuals from maturing because of the management practices in place. It is his contention that formal organizations, by their design and practice, maintain most individuals in an immature state. He argues that formal organizations, termed "bureaucratic/pyramidal," practice Theory X management that stifles individuals in their development. This type of organization focuses on task specialization that is incompatible with human growth. The environment maintains staff in childlike roles because it is easier for managers to control their performance. Argyris firmly believes these management practices prevent individuals from progressing and reaching their self-actualization goals.

The more enlightened organization, according to Argyris, is the humanistic/democratic one in which individuals increase their own competence and that of collective work groups. These organizations are more effective because individuals are encouraged to reach their fullest potential.

What Is the Motivation-Hygiene Theory?

Maslow's and Argyris's theories are not all you need to know to understand and influence the behavior of individuals within an FM department. While several other behavioral and motivational theories emerged after Maslow and Argyris developed their theories, the final one that I find useful as an FM organization assessment tool is the Motivation-Hygiene Theory. Frederick Herzberg developed this theory from a series of management studies he conducted in the late 1950s.[8] When Herzberg died in 2000, his *New York Times* obituary cited him as "one of the most influential management teachers and consultants of the postwar era. . . ."[9] He has been noted as both an icon and a legend by many postwar management theorists and visionaries, in the same category with Abraham Maslow and Douglas McGregor. He is best known for his study, along with two colleagues, of 200 engineers and accountants to examine why their attitudes about jobs showed a "difference in the primacy of factors contributing to attitudes, depending upon whether the investigator was looking for things the worker *liked* about his job or things he *disliked*."[10]

Herzberg and his colleagues found a fundamental distinction between 2 sets of factors:

1. *Job Content Factors*—The first set of factors concentrate on the actual "doing" of the job, the job content, or the intrinsic aspects of the job. These content factors include such things as achievement, recognition, responsibility, the work itself, and advancement.

2. *Job Context Factors*—The second set of factors involve the "environmental setting" of the job, the surrounding conditions, the job context, or the extrinsic aspects of the job. These extrinsic factors include company policies, working conditions, supervision, interpersonal relations, and wages.[11]

In the "doing" realm, the study team found that some job factors contributed to periods of peak performance and positive attitudes about the work. Herzberg and his team labeled these factors *motivators*. When work condition factors were explored and found to be at a low level, however, individuals had poor attitudes about their work. The researchers further discovered that while high work condition factors had the effect of preventing poor attitudes about jobs, they didn't necessarily contribute to superior job performance or satisfaction with the job. They adopted the medical term *hygiene* to describe these factors. A hygiene factor represents a health hazard that needs to be absent in the environment in order to prevent the onset of disease, rather than the curing of the disease after it has occurred.[12] So, while high marks regarding hygiene factors may not ensure positive job attitudes, they are a necessary component in preventing poor ones.

Most people are curious about the pay factor and wonder if it is a motivating or hygiene factor. Pay occasionally shows up as both a motivating and a hygiene factor so I tend to call it the "crossover factor." Although pay can be found in both categories, Herzberg's research indicates it serves primarily as a hygiene factor but also has been shown to have properties similar to a motivating factor, mostly when it is an accompaniment to recognition for achievement.

Another way to think about the factors identified by Herzberg is that hygiene factors help to *reduce* worker dissatisfaction with a job while motivating factors help to *increase* satisfaction. The graphical representation of these factors in Figure 2-2 helps to understand them.[13]

Is There a Link Among the Various Theories Affecting Motivation?

The foundation for leading thinking on motivation was provided by Abraham Maslow, who first described the various needs of individuals and made the correlation between motivation and need. His work was reinforced by McGregor in his Theory Y for management through which he provided an enlightened approach to the role managers play in ensuring their staff are motivated. Argyris, like Maslow, felt individuals have a progression to their development, and often organizations, by design, inhibit this growth. Finally, Herzberg concluded that certain factors reduce employee dissatisfaction in the workplace, thus limiting their development and helping them at lower levels of need satisfaction, while other factors

Figure 2-2. Motivation and Hygiene Factors.

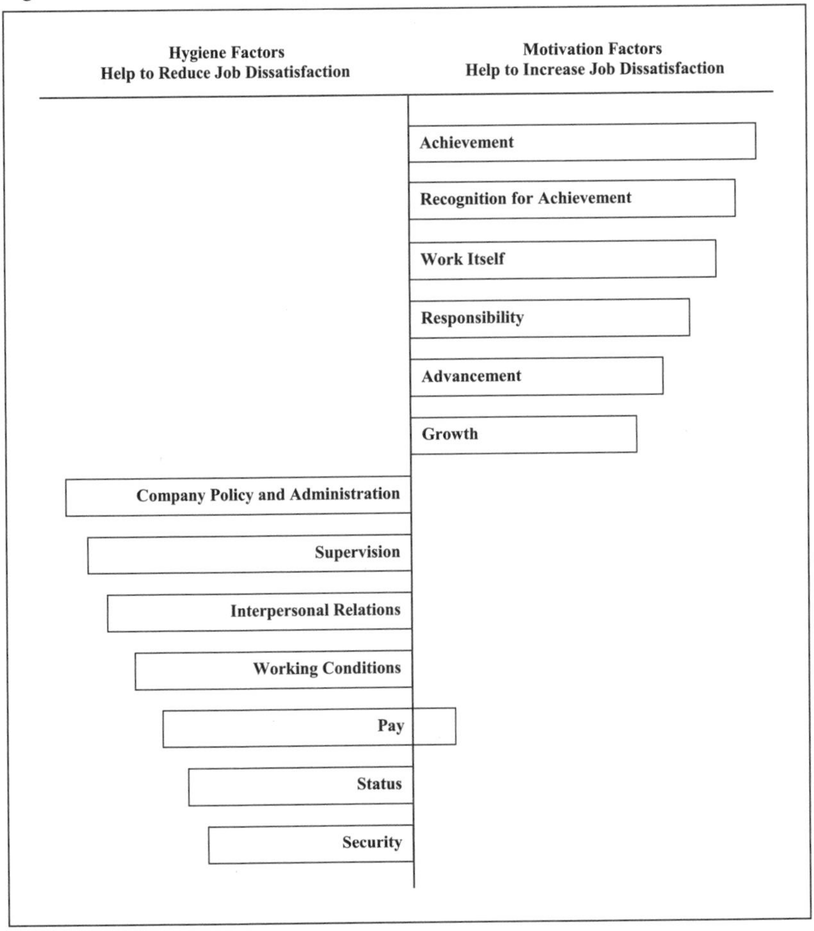

Hygiene Factors Help to Reduce Job Dissatisfaction	Motivation Factors Help to Increase Job Dissatisfaction
	Achievement
	Recognition for Achievement
	Work Itself
	Responsibility
	Advancement
	Growth
Company Policy and Administration	
Supervision	
Interpersonal Relations	
Working Conditions	
Pay	
Status	
Security	

stimulate motivation and satisfaction, allowing staff to attain higher levels of achievement.

Figure 2-3 is a visual reminder of how these motivational theories interrelate.

What Do Individuals Expect from Their Work Environment?

Saul Gellerman, another sage OD theoretician and practitioner, has written, taught, and consulted extensively on motivation and

Figure 2-3. "Need" theories relationships.

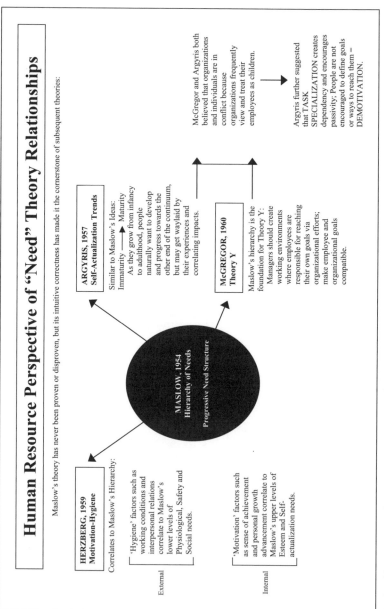

Human Resource Perspective of "Need" Theory Relationships

Maslow's theory has never been proven or disproven, but its intuitive correctness has made it the cornerstone of subsequent theories:

HERZBERG, 1959
Motivation-Hygiene

Correlates to Maslow's Hierarchy:

External
'Hygiene' factors such as working conditions and interpersonal relations correlate to Maslow's lower levels of Physiological, Safety and Social needs.

Internal
'Motivation' factors such as sense of achievement and personal growth advancement correlate to Maslow's upper levels of Esteem and Self-actualization needs.

MASLOW, 1954
Hierarchy of Needs

Progressive Need Structure

ARGYRIS, 1957
Self-Actualization Trends

Similar to Maslow's Ideas:
Immaturity ——▶ Maturity
As they grow from infancy to adulthood, people naturally want to develop and progress towards the other end of the continuum, but may get waylaid by their experiences and correlating impacts.

McGREGOR, 1960
Theory Y

Maslow's hierarchy is the foundation for Theory Y: Managers should create working environments where employees are responsible for reaching their own goals via organizational efforts; make employee and organizational goals compatible.

McGregor and Argyris both believed that organizations and individuals are in conflict because organizations frequently view and treat their employees as children.

Argyris further suggested that TASK SPECIALIZATION creates dependency and encourages passivity; People are not encouraged to define goals or ways to reach them = DEMOTIVATION.

Reprinted by permission of Natalie P. Green, 2002.

productivity within organizations. In one of his earliest books, *Management By Motivation,* written in 1968, he described research funded by the Menninger Foundation conducted at a utility company in the Midwest. The study, often called the "Menninger research," was designed to assess the impact of emotional interaction among employees within a workplace.[14] According to Gellerman, findings from the research provide tremendous insight into the feelings employees have toward each other within an organization and toward the organization itself.

Gellerman describes how the Menninger findings show a deeper understanding of the term *interdependence* within an organization, which is defined as the expectations both the organization and the individuals have of each other.[15] While these expectations are seldom articulated by both parties, they are part of the glue that holds an organization together. Individuals have the tendency to assume the organization has tacitly accepted the responsibility to enable them to fulfill these expectations about unstated aspirations. The unspoken, unwritten agreement assumed by employees is called the *psychological contract.*[16] This psychological contract, rooted in individual expectations about what the organization has agreed to provide, has tremendous impact on the level of commitment an individual, as an employee, makes to that organization.

At the same time, organizations have needs and goals they expect individuals, as employees, to fulfill. When these goals are not the same as or are at odds with those of the individual, the psychological contract is in jeopardy or can even be broken. In other words, when expectations fail to be realized, one or the other party is dissatisfied, and often both the individual and the organization are unhappy.

What Does the Psychological Contract Mean for FM?

The notion of a psychological contract is important to our discussion of behavior and motivation within FM departments. Employees of FM departments and the department expect to receive something from each other that will satisfy certain expectations. Unless there is real communication about these expectations and a more formal agreement about how these expectations will be achieved, both parties could end up unhappy and dissatisfied. The implications associated with the communication process necessary to execute the psychological contract are tremendous for FM managers and staff. A manager not only has to be able to understand what motivates his employees, he also must be able to articulate what expectations he and the company have for them. At the same time, employees need to have a clear picture of what they want out of the work experience in the department and be able to describe it to management.

Within an FM department, if the articulation of these expectations fails to happen, yet both parties assume they are understood, a gap is created. As less and less communication takes place to address these expectations, the gap widens and both parties become increasingly dissatisfied. The role of the facility manager is to make certain this communication takes place. It is the job of the FM manager to identify goals and objectives for the department and communicate them to staff. At the same time, the FM manager must ensure there are formal mechanisms in place within the organization to allow dialogue about organizational and individual goals to take place. One of the most important jobs of a facility manager is making certain the gap gets closed. Figure 2-4 depicts the role of the facility manager.

In Chapter 3, we discuss the implications of the psychological contract on the activities of work groups and teams.

Is There Recent Research on What Motivates People?

The Introduction states that I am sharing OD concepts and theories with you that are timeless—those that have survived application within organizations and are relevant to current work environments. Whereas the theories of Maslow, Herzberg, Argyris, and Gellerman fall into this category, I find it reassuring to know that contemporary research validates their early findings.

When the economy is booming, human resources research and consulting firms and associations conduct studies to determine what motivates employees. They try to find innovative ways for

Figure 2-4. Role of the facility manager.

companies to retain their most valuable staff. During particularly lucrative economic times, companies try every conceivable strategy to attract and retain talent, particularly in the high-tech market. The Friday Group heard about companies offering outrageous signing bonuses, outlandish personal services such as pet-sitting, extensive cafeteria-style benefits packages, extraordinary vacations, and luxurious automobiles. While these measures are necessary during an economy in which potential candidates are in the driver's seat, they do not fall into the time-tested category of hiring and retention motivators that help you on a long-term basis within your FM departments.

What follows are findings from recent studies that have staying power and are relevant within the context of a more typical business environment. These findings affirm what The Friday Group has learned over the past 10 years from conducting focus groups and interviews with FM professionals.

The HayGroup Research—Attrition Linked to Job Satisfaction

When contemporary researchers study the issue of employee motivation, they often find the correlation between attrition and job satisfaction to be the most informative. Over the course of a 4-year period (1996–2000), the HayGroup, a human resources consulting firm, conducted research from surveys of over 1 million employees at more than 330 companies in over 50 countries.[17] They used a research approach similar to that used by *Fortune* magazine when it conducts an annual survey to develop its World's Most

Admired Companies list. To assess the relationship between job satisfaction and attrition, the HayGroup compared committed employees within companies with those who were planning to leave
within 2 years. The HayGroup defined committed employees as
those who were planning on staying in the company more than 2
years.

Their findings showed "satisfaction gaps," or percentage differences, among employees with respect to certain satisfaction factors. For example, 83 percent of committed employees felt satisfied
their knowledge, skills, and abilities (called *KSA* in human resources terms) were being used to the fullest. Only 49 percent of
employees planning on leaving in less than 2 years, however, felt
their KSA were optimized.[18] We spend more time discussing the
relationship between staff, KSA, and effective FM organizations in
Chapter 5.

From the HayGroup research it is interesting to note where
the question of pay falls with respect to job satisfaction. As we
learned from Herzberg, sometimes pay can hover on the border
between being a motivating and a hygiene factor. We also know
that pay ends up being in the hygiene factor column most of the
time. The HayGroup research confirms the latter: Pay ranks next
to last on the satisfaction gap scale, way below use of KSA, opportunities for advancement, and confidence in upper management.

In addition to supporting Herzberg's factors concept, the
HayGroup research findings also support the Maslow Hierarchy of
Need Theory in that the individuals polled cite meaningful work
and the desire to be part of a team as critical to their job satisfaction.

Seven factors were identified by the HayGroup respondents
as contributing to their gaps in satisfaction at work. These factors
are shown in order of the largest satisfaction gap size to the
smallest:[19]

Confidence in the ability of upper management

Company has a clear sense of direction

Opportunity for advancement

Opportunity to learn new skills

Availability to learn and be coached by one's supervisor

Pay

Training

Of all the findings from the HayGroup research, there is one that links most dramatically to our focus in this chapter. Their work revealed that if a manager tries to adopt a universal strategy to motivate and retain employees, the manager fails to attain the desired goal: The types of things that motivate individuals in sales, for example, are not necessarily the things that motivate staff in manufacturing. Their study also revealed that salespeople have a high need for self-esteem, while other employees, such as engineers, do not view the need for recognition as a priority need.[20] Understanding what motivates people and having the ability to influence their behavior is situational and personal: There is no single motivation formula that can be adopted for all individuals.

The HayGroup study also identified methods for reducing attrition and noted 7 concepts that can aid in this effort:[21]

1. *Demonstrate organization commitment*—Employees typically hear they are in charge of their own career and the organization isn't going to do much to help them advance or find challenging opportunities. Employees often feel management is not anxious or willing to help them achieve self-actualization. When an organization makes a commitment to employees that demonstrates an interest in their career development, both job satisfaction and the desire to be more productive increase.

2. *Balance efficiency with concern*—An organization needs to nurture good people in order to keep them around. While an organization needs to consider how to maintain a productive workforce in the most economical way, the organization also needs to treat employees with compassion and nurture those it hopes will stay committed to long-term involvement.

3. *Eliminate poor managers*—Too often organizations tolerate managers who have been given adequate opportunity to learn or improve management skills but fail to demonstrate capability to perform.

4. *Follow through on commitments*—While employees must understand an organization's strategic goals and objectives, the behavior of management in terms of rewarding employees for

achieving these goals and objectives must reflect what is stated. Sometimes, there is a disconnect between an organization's strategy and its reward systems; managers tell employees that they want one thing, but the incentives say something very different.

6. *Assess nonmanagerial staff performance*—Organizations also tolerate poor performance by staff and do not take appropriate action, which leads to job dissatisfaction for those who are working productively.

6. *Measure soft skills*—Organizations need to measure the people skills of their staff, not just the technical or financial capabilities.

7. *Train employees for their jobs*—Organizations need to ensure that training is provided to allow staff to meet job expectations.

We talk more about strategies for enhancing job satisfaction later in this chapter.

The Segal Company Research: Work/Life Programs Linked to Motivation

Other human resources research groups, including The Segal Company, have determined that work/life programs are highly valued by employees, rank high on the motivation scale, and can be of low cost to a company when implemented thoughtfully.[22] By work/life programs, we mean those that actively promote a balance between an employee's work and the life of the individual outside the organization. These programs include flexible work arrangements, family care, personal convenience services, paid time off, tuition and financial assistance, wellness, and career counseling. The Segal Company found trending information that showed more organizations are using such programs as part of their rewards management strategy and finding them to be successful motivators.

According to The Segal Company research, these types of programs make employees feel cared about and valued, not only as employees but also as individuals who have a life outside of work. This caring feeling feeds into one's career path and personal development.

Fortune Magazine's "Top 100 Companies to Work For": Valuing Employees Linked to Top Ranking

Since 1996, the human resources firm Hewitt Associates annually conducts research for *Fortune* magazine to identify the best 100 companies to work for in America according to their employees. Despite fluctuations in the U.S. economy over the course of the studies, their findings overwhelmingly point to corporate strategies for maintaining and retaining employees as the reasons for making these companies the best.[23]

The top three characteristics for *Fortune*'s 2000 list of the 100 best companies to work for in America included creating a supportive and inclusive corporate culture (see Chapter 4), providing greater consideration to employees' quality of life (the work/life program concept), and taking steps to engage employees in the business (providing a challenging work atmosphere). The Hewitt research consistently determines that in order for a company to rank as one of the top 100 in the minds of employees, it must recognize and take steps to value the importance of its employees and the contribution the employees make to the success of the company.[24]

Have We Learned Anything Specific About Motivating Individuals in FM Organizations?

The process used by The Friday Group to assess FM departments and provide recommendations for strengthening or reengineering them includes focus groups with staff and managers to determine issues, concerns, and challenges associated with the department's overall health and operational effectiveness.

Over the past 10 years, The Friday Group has asked FM employees what they feel the most critical motivational factors are and what factors provide them with the highest job satisfaction. As you read about these factors, think back to Maslow, Herzberg, Gellerman, and the more recent HayGroup, Segal, and Hewitt studies. You will notice that FM staff findings track with those of past and current research findings. You also will see that many of the FM staff factors follow the self-esteem and self-actualization needs identified by Maslow. For the most part, staffs within FM departments are striving to achieve goals both for the organization and for themselves (synchronizing the psychological contract) while, at the same time, looking for more opportunities to balance the quality of work with life outside the work environment.

Challenging, Meaningful Work, and Acknowledgment of Efforts—FM staffs want meaningful work and managers and supervisors to acknowledge that often within an FM environment, staff fall into what they describe as dead-end jobs. FM staffs consistently tell us that when their work is not rewarding and they feel they have no place to go within the department, they no longer are motivated. Sometimes, they feel that they have mastered their present job and are looking for more challenging opportunities.

Fair and Equitable Dealings—FM staffs want managers to be fair and equitable in dealing with staff. Not one individual over the years has said that he wants preferential treatment; he just wants to be treated fairly and equitably. I often use the example provided by individuals within one FM department who had worked every weekend for 6 months to relocate employees to a new building. After the move was completed, instead of congratulating them on a job well done, their manager said that they could start on another relocation project the following weekend. These individuals said that they didn't feel they were being treated fairly or equitably when compared to others within the department.

Voice in the Decision-Making Process—FM staffs say they want to have a voice in the decision-making process. They want to feel that their opinions count. More than any other type of reward, staffs consistently tell us that recognition for making a contribution to the department's decisions is a motivational factor. Often when we assist an FM department with reorganization, we are asked to interview candidates for positions in the department. When individuals are considering employment in an FM department, they tell us that they evaluate how much they will be involved in the department's decision-making process before they accept the position.

Appropriate Compensation—FM staffs also say they want appropriate compensation for the work they perform. They tell us that it isn't just money alone that is a motivator. Most FM staffs say that they want their FM positions to be respected within the corporate pay structure such that their compensation is commensurate with other professional positions throughout the company.

Flexibility in Working Conditions—Flexibility with respect to work hours is another factor that contributes to employee satisfaction within an FM department. As an example, FM staffs, like those in most companies, want to have more flexible hours and also have a balance between work and life outside the FM environment. FM staffs want flexibility in their working conditions and they want time off as a means of reward for a job well done. Employees say with the technological advances associated with building systems, such as infrastructure systems controls, they can have the ability to monitor and change building systems from remote locations. They often say the need to have FM staffs on-site at all hours of the day can be reduced, which gives them more ability to have flexible hours.

Recorded Success as a Group Within the FM Field—The final motivational factor we hear about from FM staffs involves documentation of the FM department's success. FM staffs indicate they want to know where their FM department stands in relation to other FM departments. They want to know if the FM department has achieved ultimate effectiveness when compared with similar departments. Often FM staffs suggest their departments aren't doing enough benchmarking to determine how they stack up. When benchmarking occurs and a department learns that it is performing at the same or higher level than other FM departments, staffs indicate they are gratified for their hard work. They want theirs to be the best FM department.[25] We learn more about organization benchmarking in Chapter 6.

How Do We Create a Motivational Environment?

Many who write about techniques that supervisors and managers can use to motivate employees emphasize they actually *cannot* motivate individuals; only individuals can motivate themselves. If we investigate this further, we find that the previous statement really refers to the hygiene factor we discussed earlier. Employees can't be motivated because the environment or the atmosphere is not conducive to motivation. The job of the supervisor or manager is to create an environment in which individuals are willing and interested in motivating themselves.

To be knowledgeable about what motivates individuals and influences their behavior, you have to be able to create the appropriate environment to stimulate positive behavior. When employees are not working in an environment that affords the opportunity for meeting some of their needs, the working climate evolves to one of anger, mistrust, and frustration. In this situation, employees take out their anger and frustration on something or someone, usually the organization and the people in it. When I visualize an FM department with an atmosphere to stimulate employee motivation, I consider the conditions presented in an older, 1997 article that appeared in *Supervision* magazine.[26] The article, "Creating a Motivating Environment for Employees," provides an excellent summary of what conditions need to be in place in order for a motivational environment to exist:

High standards and a challenging work environment—The standards individuals are expected to meet need to be high, but not so high that employees can never reach them. If low expectations are established, individuals generally produce to that level and no higher. Employees also want to be challenged, so an organization needs to make certain that there are opportunities to grow employee talents.

Clear objectives—Employees want and need to know exactly what is expected of them. If individuals do not know what the objectives are, they won't know what they are expected to produce. They also need to know the objectives of the total organization and how their particular task fits into the scheme of the overall picture.

Adequate training—Employees become angry and frustrated when they don't know how to do the job. They need both training to do their jobs and the proper tools and resources to complete their tasks. Read more about training in Chapter 7.

Adequate management contact—Employees want to know management is concerned about them, their problems, and their interests (both within and outside of the work environment—the combination work/life aspect). Individuals don't want to feel they are just a number within an organization. When this happens, employees start to feel isolated (social need according to Maslow) within the organization. When a supervisor talks with individuals, he should do more listening than talking.

Adequate feedback—If an individual employee is doing something wrong, he needs to know about it. Conversely, if he is doing something right, he needs to know that too. Often feedback is given only regarding what the individual is doing wrong and not what he is doing right. If employees are always being criticized, they will get the idea it doesn't make any difference what they do; only the things they do wrong will be recognized, so why do anything? The message here is, constructive feedback needs to be given on a regular basis.

Adequate working conditions—The equipment and other tools employees need to do their work must be in good working order and up to contemporary standards. If individuals are constantly working in an environment in which their technologies and systems are outmoded or in need of repair, they may not be able to do their jobs properly.

Rewards that are valued by employees—Since we know monetary rewards are somewhat important, we must ensure that fair and adequate compensation is provided. Beyond monetary rewards, organizations also need to determine if there are other things considered by employees to be appropriate rewards and incentives.

Effective leadership—Above all, as discussed in Chapter 1, leadership is an important contributor to a motivational environment. Employees want, expect, and need effective leadership. Active leadership is part of the responsibility assumed when an individual takes on a management position. Employees want to trust their leaders and know that what the leader tells them is true.

How Do We Create a Motivational Environment for FM Employees?

In FM, if you want to enhance productivity through the behavior of individuals, you must think of motivation as an ongoing process, not a one-time event. Motivation is an iterative process. You must evaluate on a regular basis what it takes to motivate yourself and your colleagues to achieve both personal and organizational goals.

As we learned, the needs of individuals change, just as their personal and professional lives evolve.

To motivate each and every individual within an FM department, everyone within the department, not just a manager, must look for innovative ways to stimulate the environment. The more everyone understands what it takes to keep a team motivated, the greater chance the organization will maintain the right atmosphere to stimulate individual creativity and satisfy personal and organizational needs. Some examples of innovative techniques that work well for FM departments follow.

Empowerment

Empowerment can be the creative force behind motivation. It supplies one of the ingredients described by FM professionals as key to their desire to achieve and perform. Empowerment provides the framework for staff to be influential in the decision-making process of an FM department and be recognized as making a positive contribution to the department's success.

We often hear FM professionals say they want to be empowered without truly understanding what empowerment means. Empowerment involves making independent decisions as well as taking responsibility for their accompanying risks and assuming accountability for outcomes. To give you an example, most FM professionals interviewed by The Friday Group say empowerment means the ability to make independent decisions on the spot when they are interacting with internal customers. They want to be able to resolve unanticipated issues with customers that arise while they are responding to known problems. They feel being able to exercise sound judgment on the spot gives added capability to maximize assistance to customers. To make this happen, FM staff and managers must work together in good faith. It is the responsibility of managers to ensure that individuals understand what empowerment means and to create an environment that encourages its effective implementation. The corresponding FM staff responsibility is to exercise their best judgment and accept accountability for the results of their decisions.

In FM, one empowerment strategy with demonstrated success is treating FM staff like entrepreneurs who behave as if the FM organization were their own business. When individuals within the department become stakeholders who have a vested interest in furthering the department's success, they usually are more highly motivated. If they feel that what they do personally has an impact on the success or failure of the total FM department, they are more likely to invest in achieving success. This entrepreneurial strategy helps to synchronize the psychological contract between the department and the individual, thus increasing opportunities for rewards associated with performance for both the individual and the department.

Chris Argyris, the OD writer we identify with the Immaturity-Maturity Theory and the relationship of formal organizations to personal development discussed earlier in this chapter, also writes about the subject of empowerment. In the May/June 1998 issue of the *Harvard Business Review,* he speaks about empowerment as a concept with tremendous potential to be a successful OD tool to transform organizations, but one that has not had the results it should. Argyris feels managers embrace empowerment in theory, but in practice they follow the command-and-control model he calls the bureaucratic/pyramidal organization. He feels empowerment allows employees to take control of their own destiny, but only when managers understand individuals commit themselves in only two ways: externally and internally.[27]

External commitment means an organization receives exactly what is has "contracted for"—when employees have no control or input into decisions made about the work they are performing. The less power individuals have in an organization, the less committed they are to the organization's goals. They have more difficulty closing the gap between the organization's "psychological contract" and their own. At the opposite end, in keeping with Argyris's humanistic/democratic organization model, is internal commitment, whereby employees are very participatory with respect to decision making. Argyris believes that when individuals have a say in their own destiny—when they are empowered—they are much more committed to its outcome.

Performance Indicators

As the "Creating a Motivating Environment for Employees" article mentions, one successful strategy is to ensure performance indicators have been discussed and negotiated up front with each individual within the FM department. In instances where The Friday Group has guided FM departments to develop performance indicators against which individual performance is measured, overall performance within the organization has increased dramatically.

Flexibility

Flexibility to manage their own time also is being used more and more by FM departments to motivate staff via the work/life balance concept. As an example, technological advances provide more freedom for FM employees by allowing them to monitor and operate building systems from remote locations rather than restricting their work to a particular facility. We also have found that some FM departments are staggering work hours and using flextime, which varies the work schedule and gives employees more concentrated time away from the job.

Another aspect of flexibility is streamlining FM policies and procedures. The more rules and regulations you create within an FM department, the more they will be broken and the more staff will become disappointed and frustrated. Once clear expectations are established and agreed on, an FM department doesn't need as many rules. FM managers and supervisors who are effective motivate their FM staff by an enlightened "This is what I want you to achieve," rather than "This is what I want you to do."

Open Book Management

Perhaps the most dramatic examples of motivational work environments occur in those organizations that practice open book management. Unlike the long forbidden practice of breaking the spine on a book to use it better, open book management stems from the premise that everyone in a company, from the CEO to the mail-clerk, should have access to key information about the company in order to do his job more effectively. This means sharing all available information with each and every FM staff member, not on a need-to-know basis, but as a general rule. The Friday Group has heard from some FM managers that when they practice this philosophy, it is like capturing lightening bugs in a bottle because it sharpens employee investment in the department.

When an FM department doesn't practice open book management, the department suffers in many ways. First, FM staff build up resentment. They don't understand why they can't have access to more information and wonder why it is being withheld. Second, absence of full disclosure often contributes to bad decision making by FM employees; a single piece of information may make the difference in deciding a critical issue. Finally, not knowing what is going on takes some of the fun out of being involved in a business. You remember, individuals have a need for belonging in the workplace, and part of belonging is knowing what is happening within the business and feeling part of the team. If they have sufficient information about how to contribute to the profitability of the FM department, staff members assume a direct stake in helping the group succeed.

Absent open book management, FM staffs merely do as they are told. In an enlightened and informed mode, FM staffs act as true entrepreneurs, figuring out what needs to be done and doing it. We have seen dramatic turnaround in FM departments that have a practice of making certain that every staff member understands the business side of providing FM service.

Monetary Rewards Recognition

The debate over how important monetary rewards are for individuals in terms of motivation and increasing productivity is likely to rage forever. We know that it can be both a motivating and hygiene factor. We also know that when individuals consider their pay to be equitable, most employees need a more significant reason to get up and go to work each day. I once heard someone explain why money isn't always a motivating factor: When money isn't tied to recognition or achievement, it has no lasting "trophy value." In other words, employees will talk longer and feel better about the letter of congratulations accompanying a monetary reward than they will about the amount of money received. Often monetary rewards get absorbed in everyday expenses so they are readily forgotten. Unlike letters to a personnel file or to an employee's family, money doesn't always serve as a lasting reminder of a job well done. That's not to say that monetary rewards aren't welcomed; they often don't have as much staying power.

If you look again at *Fortune* magazine's leading 100 companies to work for and what makes them so esteemed, the answers range from cutting-edge technology, exciting work, the chance to change careers within the same company, advancement, flexible or reduced work hours to work/life benefits. In these companies, NO ONE MENTIONED MONEY. For some respondents participating in *Fortune*'s survey, money as a reward for productivity seemed rather devoid of imagination. Several years ago, The Friday Group had a long conversation with a senior corporate real estate executive who was job hunting as a result of a series of mergers and acquisitions. He had interviewed with a few excellent companies and all were willing to throw money at him, but that wasn't what he wanted. He assumed he would be adequately compensated for his experience and business skills—he wanted prospective companies to tell him how they would provide challenging and meaningful work.

Monetary rewards can be a great stabilizer in terms of making pay equitable by leveling the field. There are some innovative ways in which monetary rewards can have a positive impact on individuals within FM departments:[28]

Bonuses Instead of Merit Increases—More and more we see FM departments giving employee bonuses tied to performance rather than routine salary increases. The concept of bonuses may be one way to counter the "entitlement syndrome" that has employees disassociating monetary rewards from performance in some FM departments. We are finding FM departments awarding bonuses tied to specific performance criteria, which is the incentive for individuals to excel.

Pay for Knowledge—The concept of compensating individuals more for the KSA they provide to an organization is a popular idea. We see FM departments offering incentive dollars for staff who take it upon themselves to obtain additional knowledge or multiple-skills levels in addition to the training and educational opportunities made available. The concept is, the more valuable employees become to the department and their teammates in terms of KSA, the more the department is willing to reward employees. Using pay for knowledge as a motivating influence can be viewed as an investment strategy for both parties by helping to fulfill the psychological contract.

Gain Sharing or Profit Sharing—While still a relatively new concept within the FM world, gain sharing is where workers generate cost savings for an organization and then share in the benefits of those savings. If this approach is sold correctly to senior management within a company, it is a very attractive proposition for FM staff and a huge motivator because staffs are driven to identify and implement new approaches to achieve these savings. When management agrees with this approach, another problem is resolved. Typically, when an FM department generates savings through such means as energy management, outsourcing, consolidation, and reduction of churn, they never see any of the savings because they end up in the corporate coffers. Under this scenario, a portion of any savings (or in some instances, profits) accrue back to the FM department.

Job Security—When pressed, FM professionals still would rather have job security than more dollars. Despite the trend in corporations for less security and loyalty, many FM departments strive to prevent layoffs instead of providing salary increases.

Individual Recognition

Frequently, when successful executives such as Jack Welch, Bill Gates, and Herb Kelleher are asked about their management styles, they invariably talk about their practice of recognizing individuals as one of the most critical and easiest ways to encourage productivity and make a statement about employee value. Research statistics on the reasons employees leave companies support their argument. The statistics indicate that roughly 34 percent of employees who leave an organization feel they aren't personally recognized for their work. Other employees, over 63 percent, also say that a personal thank you for a job well done is the most successful personal motivator of all.[29]

With every approach—from handwritten notes to employee of the month to privileged parking spots to memos in personnel files to letters to an individual's family—individual recognition is a powerful motivating tool. In his latest book, Jack Welch includes many of his handwritten notes as examples of how effective this approach can be. Welch was well known within GE for his notes to everyone in the company, from supply clerks to executive vice presidents. Employees say these framed notes will be sitting on their desks as a reminder of how much Jack Welch valued their personal contribution years after he has gone.

Another way to recognize individuals is to acknowledge their need to have a rewarding life outside the office. We have seen many FM departments honor staff who give countless hours of their valuable "life" time to civic/charitable organizations and their own children's educational institutions. Recognizing these activities is designed to let people within the FM department know their external contributions are valued and that people need to take a break from work to be well rounded, productive, and fulfilled.

What's Next?

Although we haven't exhausted the topic of understanding and influencing individual behavior, we have covered some fairly extensive ground. We learn in Chapter 3 that one of the greatest challenges for any FM department is understanding and influencing the behavior of groups of individuals such as a whole FM department, a work unit, or a team. Armed with valuable knowledge about yourselves and other individuals within FM departments, we can turn our attention to the next DNA link, groups.

■DNA Link: Individuals

Company: Adaptec (computer peripheral technology)

Background

Adaptec provides highly available storage access solutions that reliably move, manage, and protect critical data and digital content. Adaptec's storage solutions are found in high-performance networks, servers, workstations, and desktops from the world's leading manufacturers and are sold through

OEMs and distribution channels to ISPs, enterprises, small to medium-size businesses, and consumers. The organization chart below (Figure Adaptec 1) describes the Facilities department at Adaptec. This department currently reports to the CFO, but has at times reported to senior VPs of Human Resources. It does not matter where Facilities reports; as long as the group is capable of performing its responsibilities and marketing its value, then any management tends to leave it alone. When reporting to Human Resources (HR), there is slightly more emphasis on the workplace environment as a recruiting tool and on the new employee orientation and concierge services. This strategy makes sense because HR is part of the "three-legged stool" that, along with Information Services and Facilities, affects employees on a daily basis. When reporting to Finance, there is more emphasis on budgets and capital spending. As long as Finance understands that Facilities cannot flex all of its spending on a quarterly basis, this is a good home for the large assets holdings and capital spending typical of Facilities departments.

Their Story

Driving Factors

The 3 driving factors in the development of Adaptec's Facilities organization have been the corporate culture, the customer requirements, and the general business environment:

1. *Corporate Culture*—Do what you say you will do, do it right, and do it on time.

2. *Customer Requirements*—Provide the environment needed by each customer based on his individual needs; standards are a guideline and should not get in the way of serving our customers.

3. *Business Environment*—Maintain an entrepreneurial spirit and compete for the most talented knowledgeable workers.

Figure Adaptec 1.

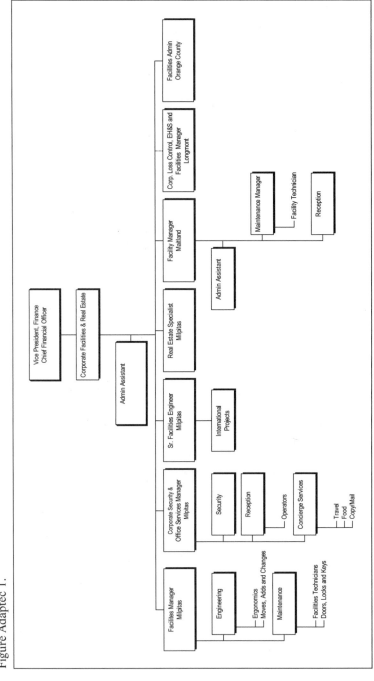

There is a fourth driving factor to consider: *Career Development*. Each individual in Facilities needs to be successful, not only in his role at Adaptec but also in managing his own career.

Core Competence

The core competence of the Adaptec Facilities organization is the ability of the group to identify and respond to the individual needs of each customer. Facilities individuals provide what their customers want—sometimes before customers recognize their own needs.

Service Providers

The Adaptec Facilities group is 92 percent outsourced. Only 8 percent of the full-time workers in the Facilities area carry an Adaptec badge. Each outsourced resource reports to the Adaptec Facilities employee who is responsible for his particular area. For example, the Adaptec HVAC mechanic is responsible for the two full-time and numerous part-time outsourced HVAC mechanics. The outsourced plumber, electrician, and grounds maintenance personnel report to the Adaptec lead mechanic, and the outsourced food, copy, mail, and travel personnel report to the Adaptec Office Services Manager.

Each Adaptec employee has the equivalent of his own business, with outsourced personnel to assist in delivering services. This strategy is further illustrated in the Best Practice described below.

Best Practice

In February 2000, the entire Adaptec Facilities organization attended a Tom Peters presentation at Santa Clara University. Peters painted a picture of the future where all employees were viewed as independent contractors, going from job to job and surviving based on their own abilities and on having something of value to sell. This concept has been the main organization plan for Facilities at Adaptec for the past 5 years. Individuals within the company are encouraged to perform as if they are running their own businesses as outsourced contractors. This allows individuals to become more efficient and valuable to themselves and to the company. According to Tom Peters, this approach is no longer an "option" but a "necessity." It was time for the Facilities organization to convert a management style into a formal training program. In conjunction with the California Leadership Center, a class was created to train people in the Adaptec Facilities department to run their individual areas of responsibility as if they were outsourced businesses. This class is called "Me, Inc." to enforce the concept of individuals becoming the CEO of themselves, but it could have been named "Customer Focus, Inc." since the whole class focused on meeting and exceeding customer expectations.

The program emphasizes that each individual has a responsibility to take charge of his own career and career opportunities. Employees need to become more than excellent taskmasters. They are required not only to do the task but also to take care of the soft requirements of running a business. The goal is to teach each individual in Facilities how to run his own business within the walls of Adaptec. The most important distinctions between doing a job and leading a business are in these 4 areas:

1. *Customer Focus*—When you own a business, your customers are not captive, so you need to be more aware of their needs and recognize that they can choose whether or not to hire you.

2. *Marketing*—Excellent taskmasters often believe their customers know how good the FM people are, but this is not always true. Outstanding facility task accomplishments are frequently invisible; only the errors or defects are obvious. Tell customers how good you are at what you do. Concentrate on both doing the task well and on making sure the customer can acknowledge that the proper result was achieved.

3. *Finance*—If how you spend the company's money directly influenced your income, would you make different decisions? When you can relate your performance to the bottom-line financial performance of the company, management up through the CFO will listen to you.

4. *Career*—The company is not responsible for your training. You are responsible for keeping current with the latest advances in your profession and for convincing the company to help you in that quest.

The director of facilities, then, is the adviser and cheerleader to a conglomerate of companies: a grouping of "Me, Incs." that comprise the Adaptec Facilities organization. All of the individual Adaptec "Me, Incs." have the same main purpose (to provide a workplace where productivity is maximized) and main strategy for accomplishing that purpose (tailoring performance guidelines to meet individual needs). It is how they fit into the conglomeration that changes. Part of the director's job is also to ensure that the individual "Me, Incs." work together in a synergistic fashion.

Adaptec "Me, Inc." Examples

An example of an Adaptec "Me, Inc." is John. John is a mechanic with a specialty in door maintenance and locks and keys. He refers to his business as "John's Lock and Key." His tag line is "Service and Professionalism." That is what he wants to be known for. Every new employee at Adaptec is allowed to do some customization to his cubicle by selecting any combination of peds, laterals, and flippers. John ensures that all locks on the new employee's chosen mix of units can be opened by a single key and then presents that key to the new employee on a key chain that includes the Facilities service line extension and his tag line. John is also responsible for door maintenance and repair. If the workload exceeds his time available, he calls in an outside firm to supplement his work. He does this on his own and isn't required to seek management approval. John is often given the opportunity to be a hero to his customers. When someone locks his or her keys in the car, John treats it as his highest priority. He knows that the person is embarrassed by, and anxious about, the situation. He quickly unlocks the car and then gives them a magnetic key holder and a certificate for a free spare key from a local shop. The key holder, of course, has his tag line on it.

Another "Me, Inc." example is Nita. Nita is responsible primarily for moves, adds, and changes, but she also does new employee orientation and a preliminary ergonomic assessment for new hires. Nita has a marketing giveaway—stress balls with the Facilities service line extension and her tag line on them. Her tag line is "Taking care of the things that matter most to you." Nita has also produced a flyer that introduces herself to the new employee and lets him know how she can support his needs. Making good on her claim, Nita took the time to learn the basics of Feng Shui and how to apply them to the office environment after receiving a number of customer inquiries about how to incorporate its principles into their work areas. She is often asked for consultations and once received a phone message from an eager new employee who stated how exciting it was to have an appointment with Nita to come and "Kung Fu" her cubicle.

A third example of an Adaptec Facilities "Me, Inc." is Chris, responsible for office services and security. She has always done a great job of adding concierge services, and after taking over Security, made an impact by offering customers something they wanted but did not necessarily realize they wanted. Chris did two things. First, she found a way to positively impact the customer's family using security and organized a child safety fair. She offered child CPR classes, child fingerprinting and photographs, and car seat safety inspections. She also purchased car seats before the fair, and if one was found to be defective, it was replaced for free. Chris created 52 lifetime fans of Facilities that day. During the safety inspections, one of the car seats—virtually new and a top-of-the-line model—was deemed defective. It had been in a minor accident, but the restraining straps were stretched and would not have been effective in a second crash. The mother had brought her child in for fingerprinting and only had the car seat inspected as an afterthought. This episode reinforced that an effective way to win loyal fans is to positively impact their families.

Chris's second new customer-focused event was something called "dump your junk." Chris organized a cleanup day and arranged for four large dumpsters to be brought to the Adaptec facility during Memorial Day weekend. All four were filled by 10:00 A.M. on Saturday morning. It took an entire week and twenty full dumpsters to clear the parking lot. Anticipating customer needs and responding before asked to shows real customer focus.

And, finally, "Me, Inc." Dolores, who struggled with the requirement of our Facilities customers that rooms not be kept too hot or too cold. How do you tell a customer that he is not hot when the temperature in the room is 70 degrees? The customer knows he is hot! Her solution to the HVAC question was created through the Facilities home page. Dolores used a link to the HVAC control system to create a live feed to the intranet site. Occupants of the building can click on their work area to see the room temperature, set points, and other parameters. Even engineers visit the Web site before calling Facilities for help. Trouble calls for one building were reduced by 30 percent simply by giving employees access to the HVAC data. Dolores created an innovative solution to a particularly difficult problem—keeping people comfortable in Adaptec facilities.

Some people wonder if there is a downside to training individuals in an organization to be independent—if people might choose to leave and start their own businesses. At Adaptec, this happened only twice in the past 6 years: The maintenance supervisor left to start his own HVAC maintenance company, and the senior Facilities engineer left to start his own outsourced facility and project management company. The HVAC maintenance at Adaptec is under the direction of an Adaptec HVAC mechanic utilizing the prior supervisor's new company, and the large project work is outsourced to the project management company that was founded by the senior Facilities engineer. The majority of Adaptec customers do not realize that these two individuals are no longer employees of the company.

Learning Points

❏ Creation of entrepreneurial environment to motivate individuals

❏ Individuals are the best marketing agents for FM organizations

❏ Empowered individuals make smart decisions with customers

About the Author

Bob Kraiss, CFM, is Corporate Director of Facilities and Real Estate for Adaptec. He has a mechanical engineering degree from Illinois Institute of Technology and an MBA from Loyola University. Bob has championed the City/Industry partnering in Silicon Valley and was instrumental in the creation of Smart Permitting, the use of the Internet to conduct City business. Kraiss has been a leader of the International Facilities Management Association (IFMA) Silicon Valley Chapter since its foundation in 1992.

Endnotes

1. John D. Rockefeller as quoted in Garrett L. Bergen and William V. Haney, *Organizational Relations and Management Action* (New York: McGraw-Hill, 1966), p. 3.
2. The Friday Group.
3. Judith R. Gordon, *Organizational Behavior: A Diagnostic Approach*, 6th ed. (Upper Saddle River, NJ: Prentice Hall, 1999), p. 11.
4. Paul Hersey and Kenneth H. Blanchard, *Management of Organizational Behavior: Utilizing Human Resources*, 5th ed. (Englewood Cliffs, NJ: Prentice Hall, 1988), pp. 10–12.

5. Paul Hersey and Kenneth H. Blanchard, *Management of Organizational Behavior: Utilizing Human Resources*, 3rd ed. (Englewood Cliffs, NJ: Prentice Hall, 1977), pp. 30–45.
6. Ibid., p. 33.
7. Chris Argyris, *Personality and Organization* (New York: Harper & Row, 1957).
8. Frederick Herzberg, *The Managerial Choice: To Be Efficient and to Be Human* (Homewood, IL: Dow Jones-Irwin, 1976), p. 250.
9. Barnaby J. Feder, "Frederick Herzberg: Challenged Thinking on Work and Motivation," *New York Times* (February 1, 2000), p. 8
10. Herzberg, op. cit., p. 250.
11. Ibid., p. 251.
12. Ibid., p. 252.
13. Ibid., p. 71.
14. Saul W. Gellerman, *Management by Motivation* (New York: American Management Association, 1968), p. 49.
15. Ibid., p. 50.
16. Ibid., p. 51.
17. Hay Insight, Dawn Sherman, William Alper, and Alan Wolfson, *The Retention Dilemma: Why Productive Workers Leave—Seven Suggestions for Keeping Them* (Philadelphia: HayGroup, 2001), p. 6. http://www.mediafiles/downloads/Retention%20Dilemma%20Working%20Paper.pdf.
18. Ibid., p. 7.
19. Ibid.
20. Ibid., p. 9.
21. Ibid., pp. 9–16.
22. WorldatWork and The Segal Company, "1999 Survey of Performance-Based Work/Life Programs," http://www.worldatwork.org/research/generic/html/worklife-survey-home.html. (October 26, 2001).
23. "The 2000 100 Best Companies to Work for in America," *Fortune* (January 10, 2000), p. 70.
24. Hewitt Associates, "Hewitt Shows What Separates Fortune's 100 Best Companies from the Rest," January 7, 2000, http://www.was.hewitt.com/hewitt/resource/newsroom/pressrel/2000/01–07–00.htm (November 11; 2001).
25. The Friday Group research, 1991–2001.

26. Thomas K. Capozzoli, "Creating a Motivating Environment for Employees," *Supervision* (April 1997), p. 16.

27. Chris Argyris, "Empowerment: The Emperor's New Clothes" in *Harvard Business Review on Managing People* (Boston: Harvard Business School Press, 1999), pp. 101–120.

28. David I. Levine, Reinventing the Workplace: How Business & Employees Can Both Win (Washington, D.C.: The Brookings Institute, 1995), pp. 48, 53, 54, 55, and 58.

29. Bob Nelson, *1001 Ways to Reward Employees* (New York: Workman Publishing, 1994), pp. 3, 25.

CHAPTER THREE

Understanding and Influencing Group Behavior in FM Organizations

DNA Link: Groups

Why Do We Need to Understand Groups?

Facility managers have to make choices about how certain work is going to be accomplished in their departments. They have to decide whether to distribute work to individuals on their staff or to ask a group of individuals to accomplish work collectively. Making the right decision about the deployment of work involves an under-standing of individual behavior, which we covered in Chapter 2, and the dynamics of individuals in a group setting. The value of groups to the FM department, how individuals in groups relate to one another, what motivates them, and how to influence their be-havior are the essence of our discussion in this chapter.

What Value Do Work Groups Bring to the FM Department?

To begin this chapter, we need a definition of a work group.

> A work group is two or more people in a work set-
> ting with a common goal.[1]

Groups bring substantial benefit to the process of implementing FM work activities and help build FM departments with strong DNA.

1. Groups Bring Different Perspectives—One of the most important aspects of group interaction is that when individuals are together within a group, they bring different perspectives on the same subject. These perspectives allow the group as a whole to have broader consideration of an issue than they would if they were acting independently. Diverse groups in which there is a mix of age, culture, and experience, as an example, have the advantage of being able to more fully explore a particular topic before they reach closure and make a final decision, unlike individuals who make decisions based on their own points of view.

2. Groups Allow Individuals to Step Outside the Box—When individuals work independently on a project or problem, they develop a particular mind-set about how things should be done. They become accustomed to approaching a problem in much the same way they have in previous efforts, especially when a particular approach or methodology worked successfully in past endeavors. The more individuals work in this mode, the more they affirm that this is the only way of doing business. Though this approach isn't always bad, too much of the this-is-the-way-I-have-always-done-it attitude leads to tunnel vision. In the end, organizations become dysfunctional if staffs are unwilling to entertain change as having any potential for positive impact. We know from Chapter 2 that it is the responsibility of facility managers to create an environment favorable to FM staff stimulation. When an effort is being made by a manager to transform a

department, using group process often serves as a vehicle to initiate change.

3. Groups Reduce Territorial and Turf Barriers—The more individuals function alone, the more they are inclined to feel territorial about the work they are performing. When they come together in groups for the first time, there is a tendency to be highly protective of turf, such as customer data, procedural and managerial information, and informal news that may have an impact on the way in which the individuals perform their jobs. A group charged by a manager with solving a problem, working on a project, or developing recommendations has to dismantle the territorial barriers eventually if the group wishes to achieve its charter and succeed. As individuals become more and more familiar with one another and there is evidence to suggest that information sharing and trust are synonymous, they become more cohesive and less protective of their own particular turfs.

4. Groups Strengthen Networks—This benefit of work groups is of particular importance to FM departments in which so much of the activity is dependent on knowledge of external components within the company as well as resources outside the department. When individuals come together to work in a group, they bring their network with them, and once the territorial issues are eliminated, their networking capability grows in proportion to the number of individuals contained within the group.

5. Groups Hold Peers to High Standards—Another positive aspect of groups and group process is that when individuals come together, they have a tendency to develop both formal and informal norms or standards of conduct that each individual must accept as a condition of participation. In some group situations, these norms are written as a code of conduct, while in other groups they are simply understood. In the case of FM departments, the high standards that are adopted by the group serve the total department because customers and others perceive all staff to be performing at the same peak level.

6. Groups Foster Institutional Change—Although groups may not perceive themselves as having any impact on the FM department or the ability to initiate institutional change, their collective strength has tremendous power to influence decision making.

Because a group typically develops a more synergistic approach to an argument for or against a particular issue through the process of consensus-building, the comprehensiveness of their effort affords a greater chance to control or influence a particular outcome than any one staff member operating independently would have.

Are There Any Negative Aspects Associated with Groups?

Of course, there are some downsides to bringing individual staff members together to interact in a group setting. Although these negative aspects are not severe obstacles, they are considerations that should be taken into account when a facility manager is determining whether or not group process is appropriate for a certain activity.

1. In Groups, Individuals Often Get Overlooked—Particularly when a group is first working together, individual expertise within the group may be overlooked because of the dynamics of the individuals involved. Sometimes dissenting opinions about a particular issue that may have validity in the final analysis get pushed aside in the name of group consensus-building. Unless individuals are able to voice their opinions and make convincing arguments, important points may be overlooked as groupthink prevails. *Groupthink* is the phenomenon that occurs when members of a decision-making group avoid the evaluation of alternatives presented by others just so they can preserve the sense of group unity and consensus.[2] In other words, consensus becomes the overarching goal at the expense of individual opinion and input.

2. In Groups, Decision-Making Time Frames Often Are Prolonged—When individuals are first getting used to working together in a group environment, the tendency is to take a longer time period to reach a conclusion or final decision. Often this occurs when the group is focusing so hard on developing a consensus within the group, they prolong their deliberations until

they have agreed. This process typically takes longer than an individual working independently.

When Is a Group Appropriate?

The purpose of this chapter is to give facility managers the insight into when groups and work group process should prevail over individual assignments. Groups are not appropriate for every situation and should not serve as a substitute for individual responsibility and accountability with respect to performance. Although there are no concrete rules for determining when to use a group versus an individual assignment, there are 4 guidelines that are applicable to FM departments.

1. Consider the nature of the assignment—Some FM situations lend themselves naturally to individual work, whereas others make sense for group interaction. To use a simple illustration: If a customer has a problem with a light in an office, facility managers probably wouldn't ask a group to study the problem and make a report; they would have someone go to the office to try and fix the problem. If, however, a manager wanted to know what best practices were in place in new facilities with respect to types of lighting, the manager might task a group with this assignment; the group would sort out how to collect and analyze the information and present it to their manager. The group might consider conducting research, talking with lighting experts, visiting state-of-the-art buildings, and a host of other activities that would be divided up among the group members who would then come together and make their recommendations. Discrete tasks, in which there are specific guidelines, standards, or policies, lend themselves more readily to individual assignments. When managers are looking for a compilation of opinion and diverse expertise, they probably would use group process for this effort.

2. Maturity of the organization—When an FM department consists of highly sophisticated, mature thinkers and doers, using group process affords the best results. Mature staffs with a high degree of experience and expertise are more likely to be able to

manage a problem in a group environment without assistance from the facility manager. Less mature organizations work best when assignments are handled individually, because individuals feel more comfortable coming to the manager for advice and guidance when they run into a problem. Staffs who are less experienced will flounder in a group environment but will not want to demonstrate their inability to function as a group by going to the facility manager for assistance.

3. Culture of the FM department—Although a thorough discussion of culture doesn't take place until Chapter 4, it is important to point out its significance here in relation to the use of groups. If facility managers have provided leadership to their departments and developed a culture in which entire staffs understand, accept, and participate in the development of norms, standards, values, and other organizational guidance, then they have created an organization culture that supports teams as problem-solving entities. In any other type of organization culture, the team process struggles because there are no agreed-upon ground rules for conduct and decision making.

4. Impact of outcome—A savvy facility manager understands that if the end result of an assignment is implementation across the FM department, the more the FM staffs have participated in the development of the processes, procedures, and guidelines, the more likely they will be accepted and adopted. Because most work groups strive for consensus-building as their decision-making process, having them participate in the front end of an effort that ultimately affects the entire FM department provides a distinct advantage toward achieving this goal. Using a work group as an instrument for consensus-building early is an insurance policy for the department's commitment to the effort.

What Is the Difference Between Work Groups and Work Teams?

There is a subtle, yet distinctive, difference between groups and teams within FM departments and one that is important for facility managers in particular to understand if they are to use the two wisely. Work groups do not become teams automatically and may take on a number of different forms before they become known as teams. The various forms of work groups include:

Committee—a work group used to investigate, advise, and report on findings

Task force—a work group used for the purpose of solving major problems on an immediate basis

Process improvement—a work group used to qualify a process, improve its quality, decrease waste, or improve productivity

Department improvement—a work group created as a focus and means for employees to contribute to an ongoing activity directed at increasing the quality and productivity of a department[3]

When a work group emphasizes collaboration to achieve its stated goal, then it becomes a team. Teams attack and resolve problems, creatively explore possibilities and alternatives, and execute well-developed plans.[4] Teams usually work hard to avoid the groupthink syndrome because the group process they have learned encourages idea and input sharing from all parties. Teams learn there is no such thing as a bad idea put forth by a team member and develop ways to ensure all team members have a voice in decision making. We focus more on group process later in the chapter.

Teams are work groups that develop their own personalities. They create norms, customs, standards, and traditions for their interactive process. These traits serve to distinguish one team from another, and as the traits mature, team behavior becomes more and more cohesive. Usually, the patterns of behavior become so finely tuned that a particular team develops its own image and style, which are recognized by others outside the group.

Teams also may be created for the same reasons that committees, task forces, and process improvement and department improvement work groups are established except that they become much more deeply involved in collaborative group process. Some teams come together for a single purpose, disband for a time, and then regroup for another project or purpose, whereas other teams work on issues and problems over a prolonged time period.

There are several different types of teams that form within any one organization:

Formal teams are those that have been officially established or sanctioned by management for a specific purpose. They are created to accomplish a specific organizational goal that has been articulated by management. Formal teams also may be hierarchically determined such as management teams, administrative support personnel teams, or supervisory teams.

Informal teams are those formed either within existing formal groups or separately for a variety of purposes. They may form around friendships or shared interests such as teams that work out at the health club at the same time each morning or teams that are attending a company-wide computer class, for example. These teams are more spontaneous in nature and may also have a social aspect that is not related to work. Sometimes these types of teams satisfy the social need on the hierarchy of needs we identified in Chapter 2.

Single-function teams typically have individuals from one area or discipline. They often consist of groupings of individuals by the nature of the work they perform. FM departments often have design teams, engineering teams, housekeeping teams, as well as single-dimension teams.

Multifunctional or cross-functional teams are those groups of individuals who come together from diverse disciplines because they each bring a particular expertise or experience to the team environment. A cross-functional team within an FM department charged with working on a plan to relocate a customer organization, for example, may consist of representatives from operations and maintenance, real estate, space planning, design and construction, and telecommunications who provide highly specialized technical expertise on one facet of the project.

Traditionally managed teams are those in which management appoints a staff member to serve as the team manager, leader, or facilitator. It is the responsibility of that individual to organize the team's activities and ensure that the tasks are executed according to a plan established by the team leader.

Self-directed teams are those in which all team members have responsibility for management of the team, and they typically elect, on a permanent or rotating basis, a member to serve as manager, leader, or facilitator. Self-directed teams were widely used first in

Japan in a manufacturing environment and became popular in North America as an outgrowth of the Total Quality Management (TQM) movement. When FM departments are faced with outsourcing, rightsizing, and downsizing, self-managed teams often are the solution for maintaining in-house service levels when having to perform them with a fraction of the staff. Self-directed teams would form to develop a plan for executing work in multiple disciplines and then come together to monitor and exchange information on work performance as well as implement the plans they develop as a group. If we look back at our discussion about empowerment in Chapter 2, the self-directed work team is the embodiment of empowering individuals to harness their power and share it with others as a resource in a group setting. The practice of using self-directed work teams within FM departments has the potential to promote increased productivity, commitment to quality service, streamlining or reengineering FM service delivery processes, and customer service/satisfaction. We learn more about self-directed teams later in this chapter.

To summarize, a helpful way to remember the differences between work groups and work teams is to key on the number *three*. There are 3 key elements that need to be present for a work group to be a team entity:

1. Structure—A team, unlike a work group, has to have structure. Teams have to have both formal and informal authority and leadership, as well as a procedural scheme for meeting times, physical location, agenda processing, and work environment.
2. Task—A team needs to be certain about purpose, goals, output, and success factors.
3. Process—Teams develop work processes, both formal and informal, to accomplish tasks.

In addition, there are three more elements for team members as individuals that have to be present at all times if a work group is going to function as a team:

Task Achievement—Individuals on the team must have a strong sense of task orientation.

Group Well-Being—Individuals have to understand and support the needs of the group. When individuals recognize the collective good of the group, there is team cohesion.

Individual Expression and Satisfaction of Interests—Teams are differentiated from work groups in that members understand the need to balance group well-being with individual need. They are aware and make provisions for individuals to express their desires and personal interests without sacrificing the team's best interest.

Is Behavior of Work Groups Predictable?

Some of you may have knowledge and experience with the concept of group process or how individuals within a group setting initiate their charter and proceed to a conclusion. Remember, we first reviewed group behavior in Chapter 1 during our discussion about Kurt Lewin who dubbed the terms T-Group and group dynamics in the late 1930s. Since his work, many researchers in the organization development (OD) field have looked at group development and produced numerous theories.

Among the most highly regarded of these researchers is Bruce W. Tuckman from Ohio State University. In 1965, he published an article in the *Psychological Bulletin* entitled "Developmental Sequence in Small Groups," which delineated four stages of group development: forming, storming, norming, and performing with a fifth stage he labeled adjourning.[5] Much of the group process and team-building training used today is based on Tuckman's model. It is worth spending a few moments on Tuckman's model, as it is a helpful tool for facility managers to use in assessing how various work groups in the department are functioning and where they are in their development as a group.

Stages of Tuckman's Model

1. *Forming, or First Stage*—At this stage, group members are becoming oriented toward each other. They seek a strong leader and depend on the leader while getting to know one another. Group members typically are anxious and trying to figure out why they are there and how to move forward. Impressions of

individuals are formed at this stage, and there is a general desire for acceptance within the group. Courtesy and rules of behavior apply, because no one wants to step on toes or hurt feelings of team members. Two things must occur at this stage in order for a group to move forward. First, the group must ensure the maintenance concern is satisfied. *Maintenance concern* is making sure individuals feel welcome and involved and that their input is valued. Second, the group needs to make certain there is agreement about the mission or goal in order to satisfy the task concern. The forming stage can be thought of as depicted in Figure 3-1:

2. *Storming, or Second Stage*—This stage is a personal favorite of mine. When The Friday Group is involved with client group process, we typically refer to this stage as "the hurricane portion" of group development. At this stage, everyone has an opinion about what should happen and how it should be accomplished. Power plays are common and leadership is challenged as special interests of individuals and small cliques become clearer. There is high energy in the group, but often it is conflict-oriented rather than productive. Individuals and small factions test the waters to see how far they can push the rest of the group to get them to agree with their ideas. Some people in the group become highly opinionated and vocal, whereas others are intimidated and remain quiet. If the leader or facilitator of the group is not skilled at coaching during this stage, the group may lapse into a fear-of-failure state. Since everyone is uncomfortable, the leader needs to insist on a high degree of listening within the group if clear roles and responsibilities for group members are to emerge. The storming stage can be remembered as shown in Figure 3-2:

Figure 3-1. Tuckman's model: The forming stage.

Source: The Friday Group.

Figure 3-2. Tuckman's model: The storming stage.

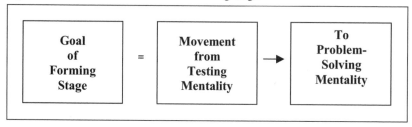

Source: The Friday Group.

3. *Norming, or Third Stage*—This stage often differentiates a work group from a team. It is essential for the group to establish norms of conduct, build consensus, give positive feedback to one another, and become cohesive. During this stage, differences of opinion are discussed and negotiated such that compromise among individuals occurs. Leadership is shared, and small factions tend to dissipate as trust in the group's collective ability takes shape. There is a sense of group belonging and high creativity. The potential downside to this stage is that groups sometimes focus on unimportant issues, which prolong their progress, or they get bogged down in groupthink. Sometimes the group also worries about accomplishing tasks too quickly and the fear of group disbursement. The norming stage is characterized in Figure 3-3.

4. *Performing, or Fourth Stage*—When groups reach this stage, they become sophisticated teams that are highly productive. Team members understand the importance of task and people orientation, and there is strong group loyalty. Often the group can form subteams to work on particular issues while problem-

Figure 3-3. Tuckman's model: The norming stage.

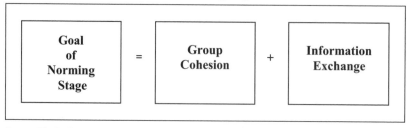

Source: The Friday Group.

solving skills are finely tuned and the group deploys resources necessary to optimize goal achievement. Leadership becomes more distributed across the group as they become less reliant on designated leaders. We characterize this stage in Figure 3-4.

5. *Adjourning, or Fifth Stage*—This stage often is the most difficult for high-performance teams because they have achieved their goal and need to terminate their activities as a group. One of the most important aspects of this stage for the team leader, as well as the facility manager, is to ensure that both a debriefing to discuss lessons learned takes place and the group is recognized for a job well done. Sometimes at adjournment, group members feel a sense of loss, especially if there has been satisfaction of the self-actualization and social needs for individuals in the group. When natural leaders have emerged through group process, they, too, may experience panic or crisis at the prospect of group disengagement. Members of the group need to have an opportunity to say goodbye to each other, often in a formal way. If some members have hesitation about leaving the group, they may try to procrastinate, or even sabotage, the project. We should think of adjourning in terms as represented in Figure 3-5.

Though the five stages of development we identified are typical, not all groups move in linear fashion from one to another. Just as we found that individuals do not necessarily have to satisfy each of their needs before moving on to another, groups may skip certain stages of group process as they work to achieve their goals. The key for a group leader and facility manager is to ensure the group doesn't get hung up in one stage or move backward to a previous stage and lose momentum as a group.

Figure 3-4. Tuckman's model: The performing stage.

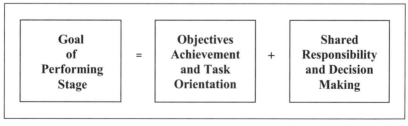

Source: The Friday Group.

Figure 3-5. Tuckman's model: The adjourning stage.

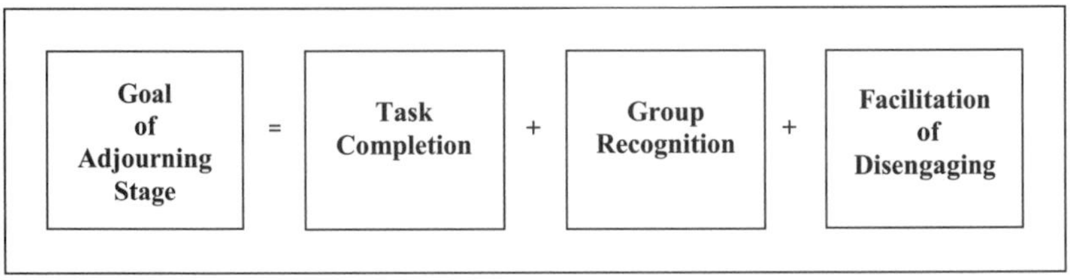

Goal of Adjourning Stage	=	Task Completion	+	Group Recognition	+	Facilitation of Disengaging

Source: The Friday Group.

Do Individuals Play Different Roles When They Are Interacting in Groups?

Our discussion about the various stages of group development is important to facility professionals and especially facility managers to evaluate the health of group process at any given time and to determine if intervention measures or corrective action is necessary to move the group forward.

How leaders, facilitators, and facility managers monitor and adjust the various roles individuals play inside a group requires adroitness and extreme sensitivity to the dynamics of the group. This skill is referred to as the ability to strike a balance within the group between the task role (or getting things accomplished) and the maintenance role (or developing members of the group). Remember, both people and tasks have to be respected by all group members in order to achieve team success. Figure 3-6 will help you understand the nuances of each role.[6]

The team roles we just reviewed are all positive ones in that they further the work of the group and support the group's well-being. Just as important for the leader and facility manager to check, however, is a role that undermines the team, ultimately resulting in the team's demise. This role is referred to as the self-interest role.[7] See Figure 3-7.

What Are Some Ways Facility Managers Can Foster Success for Their Teams?

The good news for facility managers is there are some practical tools that can be used to assist teams in driving toward successful

Figure 3-6. Positive team roles.

Accomplishment (Task Role)	People Development (Maintenance Role)
Initiator—Identifies group problems and issues; suggests policies and procedures; proposes goals/objectives, tasks and action strategies.	Gatekeeper—Makes sure all members participate; stimulates participation by reticent members; acts as timekeeper; helps a group stay on track.
Informer—Provides opinions and factual information; expresses emotion and feelings.	Harmonizer—Acts as peacekeeper by encouraging members to investigate and resolve differences; mitigates tension and disagreement.
Clarifier—Restates things in a way to assist understanding; interprets member ideas; restates questions and suggestions.	Encourager—Looks for positive aspects of member input; entices quiet and shy members to participate.
Summarizer—Proposes conclusions and restates member input; ties related information/ideas together for group to grasp.	Consensus tester—Works to get buy-in from all members; tests group's level of comfort with potential decisions.
Reality tester—"Run-it-up-the-flag-pole" approach to test feasibility of proposed ideas against known data, environment and politics.	Compromiser—Provides alternatives when group is stalemated; encourages group to relinquish ideas when conflict impedes progress.
Energizer—Acts like the pink bunny to charge the group to move forward and visualize impact of decisions on end result; reinforces quality of decision making.	

outcomes. In order for facility managers to establish teams that are highly productive, they need to understand how to structure and manage them.

Perhaps of all the characteristics of highly successful teams, the one that is of single importance is the ability of the facility manager and the designated team leader to provide clear direction. A clear sense of purpose seems to be one of the most sustaining conditions for effective teams. The Friday Group has found that when a facility manager is able to articulate exactly what he wants the team to accomplish and the team leader, in turn, reinforces this goal, the team moves forward at a quicker pace, spending less time in the storming and norming stages.

Figure 3-7. Self-interest (negative) role.

NEGATIVE TEAM ROLE

Self-Interest Role

Dominator—Tries to control the group by monopolizing discussion, determining who has "airtime," interrupting when members talk; acts superior and withholds information; forces group decisions at inappropriate times; patronizes or belittles group members.

Blocker—Consistently uncooperative; votes against group decisions; has hidden agenda; refuses to compromise; acts disagreeable most of the time.

Aggressor—Bullies individuals into submission; "shoots down" ideas in front of others; uses personal and character assaults; acts sarcastic and uses caustic humor.

Avoider—Goes off on tangents and sidetracks group with irrelevant information; uses stall tactics to avoid decision making.

Comedian—Hides behind humor to throw group off course; uses humor in inappropriate situations to belittle teammates.

You recall in Chapter 2, I quoted findings about individual motivation from studies performed by the HayGroup. This same firm in collaboration with researchers Richard Hackman of Harvard University and Ruth Wageman of Dartmouth College also has documentation about the importance of clear direction on the outcome of teams.[8]

The HayGroup research shows that although top executives are capable of communicating their overall vision and goals for an organization, they often fail to do the same for teams that are established for specific purposes. When this oversight occurs, team leaders who either are appointed or selected as part of group process cannot properly mobilize the team toward a cause of action to achieve a goal.

Failure to provide leadership and guidance to teams is a common mistake all managers, not just those in FM, make. All too often, managers are afraid they will insult smart staff by spelling out what they want them to achieve. Instead of recognizing that teams, even those comprised of high-performing individuals who may be leaders in their own right, want a framework that is clearcut, managers and team leaders make the mistake of giving little or poor direction. HayGroup's research clearly shows that of all the factors influencing team climate, the one that distinguishes great from average teams is clarity of direction.[9]

Another facet of leadership applicable to our development of OD skills for facility managers is how various managerial styles impact the performance of teams. HayGroup's research shows that of six potential managerial styles—coercive, authoritative, affiliative, democratic, pacesetting, and coaching—outstanding teams value a style that is both democratic and authoritative.[10] In other words, when teams can make the vision articulated by the manager and leader more substantial while at the same time being clear about purpose and objective, they become outstanding teams.

A clear picture of roles and responsibilities and operating procedures is critical to the success of FM teams. Team members want to know what they are responsible for and how their role relates to others. The HayGroup findings go even further by talking about the actual structure of teams. They found the optimum size of a team to be from six to eight members[11] since teams often become unwieldy, and competing interests tend to allow factions to develop when groups grow in size. In the experience of The Friday Group, FM managers tend to err on the side of inclusion and create teams with too many people. They are afraid of risking hurt feelings and short-changing valuable input from a variety of staff so they create large teams. We suggest having more teams with fewer people to accommodate the need for extensive participation.

Earlier in the chapter we talked about the role of norms within teams. We know teams need to establish norms as part of their governance process, but facility managers and team leaders should provide guidance on parameters of acceptable behavior and protocols when conducting team business.

Teams also need to be comprised of the right people to get the job done. Part of the responsibility of the facility manager is to select the most appropriate people to work together on a team. From time to time, the FM manager's goal may be to expose staff with behavioral problems to team process as a behavior modification opportunity. When this situation is the case, it is imperative for the facility manager to stay closely involved with the team's activities to ensure the right climate to foster frequent, open, and honest dialogue. The HayGroup research finds outstanding teams emphasize membership in which individuals have strong empathy and are sensitive to unspoken emotions of their colleagues.[12] Outstanding

FM teams The Friday Group has worked with emphasize trust and respect as their key characteristics. We have observed teams that go to great lengths to develop team integrity such that individuals have a well-developed sense of ethical responsibility to one another.

Another condition for the creation of outstanding teams is the development of team skills and capabilities to function as a team. Team problem solving involves the diagnostic skills we have been addressing throughout this book, and when facility managers want to have teams with their own strong DNA, they need to develop these skills. All too frequently The Friday Group has witnessed teams struggling with a problem or project because they haven't been exposed to the tools and techniques associated with team dynamics. In order to have effective FM teams that utilize the best aspects of group process, it is necessary for facility professionals to be equipped with skills to function on and lead a team. Facility managers should ensure that team members know the following techniques, at a minimum, to enhance their problem-solving and decision-making skills:

Nominal group process—Team members should know how to conduct team decision making using a variety of techniques. Nominal group process takes advantage of brainstorming as a means of obtaining a battery of ideas from each team member and then having the group discuss and rank/order the ideas to come up with a final group decision. Facility managers need to provide training for staff to help them understand the rules associated with brainstorming and how individuals within the team have to be encouraged to participate and present their ideas. Unless a team has been provided with the tools to structure their decision making, they will flounder and have little direction.

Delphi technique—Another method for conducting group decision making is that of using a structured rating system to obtain input and opinion on certain issues. This technique relies heavily on the use of surveys and questionnaires as a means of obtaining data from a larger group that then can be reviewed by the team. This technique works well when a team is tasked with performing research outside the FM department that requires data collection from a variety of individuals within the overall company. The team can create a survey instrument to gather data and then perform the analysis as a group.

Flowcharting, mapping, and force field analysis—These are all techniques a team can use to assess a particular issue or solve a problem and reach a conclusion as a group. Flowcharting and mapping work well when a team is asked to analyze a particular process for the purpose of streamlining or revamping the way in which the process is performed. Force field analysis typically is used as a change agent by looking at a particular problem or issue as a series of forces that are either propelling an issue ahead or holding it back. Organizations usually do not make any forward progress if the forces for and against are at absolute zero. This analytical tool is one that allows a team to look at these forces and potential for change.

Software techniques—Over the past few years, a whole host of software packages called *groupware* or *shareware* has allowed groups to analyze issues/problems and reach decisions without having to co-locate for the purposes of discussion. These software packages create a structured environment that allows teams to function on a multilocational basis by conducting group process via their computers. This particular technique also works well in team environments in which dialogue and discussion may become dysfunctions in that ideas, opinions, and decisions can be posted anonymously.

The final criteria for an outstanding team are assessment, feedback, and recognition. It is one of the jobs of facility managers to collect and assess information about the ways in which teams are functioning to determine if they are healthy or if some modification of team behavior needs to take place. In addition, it also is the responsibility of the facility manager to recognize and reward teams for achieving intended results.

The recommendation of The Friday Group to our client facility managers is to overcommunicate with teams initially and then establish a regular process for obtaining team feedback, not only from the team leader but also from the team as a whole. Many team problems stem from lack of communication both from within the team and with managers. Facility managers need to have updates on team progress and milestone achievement to check on how well the team is meeting goals. Even though teams must learn how to resolve their own problems, facility managers need to monitor activities to ensure teams aren't spinning their wheels on a particular topic or using an issue as an excuse for not reaching a conclusion. All too often teams become focused on the obstacles rather than looking for solutions and need facility managers to intervene.

It also is extremely important for teams to know that management is pleased with their outcome. Team energy and commitment are renewed through positive reinforcement that they have performed tasks well and have provided an effective output. Facility managers have an obligation to their teams to recognize their accomplishments and reward team effort. We discuss rewards in the upcoming section "What Motivates Teams?"

In summary, ensuring the well-being of teams requires facility managers to perform routine assessment of the team task and maintenance functions we discussed earlier in this chapter. As a helpful tool, The Friday Group follows a model for team well-being with FM departments developed by Dick Richards and Susan Smyth in their *Team Members Manual: Assessing Your Team* publication. Their graphic, Figure 3-8, presents the interrelationships among the characteristics of outstanding and healthy teams.[13]

❏ Purpose—As we said before, the nucleus of the team is a shared sense of purpose. It is important for all members of the team to have the same definition of purpose and a commitment to that purpose.

❏ Role—By role we are referring to the role that the team has in the overall organization, not the individual roles of team members. Agreement must be reached on the role the team will play in achieving its purpose.

❏ Strategy—This refers to how the team will go about implementing its work in order to achieve the purpose for which the team was established. The strategies of the team must be evaluated on a continuous basis to assure that the team is headed in the right direction.

❏ People—The people component is complex in that it represents not only the right mix of individuals and expertise on the team to accomplish the goal but also the way in which team members support and care for one another. Team members need to be respectful of each other's ideas and try to maximize the talents of each team member. If

Figure 3-8. Seven measures of team success.

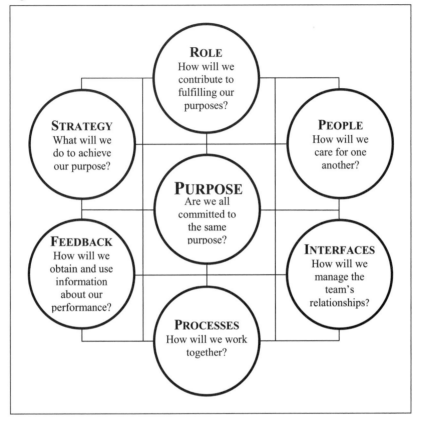

the team is to function as a cohesive unit, each member must feel his role is important to the total team.

❑ Interface—In this context, the team must determine how it will interact with external parties both within their own organization and in the company overall. This is the relationship-building and networking piece of the well-being model.

❑ Feedback—This component refers to the way in which the team processes the information it obtains about how it is performing as a team and how it is achieving its purpose. Some ground rules for continuous improvement as a team must be established at the onset of team efforts in order for the team to be successful.

❑ Processes—The team needs to decide how it will work together as a group and what processes it will employ as a
team to support its strategies for goal attainment. This is
where a team might develop codes of conduct or decide if
it wants to use consensus or majority rule as the governing
structure for decision making.

What Makes Self-Directed Teams So Unique?

We are devoting additional time to self-directed work teams because they present both opportunities and challenges for FM departments. As you remember from our discussion of the types of
teams earlier in the chapter, self-directed or self-managed teams
are an outgrowth of the TQM movement as are the use of quality
circles to analyze problems. Self-directed teams take these TQM
concepts further: They are the embodiment of group empowerment
at the maximum level.

In the purest sense, a self-directed team is *a work group that
operates with varying degrees of autonomy and without a visible
manager or leader*.[14] The team assumes the roles and responsibilities of a manager as team members learn to share these functions.
The team controls the activities of its members internally rather
than depending on controls provided externally by supervisors and
senior managers.

For organizations in which self-directed teams have been successfully institutionalized, there is evidence that staff motivation increases, thereby generating a higher level of productivity. When
staff are empowered to control their own destiny, typically they
learn quickly to self-correct when problems emerge and move forward at a more rapid speed. We talked in Chapter 2 about the psychological contract and that self-directed teams provide greater
opportunity for individuals to fulfill their predisposed ideas about
the workplace and what it will provide for them. These teams allevi-
ate many management barriers employees say inhibit their psychological enrichment and creativity. They epitomize Chris Argyris's
theory that empowerment furthers the goals of an organization.

Not all FM departments are ready for self-directed teams.
Their effectiveness requires a tremendous amount of up-front staff
training on the dynamics of group problem solving and decision

making. Self-directed teams in their infancy typically take longer to resolve issues, reach consensus, and deliver output so they are not appropriate for quick turnaround projects until they reach a certain level of maturity. Not only do they require a significant investment in training and time to get established, but facility managers have to set aside blocks of time to assist teams in the early stages of development. Facility managers also must be willing to risk a trial and error period because new teams sometimes fail to achieve the desired objective on the first attempt. In order for teams to have a positive learning experience and benefit from mistakes, they must be confident that there won't be reprisals from failed efforts. We talk more about how facility managers create a climate for fostering self-directed teams in Chapter 4.

What Motivates Teams?

Our final discussion centers on what it takes to motivate a work group to become the type of healthy team we have described previously. I stress here, as I did in Chapter 2 on motivating individuals, that facility managers need to ask the team what they value as incentives if they really want to motivate them. In other words, don't guess what is important to a team—ask the team!

Teaming and the rewards of teaming are an effective way to stimulate staff and one in which some managers have come up with creative incentives. There are numerous types of companies that have been established solely for the purpose of creating group promotion or incentive programs. Many companies have their reward and recognition programs designed exclusively for them by these firms. They believe their programs contain valuable proprietary information and guard them as carefully as they do company trade secrets.

When the economy is good, The Friday Group sees a variety of exotic group reward programs such as hot air balloon rides, kayaking trips, visits to dude ranches, cruises, fly-fishing and golf trips, fighter pilot programs, and race car driving. We also have worked with companies that provide team events such as tickets to sporting events, theater performances, and concerts. Routinely, we also find teams that want to further their training/education as a group and suggest taking classes in a subject that is of interest to all of them as a group reward.

For many FM departments, symbols of the team spirit have become popular. We see hats, shirts, jackets, mugs, pens and pencils, and bags imprinted with the logo or slogan a team has adopted. We also find FM teams participating in competitive activities with other teams inside their own department, as well as with other corporate teams. FM departments are fond of having softball, volleyball, bowling, and other competitive activities for their teams.

Another critical aspect of team motivation is that of finding a means for a team to leave some type of legacy for their efforts. Many FM teams become involved as a group in civic activities such as Habitat for Humanity projects, sponsoring children at camps, and Big Brother and Big Sister events. In addition, FM teams often like to leave their mark on facility projects by having their hand- or footprints left in cement walkways, time capsules planted in building cornerstones, or plaques hung in lobbies of renovated facilities—in other words, something that identifies the solidarity of the group and leaves an impression of how they have worked together as a team.

Finally, some FM teams simply want more job enrichment and less supervision to work more freely as self-managed teams. They may choose how they wish to reward themselves and pursue some or all of the above reinforcement mechanisms.

Groups of individuals working toward collective goals are the backbone of FM departments. They should be viewed as precious resources by FM managers and given every opportunity to grow and demonstrate their skills. To reiterate what I stated in Chapter 1, without human resources we wouldn't have FM departments or be discussing the importance of departmental DNA.

Throughout Chapters 2 and 3, references are made to the impact culture has on the well-being of FM departments. We move to our next DNA link to learn what culture entails and how it influences the way organizations function.

DNA Link: Groups

Company: Applied Physics Laboratory (scientific research)

Background

The Applied Physics Laboratory (APL) is a research and development division of The Johns Hopkins University, which supports the Department of Defense, NASA, and other government agencies. Located on 360 acres in Laurel, Maryland, the laboratory employs approximately 3,500 engineers, scientists, and supporting staff in a broad range of disciplines.

Three departments at APL provide facilities management services:

Business and Information Services Department (BISD)

Human Resources and Services Department (HRSD)

Technical Services Department (TSD)

Their relation to the overall APL organization is shown in Figure APL 1, and their individual functions are shown in Figure APL 2. This vignette, however, focuses only on the facilities management services provided by TSD because this department provides the majority of these types of services at the laboratory.

Currently, the main facilities management groups of TSD are Plant Construction, Plant Operations, and Facilities Projects Management. These groups are structured according to function or task while an Operations Center provides a single point of contact for the majority of customer interactions for smaller, day-to-day facilities projects (Figure APL 3). There are no more than five organizational levels between the worker and the director's office (Figure APL 4).

Both Plant Construction and Plant Operations personnel

(text continues on page 109)

Figure APL 1. Facilities-related departments within the APL organization.

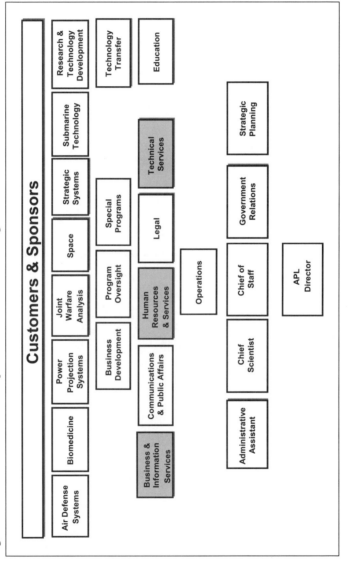

Figure APL 2. Functions of APL's Facilities Management Departments.

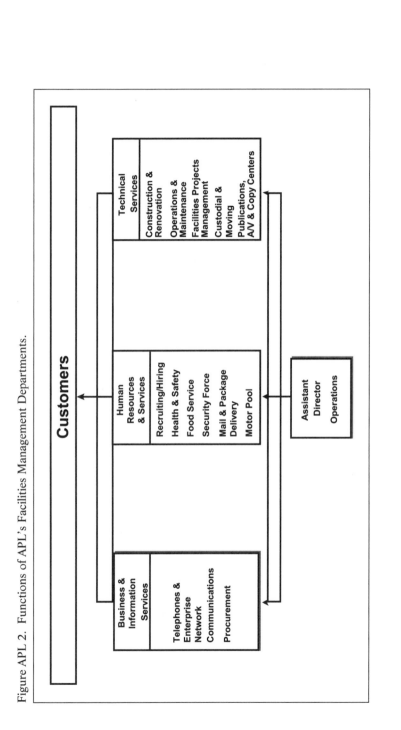

Figure APL 3. The Operations Center provides a single point of contact for customers of the Plant Operations and Plant Construction groups.

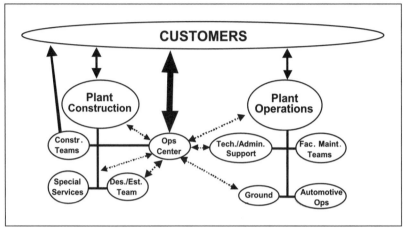

Figure APL 4. Current organization of TSD's Facilities Management groups.

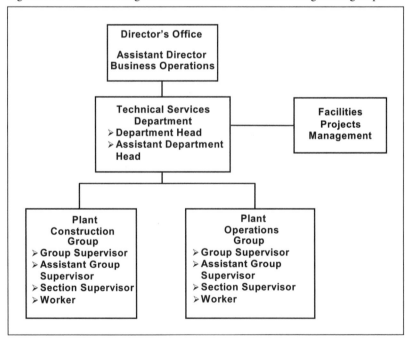

work in multicraft, self-directed teams. For a given task, a person proficient in the primary trade takes the lead in the effort and is assisted by other people proficient in other trades. For example, an electrician would take the lead in wiring lights in a room and may be assisted by a carpenter, a plumber, or a painter. On the next assignment, these staff members may serve as plumber's helpers or painter's assistants. This process allows the laboratory to use its highly trained staff efficiently while minimizing crew sizes, and it enables individuals to broaden their experience and learn new skills.

Although certain support skills and resources may be provided by only one group, specialty tools and expensive diagnostic or fabrication equipment, as well as unique skills, (finished carpentry, exotic coatings, precision welding, locksmith services, etc.) are readily shared across the entire organization.

Facilities Projects Management consists of two technical staff members reporting directly to the department office. These two individuals manage all of the major new construction and renovation work at the laboratory. They receive support from the Department Budget Office and the administrative staff. When the scope of a project exceeds in-house capabilities, selected tasks are outsourced to either a construction manager (CM) or a project manager (PM). By utilizing outside resources, the core staff can remain constant while engaging additional resources on a just-in-time basis.

Their Story

The Evolution of Facilities Management at APL

Facilities management at APL was not always structured as it is today. The previous organization is shown in Figure APL 5. Earlier, the structure was trade-based and lacked a central point of contact for the customer (Figure APL 6). Communications were complicated and marginally effective. The Plant Engineering Branch was comprised of building, electrical, and mechanical functions (Figure APL 7). Each group was responsible for both new construction and maintenance within

(text continues on page 112)

Figure APL 5. Previous APL Facilities Management Organization functions (1990s).

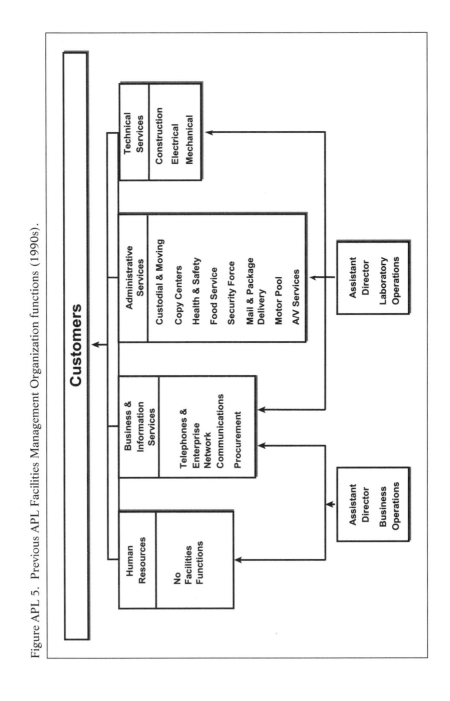

Figure APL 6. Early trade-based organization of Facilities Management Groups.

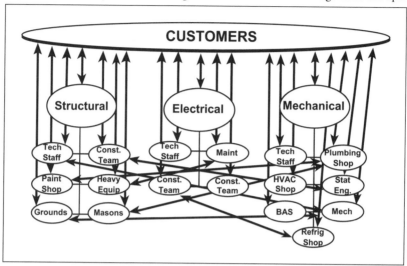

Figure APL 7. Plant Engineering Branch Organization (1990s).

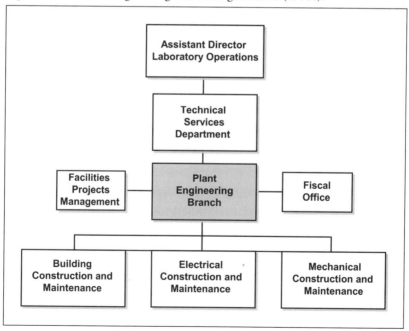

its respective trade area. The branch organization provided administrative and financial services to these three groups and administered all new construction. The branch reported to TSD, which reported to the assistant director of Laboratory Operations. This layered structure was appropriate at the time because there were 175 people in the branch.

When the laboratory was downsized in the early 1990s, the Administrative Services Department was eliminated and its functions were divided between two of the remaining three service departments: TSD and HRSD. This action eliminated a senior management position and increased the scope of responsibility for these departments. Publications, audiovisual services, and printing services became part of TSD. HRSD gained responsibility for health and safety, food service, the security force, mail and package delivery, and the motor pool. In addition, Plant Engineering Branch functions were evaluated to determine which were core competencies critical to the success of the organization. TSD then determined which tasks could be performed most effectively in-house and which could be outsourced. All tasks that required special expertise, training, or equipment and those that were performed infrequently were outsourced. By the end of 1999, all resident subcontract employees (RSEs) had been converted to staff. This was done to encourage retention and to create a stable core of critical skills. The overall decrease in Plant Engineering Branch staff from 1991 through 2000 is shown in Figure APL 8. This decrease occurred as TSD's physical responsibility increased from 1.3 million gross square feet (gsf) in 1991 to 1.7 million gsf in 2001. TSD was now doing more with less (Figure APL 8).

The functions, core competencies, outsourcing procedures, and best practices of TSD's Plant Construction, Plant Operations, and Facilities Projects Management groups are described in the following sections.

Plant Construction Group

The Plant Construction Group (see Figure APL 9) provides laboratory-wide construction services using four teams that comprise the group's core competencies:

Figure APL 8. Plant Engineering Branch staff (1991–2000).

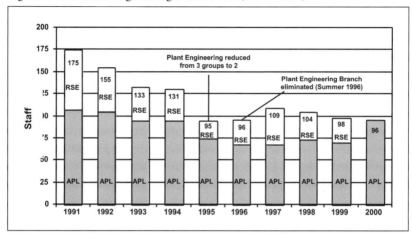

Figure APL 9. Plant Construction Group Organization.

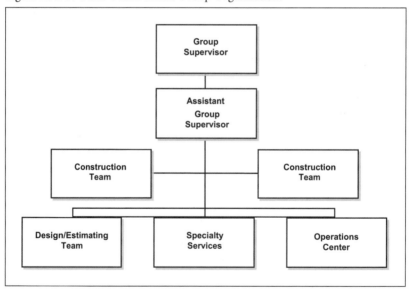

Design/Estimating—5 staff

Construction—26 staff

Specialty Services—4 staff

Operations Center—4 staff

The group's mission is to provide quality construction and operation services in a timely and cost-effective manner to support the mission of the laboratory. Its vision is to be the provider of choice for all customers within the laboratory by continuously improving the quality of services in a safe, timely, and cost-effective manner through its knowledgeable and dedicated staff.

Core Competencies

❐ *Design/Estimating Team*—The Design/Estimating Team provides structural, electrical, and mechanical engineering services to support facility maintenance as well as planning, design, and cost-estimating services for facilities improvement projects including renewal, remodeling, and new construction. The staff performs facilities audits and master planning for capital replacement projects and infrastructure renewal, ensures compliance with Howard County Life Safety and Building codes, and maintains a computer-aided design (CAD) system, as-built drawings, and a facilities database.

❐ *Construction Team*—The Construction Team provides electrical, mechanical, and structural trade skills for the construction and renovation of all laboratory buildings and infrastructure. The Construction Team plans, organizes, and monitors construction-related resources to ensure optimal customer benefit, minimal disruption, and reasonable costs. Team members inspect all work to ensure compliance with all national and local Howard County Life Safety and Building codes.

❐ *Specialty Services Team*—The Specialty Services Team contributes skills including cabinet-, model-, and pattern-making design and fabrication; furniture finishing; mil-spec and space flight coatings application; general spray painting services; and custom sign design and fabrication.

❐ *Operations Center Team*—The Operations Center is the hub of the Plant Construction Group, receiving service request calls and processing work orders. The Operations Center Team maintains the plant facilities inventory and the inventory storage areas. The team also administers material and equipment purchasing, billing records, billing reconciliation, blanket service contracts, emergency service procurement, and a computerized work order system.

In-House vs. Outsourced Services

The Plant Construction Group provides the full range of construction services from project design and material procurement through the demolition, fabrication, installation, and construction stages to final inspection, commissioning, and delivery of the finished project to the customer.

There are many specialized skills that the group has chosen not to provide using in-house staff. For example, the following services are typically outsourced: flooring, glass replacement, specialty doors, fencing, partitions, roofing, 33-kV medium-voltage electrical work, specialized piping systems, and countertops. For additional resources, APL has contracted with three architectural/engineering firms to provide design services under a blanket contract arrangement.

Plant Construction outsources these skills due to their specialized nature. It is not always cost-effective to train personnel to provide services that will be used only occasionally throughout the year. Most of these outsourced skills also require certification—an additional cost component that must be considered. Outsourcing these skills saves the customer money.

Best Practices

In addition to the use of outsourcing when required, the Plant Construction Group's best practices are cultivated by the use of multiskilled trades construction teams and a customer focus in all aspects of day-to-day activities.

❐ *Construction Teams*—The concept of multiskilled trades construction teams had been considered, and even informally used, for many years with substantial success. However, formally reorganizing the traditional trade shops into two full-service construction teams was a significant event.

It eliminated the supervision, organization, and job assignment by trade and opened up opportunities for personal growth, increased productivity, enhanced communications, and improved logistics. This "work-sharing" approach was instituted with each team modeled on the theme of a small general contracting firm with resources in carpentry, electrical, painting, plumbing, and HVAC specialties. As a direct result, the logistics nightmare is gone, job duration has been reduced by 25 percent, customer satisfaction has increased dramatically, and staff morale has soared.

In an average year, construction teams will complete 350 plant facilities work requests ranging from $5,000 to $125,000 per job. Services groups process an additional 400+ service requests, each costing less than $5,000 per job. Construction teams complete all work in their assigned zone with as little disruption to the staff as possible. Jobs are requested by every department and run the gamut from standard office renovations associated with personnel relocations to construction of major simulation laboratories with requirements for special power, air conditioning, security, fire suppression, and network cabling.

❏ Customer Focus—Project scheduling has been one of the most challenging aspects of the Plant Construction Group's customer focus strategy. In order to provide realistic scheduling information to customers, material ordering and delivery are closely monitored, long lead items are identified early in design, and shift work or overtime is used to meet operational requirements. A permanent change in the staff work schedule (from 8:30 A.M.–5:00 P.M. to 7:00 A.M.–3:30 P.M.) allows work to begin 1 1/2 hours before normal laboratory operating hours. This new schedule enables disruptive work to be completed before the arrival of most laboratory staff.

Another outgrowth of the customer focus strategy was the creation of the Specialty Services section that provides cabinetry, model-making, spray painting, and special coatings for conceptual designs, prototypes, or proposal presentations. This process is normally fast-paced with little formal documentation, but by working directly with the scientist or engineer, these craftsmen are able to turn concepts into tangible objects that support high-tech project development.

Perhaps the most frequent manifestation of the group's commitment to customer service occurs in the Operations Center, where over 100 calls are answered daily. It is the focal point for initial contact with customers, and the work reception and dispatch functions performed here set the tone for staff members to develop a one-to-one relationship with every customer calling for information or assistance. In addition, Operations Center personnel provide work order and inventory management for construction and maintenance activities using credit cards to purchase more than 90 percent of needed materials with just-in-time ordering to control on-hand inventory.

Plant Operations

The Plant Operations Group is the primary caretaker of APL's grounds, vehicles, facilities, infrastructure, and utility distribution systems (Figure APL 10). With 50 major buildings and more than 1.6 million square feet of space (28% over 40 years old), preventive maintenance performed by highly qualified and dedicated personnel is the foundation of a program that has allowed the facility to function reliably and age gracefully.

Core Competencies

Core competencies for the Plant Operations Group center around the technical skills and knowledge required to operate facilities and deliver maintenance services essential to APL's success as an enterprise. The group provides these services through an organization comprised of support staff, watch engineers, and specialized maintenance teams that make the most of individual skills, creativity, and initiative.

The support staff provides a full spectrum of administrative and technical services for both the Plant Operations and Construction groups. Their professional expertise in computer-based systems ensures that building automation and life safety systems are always functioning properly. The work

Figure APL 10. Plant Operations Group organization.

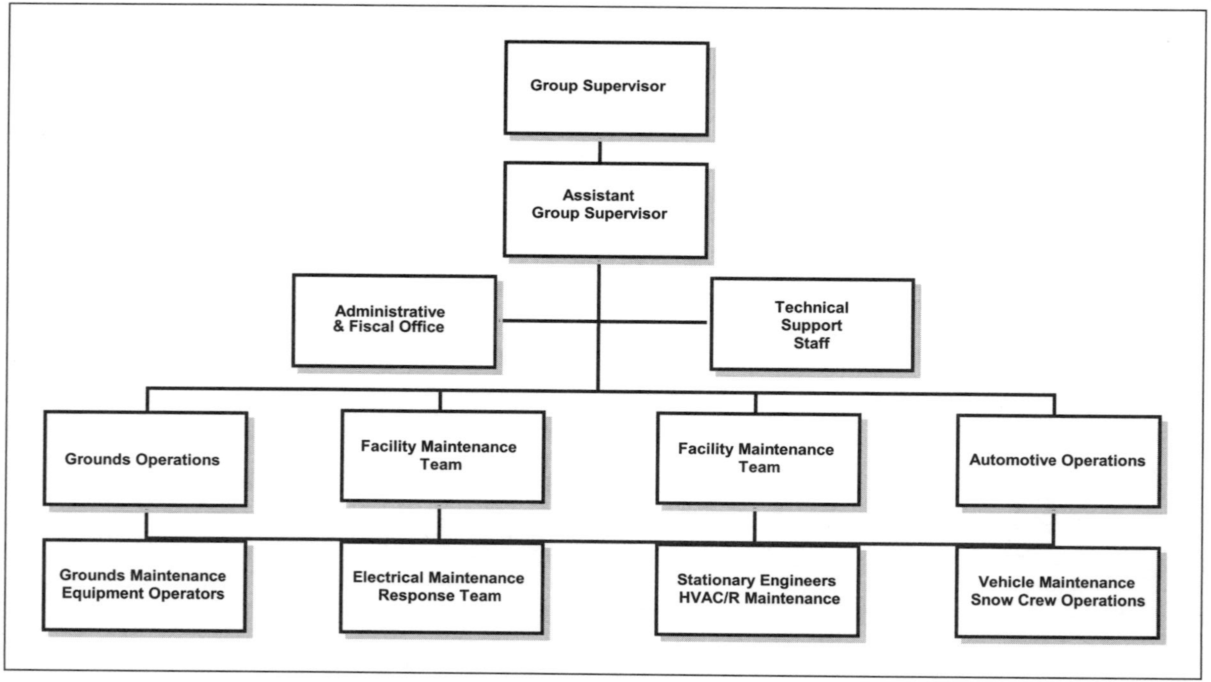

management system provides customers with timely information to track their work requests through design, review, and scheduling tasks. The group's additional responsibilities for computer hardware, property administration, procurements, budgets, time-card processing, and a chargeback system provide essential support for its work for the laboratory.

Watch engineers are available 24 hours per day, 365 days per year to monitor all mechanical systems and machine rooms. These licensed stationary engineers make prescribed rounds of the facility, monitor building automation system alarms, and respond independently to both routine and urgent situations. Their judgment and knowledge are essential to efficient plant operations and off-hours emergency response.

Two facilities maintenance teams deliver preventive maintenance and handle repairs required to restore facilities and services. With expertise in plumbing, carpentry, electrical maintenance, air-conditioning and refrigeration, stationary machinery, and mechanical and hydraulic equipment, the group's skilled staff is the key to continuous and reliable delivery of building environmental and utility services. The combination of trades within the teams supports cross training of multiskilled personnel and enhances organizational flexibility.

Automotive maintenance services are provided to keep the laboratory's vehicles and industrial equipment in top condition to meet all mission requirements. Technicians certified by the National Institute for Automotive Service Excellence employ the latest in diagnostic equipment and tools to analyze and repair the complex systems of today's vehicles. Also serving as the operations center for snow emergency response, the Automotive Maintenance Team readies snow removal equipment, stockpiles necessary supplies, solicits snow crew volunteers, and coordinates the activities that minimize the impact of snow and ice on laboratory personnel and operations.

The appearance of APL's grounds reflects not only the professional image of the laboratory to visitors and staff but also the talent and dedication of the Grounds Maintenance Team. Keeping the laboratory's external environment neat and attractive has been achieved in compliance with the requirements of legislation involving wetlands, forest conservation, soil erosion and sediment control, herbicide application, and storm water management.

In-House vs. Outsourced Services

Services provided by the Plant Operations Group are those that most directly affect facility readiness and mission requirements while delivering the best value for the laboratory. Those services provided in-house include mechanical systems maintenance, building automation system monitoring, automotive maintenance, plumbing, carpentry, electrical maintenance, and groundskeeping. Outsourced services include high-voltage testing, elevator and diesel generator maintenance, building automation system service, fire suppression system inspections, glass replacement, hazardous material handling, paved surface repair, and various testing programs, as well as the design and construction of major facilities renewal projects.

Outsourcing select services is warranted when:

Required services are readily available in the marketplace

Specialized knowledge/training is required for the task

Project schedule is not significantly impacted by outsourcing

Other projects may be impacted negatively if in-house resources are used

In-house staffing constraints exist

Best value for the laboratory is via outsourcing

Best Practices

The foundation of the group's best practices is the safe and reliable delivery of cost-effective services that support the laboratory's mission. The focus is on responsible stewardship of the facilities and resources made available to us, always keeping in mind what is important to the customer—timely response, minimum inconvenience, good communications, seamless service, and a well-maintained workplace.

A talented and dedicated staff ensures the group's success by working as a team to support the laboratory's mission. The customer is the focus of the group's service delivery system, and understanding and meeting customer expectations is Plant Operations' recognized strength, competitive advantage, and ultimate mission.

Facilities Projects Management

Facilities Projects Management staff perform key management functions from concept to completion for large-scale construction projects (greater than $1 million) at the APL campus. Examples include renovation projects such as the $2.7 million conversion and renovation of a cafeteria into laboratories, offices, and conference rooms. Recent construction includes a 75,000-gsf building containing highly sophisticated facilities such as a Guidance System Evaluation Laboratory (with an anechoic chamber) used for end-to-end missile evaluation and a 100-seat Warfare Analysis Laboratory. Currently, the Facilities Projects Management staff, with the assistance of a contract project manager, is planning and designing a 230,000-gsf multipurpose building and a District Utility Plant. The multipurpose building will include a new cafeteria, a health and fitness facility, service and support areas, 69,000 square feet of offices, and 57,000 square feet of highly sophisticated electronics laboratories.

Two Facilities Projects managers coordinate this work with the assistance of a third project manager from the Plant Operations Group. The projects management function is under the direction of the Plant Facilities Chief Engineer (PFCE), who is responsible for the overall organization and management of all major new construction and renewal projects. The PFCE provides direction for the design and construction of the multipurpose building and associated work. Department staff, Plant Operations and Construction groups, and the Laboratory Business Office also support the two Facilities Projects managers. By sharing resources in a matrixed structure, these two individuals can effectively manage new construction and major renovation projects totaling more than $50 million.

Core Competencies

The core competencies of the Facilities Projects Management Group begin with sound project management skills. Supplementing this fundamental management expertise are:

❏ Technical skills in architecture and engineering of building systems to help establish the customer's expectations for project scope, cost, and schedule

❏ Effective communication skills for conferring with design experts to generate construction documents

❏ Risk assessment skills to qualify project goals

❏ Coordination skills to effectively harness the contributions of user and service groups during construction to expedite project completion and assess any impacts to ongoing operations

In-House vs. Outsourced Services

In-house staff is used primarily for mission-critical, information-sensitive, or time-critical projects. Using in-house resources allows a project to proceed quickly with minimal documentation, allowing activities such as design, procurement of long-lead items, and construction to occur simultaneously with the necessary quality control. This process has been highly successful for the majority of customer requests.

Typical in-house services performed by Facilities Projects Management staff are:

❏ Consulting with design experts (architects and engineers) to generate construction documents that address the needs of the customer

❏ Clearly defining the project scope, cost, and schedule with the customer

❏ Analyzing and addressing the impact of each project to all APL business operations

❏ Contracting with builders, using a variety of delivery methods such as construction management, general contracting, and design/build

❏ Coordinating with internal user and service groups, such as technical laboratory staff and the laboratory food service provider during construction to facilitate and expedite project completion

❏ Monitoring project status through work inspections and reviewing and approving progress payment applications

❏ Closing out all projects with a commissioning process prior to turning over operational responsibility to the Plant Operations Group and before the occupancy of finished spaces

❏ Benchmarking for future projects

The decision to employ outsourced resources is driven primarily by the needed degree of effort, sophistication of construction design, or availability of in-house technical resources. In general, using outsourced resources allows a large or complex project to proceed quickly, but requires additional efforts by in-house staff to meet quality control standards. The most common outsourced services include design/consulting services for generating planning and construction documents, such as the Site Development Master Plan and project-specific plans and specifications, and contracting with construction firms for project execution.

Best Practices

One of the best practices of the Facilities Projects Management staff is providing a single point of contact for customers from project inception through completion. The project manager is responsible for the coordination of all services, materials, and equipment provided by consultants, contractors, vendors, and other APL team members.

The key to this organization unit's success is the custom-tailoring of the delivery system based on the scope, complexity, and magnitude of the project at hand. Because the laboratory's capital construction program has varied greatly (from a low of $0 per year to almost $20 million per year, depending on priorities at the time), the laboratory does not staff to meet current demand only to have to lay off personnel when the wave of new construction passes through the system. By carefully matching available internal and external resources to the requirements of the project, the projects management team can leverage its limited resources and effectively manage several multimillion-dollar projects concurrently.

Summary

TSD is organized in a flat, matrixed structure and has a core of highly trained and experienced managers. As an organization, TSD is able to offer complete construction, renovation, and operations services to the laboratory with minimum staff. Because services are shared between organization subunits, redundancy is eliminated and available in-house resources can be used most efficiently. When demand exceeds the capacity of limited in-house resources, TSD selectively outsources activities that are not within its core competencies or that are too large to handle effectively. However, TSD retains ultimate responsibility for product and service delivery to its customers.

Learning Points

❐ Team-oriented approach to service delivery
❐ Use of self-directed teams to perform construction and operations functions
❐ Sharing of unique skills across organization lines
❐ Customer focus orientation created need for single point-of-contact role for Operations Center Team for work reception and dispatch

---

About the Authors

A team of experienced professionals administers the facilities management services at the Johns Hopkins Applied Physics

Laboratory. This team includes James E. Loesch (Plant Facilities Chief Engineer), Glenn M. Carey (Facilities Project Manager), Ray W. Grose (Supervisor, Plant Construction Group), and William E. Kozak (Group Supervisor, Plant Operations Group). This vignette is a product of their cumulative experience as team-oriented, customer-focused facilities managers who recognize the importance of effective teaming not only among themselves but also among the many talented, multiskilled tradesmen and technicians they oversee. This philosophy is the foundation of the efficient delivery of quality construction, renovation, and operations services throughout the laboratory.

Endnotes

1. Judith R. Gordon, *Organizational Behavior,* 6th ed. (Upper Saddle River, NJ: Prentice Hall, 1999), p. 165.
2. Ibid., p. 164.
3. Jerry Spiegel and Cresencio Torres, *Manager's Official Guide to Team Working* (San Diego, CA: Pfeiffer & Company, 1994), p. 25.
4. Gordon, op. cit., p. 165.
5. B. W. Tuckman, "Developmental Sequence in Small Groups," *Psychological Bulletin*, vol. 63, no. 6 (1965), pp. 384–399.
6. Adapted from National Crime Prevention Council, *Becoming a Better Supervisor: A Resource Guide for Community Service Supervisors* (Washington, D.C.: National Crime Prevention Council, 1996), pp. 3-5–3-9.
7. Ibid.
8. HayGroup, Richard Hackman, and Ruth Wageman, *Top Teams: Why Some Work and Some Do Not* (Philadelphia: HayGroup, 2001); http://www.haygroup.com.
9. Ibid., p. 6.
10. Ibid., p. 8.
11. Ibid., p. 9.
12. Ibid., p. 12.
13. Dick Richards and Susan Smyth,. *Assessing Your Team: 7*

Measures of Team Success, Team Member's Manual (San Diego, CA: Pfeiffer & Company, 1994), p. 9.

14. Robert F. Hicks and Diane Bone, *Self-Managing Teams: Creating and Maintaining Self-Managed Work Groups* (Los Altos, CA: Crisp Publications, 1990), p. 2.

CHAPTER FOUR

The Importance of Culture to FM Organizations
DNA Link: Culture

Is Corporate Culture Really an Important DNA Link?

Restraining myself from populating the book with personal stories, I can't resist the opportunity to use one here to illustrate the impact of corporate culture on individuals and organizations. As a relatively young consultant, after 5 years of working for a small boutique management consulting firm, I made a career move to one of the "Big Eight" firms as they were called in the seventies. Coming from a firm where I was a senior consultant with my own clients and staff to support me to a firm where I supposedly was on the partner fast-track, but nonetheless a newcomer, I was ill prepared for the culture shock awaiting me.

Mind you, the managing partner informed me at the time of my hire they were taking a big risk by asking me to join the firm since they typically didn't hire anyone who already had consulting experience. They preferred recruiting impressionable young folks right out of business school who could be indoctrinated to the firm's way. Without making this chapter about my lifetime career in consulting, suffice it to say both the firm and I knew we were treading on thin ice with my hire, but didn't know just how thin the ice was going to be.

The firm tried to indoctrinate me on the first day by putting me in the bull pen with all the other new consultants. There was a long shelf around the perimeter of the room serving as our collective desk and five phones hanging on the wall to be used by all ten of us sharing the room. Let me point out to you that in my previous life I had a private office, my own secretary, and staff so I didn't appreciate being treated as the kid with no seniority. I went berserk after only 4 hours in the bull pen!

From the first day, it was all downhill. I couldn't adjust to not being able to talk to clients on my own unless a manager said it was okay, not having my own client files and having to go to the "red robes room" to sign things out like a large law firm, and watching grown men scramble to put suit jackets on when they were summoned to a partner's office. I never could figure out the validity of these customs in the overall culture!

So I managed by the second day of complaining to the managing partner to get "promoted" to a four-person office with my own desk and two phones on the wall for all of us to share and to also get permission to discuss things with clients without being monitored, but that wasn't enough. I really rebelled. I held clandestine after-work sessions with the bull pen crowd to tell them about the culture of the firm I had come from. We discussed my previous firm's concepts of empowerment—the fact that guidance and parameters were provided to all new recruits, that they were *required* to interact with clients. How else would they learn to be consultants? My old firm's way of doing things was learning through observation and active participation. (Refer back to Chapter 1 or Figure 1-1 for a refresher if necessary.) I also told them that most of the important client decisions at my old firm were made during lively conversations by the entire consulting team, often lounging around in casual clothes by the pool on the roof of our office building with a soft drink in hand, instead of sitting stiffly around a table in a formal boardroom wearing three-piece suits (remember, it was the seventies!) waiting for a nod from an executive before anyone could express an opinion.

I rallied the troops, explaining to them there were firms where you had privacy in terms of an office and your own telephone and where you were responsible for keeping copious notes on your own clients in your own client files. I told them there was a better way of life that provided a stimulating environment in which issues and problems were debated into the wee hours of the night. I informed them that clients still respected the work accomplished by these types of consulting firms. Then after seven of the most miserable months of my professional life, I left the company. Not once did I feel guilty when several of the "kids" called me months later to tell me they had left the firm and joined smaller consulting companies!

You can't imagine how much better I feel having relayed that story to you. It has been told at cocktail parties and to aspiring consultants who ask me if there are any differences between the big prestigious firms and the little, often unknown, boutique ones, but I don't often share the story with FM colleagues. Believe me, I'm not knocking any of the big firms. Most of them have excellent reputations (this is the year 2002 as I write, though) and provide the right atmosphere for many successful consultants. My experience there, however, not in terms of the work I was doing or the clients I was working with (one of which still is a client of mine today), but in terms of the *corporate culture* left such an indelible impression on me that some 30 years later, I still get a knot in my stomach and break out in goose bumps when I tell the story.

So is there anyone out there who wants to argue with me about the impact of corporate culture? Don't even attempt it. Corporate culture plays a critical role in how individuals and groups function in organizations and is an essential DNA link to the genetic makeup of FM departments.

What Is the Big "C"—Corporate Culture—About?

This chapter seems to be one where there is absolutely no reason not to borrow concepts shamelessly from others. There doesn't appear to be much room for improvement on what others have said. Corporate culture has been studied by some of the best minds in the OD field, and what these researchers found has tremendous applicability to our discussion here. There are at least a hundred variations on definitions of corporate culture contained in books on the subject, but they all seem to say the same thing. The three best for our purposes are quoted here. These three definitions range from the most formal one found in the dictionary to the most informal one The Friday Group has heard in the halls of client companies.

> Culture is the sum total of ways of living built up by a group of human beings and transmitted from one generation to another.[1]
> Culture is the values shared by the people in a group that tend to persist over time even when group membership changes and the behavior patterns or style of an organization that new employees are automatically encouraged to follow by their fellow employees.[2]
> Culture is the way things get done around this place.[3]

Take your pick from among the three or any other definitions that sound like these because they capture the essence of culture. Culture, probably more than any other topic in our OD discussion, is the very essence of organizational DNA. Culture is like a company's genes or personality. Often it isn't formally captured in documents or processes, but it is the cement that holds an enterprise together.

Some of the experts on culture you are familiar with from previous chapters. You may remember our discussion on leadership where I quoted Harvard professor John Kotter. Kotter and his colleague James Heskett have conducted extensive research on culture and its relationship to performance of major corporations and made several important discoveries. They have evidence to support their belief that the culture of a company is so powerful that its impact supersedes all other factors when it comes to organizational economic performance.[4] This finding is a pretty strong statement about the influence of culture, yet there is a body of research to support Kotter, Heskett, and others who affirm strong culture has almost always been the driving force behind continuing success in business, not only in America but around the globe.

The work of Kotter and Heskett, produced in their book *Corporate Culture and Performance*, gives credence to my belief that being intimately familiar with the corporate culture of any enterprise is key to OD in FM. Through their work, Kotter and Heskett identified 4 critical facts about corporate culture:[5]

1. Long-term financial performance is affected by corporate culture.

2. Success or failure of a company in the future will become more profoundly affected by corporate culture.

3. It is fairly common to find companies staffed with capable people who make sound decisions that still have corporate culture inhibiting long-term financial strength.

4. It is possible to manage and change corporate culture.

It seems only logical that FM professionals who are striving to impact the financial well-being of their enterprises would want to have an in-depth knowledge and understanding of the corporate culture. How else could they influence corporate culture if it isn't understood?

Since corporate culture is considered a main ingredient to enterprise success, facility professionals should be able to identify the primary element of culture. Of all the research conducted to determine what constitutes corporate culture, The Friday Group finds the research of Terrence Deal and Allan Kennedy to be the most definitive. This research served as the basis of their first book, *Corporate Cultures* in 1982, which was revised in 2000. They conclude from extensive investigation within corporations that four elements comprise the basis of corporate culture.[6] What's going on in the business environment has the greatest impact on the shape of the corporate culture. Companies that have a solid corporate culture are keenly aware of the business environment within which they operate. They know the pulse points of the marketplace such as the competition, the economic indicators, government regulations, customer trends, and technological advances. By understanding the business landscape, companies know what they have to do to be successful. Business landscape influences the four elements of culture.

❒ *Values*—To be perfectly honest, there seems to be too much hype about values and not enough substance. Values should be similar to a company's formula for success and its philosophy about the way employees work together and produce whatever output for which the company is responsible. Sometimes values statements are sweeping and grandiose, sounding very much like platitudes or slogans, such as the Avis "We try harder." They take on a larger than life meaning both outside the company and for employees inside. Other values statements try to enlighten employees on corporate qualities they should embody, such as "We will be respectful of one another" or "We will strive to be thoughtful of our fellow coworkers." Still other corporate values address attitudes about customers, such as "Our most important people are our customers."

According to Deal and Kennedy, what makes the difference between corporate mottos and true values statements is the extent to which they are institutionalized and shared by all within the company. A system of shared values that is reinforced and practiced by everyone inside the company makes a big difference in defining what is most respected within the company. A shared value system helps recruit employees that will fit into the corporate culture. The Friday Group knows, for example, that Southwest Airlines values a sense of humor in prospective employees: At one time, candidates were asked to relay an amusing incident or story as part of the interview process.

What the company values also creates parameters for success for those who want to advance within a company. If customer service is valued highly, for example, then individuals who exhibit strong customer relations skills in their job performance should have a greater chance of receiving promotions. The downside to this, however, for many companies is that in reality, the bottom-line contributions often receive higher recognition and reward than do the achievements in customer relationship-building. When companies say they value something but fail to be consistent in applying the value system, the system is diluted and ultimately undermined.

❒ *Heroes*—Deal and Kennedy use this term for individuals within companies who inspire individuals and are viewed as the epitome of corporate cultures. From my perspective, heroes within companies possess many of the same qualities we discussed for leaders in Chapter 1, with an exception. In corporations, heroes may not necessarily have charismatic features that make them liked by all, but they typically become heroes because they have fought hard to ensure that the values and beliefs of the company are held sacred—often at the expense of popularity. These heroes make certain the corporate culture and ethics of success are upheld in extraordinary circumstances.

❐ *Ritualism*—Walk into almost any company and ask for symbols of the culture and employees will bring up company rituals. Remember my personal experience with associate consultants putting on suit jackets to meet with partners and other executives? Though no one ever told these folks to do it, the customs and rituals were handed down over the years.

One of the most dramatic examples of cultural ritualism in companies is the positioning of staff around a meeting table. Without fail, those who research the strategy of seating arrangements find there is a ritualistic approach to selecting a seat at a meeting. Once that pattern is established, rarely do employees deviate from the pattern unless the individual in charge encourages or mandates a change.

Without attention to ceremonial expressions of corporate cultures, the value system has difficulty surviving. Values are manifested through symbolism and traditions. Having retirement dinners, recognition assemblies, company picnics, and holiday parties all serve to reinforce the social and work culture of a company. If we look at *Fortune*'s list of top 100 companies to work for, we find these companies all pay close attention to rituals that inculcate the corporate culture. Managers in these companies know that it is part of their responsibility to showcase corporate culture through both social and work rituals.

❐ *Communication network*—While it seems to be an obvious one, the element communication network, or the flow of information, often is overlooked in companies. Beyond the formal communication structure that strives to reinforce culture in media, such as Web sites, annual reports, employee handbooks, E-mail, memos, and marketing materials, there is an entire underground communication network serving to reinforce or negate the company's culture. How this network is managed determines, in part, the success of the company's culture. From the administrative group that serves as the gatekeeper for the organization's communication to moles within companies who may listen to the underground network specifically to report information back to executives, the culture of a company is affected by the way communication occurs. The more overt and open communication channels remain, the stronger the corporate culture becomes. It is when employees of a company feel they need to create clandestine means, such as secret meetings after work or publications of nonsanctioned newsletters to share information, that corporate culture is weakened. Companies need to nurture individuals who become corporate folk legends, passing on stories about the rituals and behavioral patterns that have historical significance to the company. These folks, in addition to others whose job it is to promote culture in more subtle ways by acting as cultural "spin doctors," serve to foster a positive environment through which the culture is embraced.

Believing the four elements Deal and Kennedy consider to be critical for successful corporate culture—values, heroes, ritualism, and communication network—are significant but somewhat limited, The Friday Group has looked for additional culture benchmarks to share with clients. Franklin Ashby, author of *Revitalize Your Corporate Culture,* considers several other elements in addition to those found by Deal and Kennedy to contribute to great culture. I have summarized his findings in Figure 4-1.[7]

If Ashby's characteristics appear familiar to you, it is because they practically parallel the factors contributing to individual and group motivation we discussed in Chapters 2 and 3. You probably appreciate why the concept of organizational DNA is so appealing to me. Like little molecules that stick together to form the DNA, motivation and culture need to form a tight link in order for an organization to be healthy and thriving.

What Is the Relationship Between Corporate Culture and the Culture of an FM Department?

Facility professionals enjoying the previous discourse on corporate culture certainly are wondering, "What's in it for FM depart-

Figure 4-1. Elements that contribute to great cultures.

GREAT CULTURE CHARACTERISTICS

Characteristic	Description
Missionary zeal	Positive energy, zeal, or fervor permeates company.
Sense of pride, sincerity and cooperation	Actions of employers towards each other and customers demonstrate feelings about company.
Attitude of constructive discontent	Status quo and complacency aren't tolerated. Systems, approaches, programs, and processes evaluated continuously. Continuous improvement philosophy prevails.
Volume-based mind-set and management style (Deal and Kennedy's values)	Values are inculcated into management decisions about all aspects of corporate activities.
Emphasis on creativity and innovation	Encouragement to bring creative and innovative ideas to the table extends to suppliers and other external providers.
Focus on role models not only leaders (Deal and Kennedy's heroes)	Ethical standards come first, often at the expense of profitability; "practice what you preach philosophy."
Sense of high expectations and professional standards	Commitment to excellence in dealings with fellow employees, customers and output is instilled at every company level.
Fair, commensurate compensation and incentive program	Employees are rewarded for meeting and exceeding established goals and performance expectations.
Habit of celebrating success (Deal and Kennedy's ritualism)	Appreciation for accomplishments and achievements are shared and showcased by all.
Attention to golden rule	Do unto others as you would have others do unto you!

Source: Franklin C. Ashby, *Revitalize Your Corporate Culture: Powerful Ways to Transform Your Company into a High-Performance Organization,* (New York: Gulf Professional Publishing Company, 1999).

ments?" How does corporate culture influence the development of an FM department?

Our discussion of culture within FM departments begins with three statements on the nature of culture within organization sub-units such as FM departments. We need to spend time on each of these to gain a better understanding of the influences corporate culture has on FM department DNA.

❏ If the corporate culture is strong, the FM department should emulate or parallel it.

❏ Strong culture in an FM department doesn't just happen; it takes conscientious planning and hard work.

❏ It is possible to change the culture within an FM department.

Emulating Corporate Culture

We learned in the previous section about elements of culture and how they affect the way in which a company operates. When found collectively in a company, these elements form the underpinnings for the enterprise way of doing business. One additional element that is probably more critical than the rest is the need for the most senior executive to function as the cultural representative par excellence or, in some instances, the company culture icon. The success of a company's culture depends on how well the chief executive officer exemplifies the culture in place. This means, in order for culture to permeate an entire corporation, it has to come from the top of the organization.

What an important lesson for facility managers! If they want their FM departments to function as a microcosm of the corporate environment, they need to emulate the behavior and characteristics of the senior corporate official and instill the same sense of culture throughout the department. We are assuming, of course, the overall corporate culture is *positive*, incorporating the elements to make it strong and vibrant. You recall in Chapter 3 we addressed the need for facility managers to create an environment ripe for team development; that environment, in large measure, is embodied by FM department culture.

Strong Culture Takes Planning and Work

One of the biggest myths about culture is that it just happens and good culture from one FM department will work in another. There is no such thing as a "right" culture that can be applied from one FM department to another. Culture, like our concepts of OD, is not trendy and can't be instilled by implementing the newest management techniques.

The culture of an FM department only works when the facility manager is crystal clear about the enterprise business (more on this in Chapter 5) and the business of the department. Often, establishing a solid department culture is a long and arduous task, accomplished through a trial-and-error process. When facility managers establish a vision for what the department's culture should be, they need to be prepared to commit the time and resources necessary to develop and sustain it.

Changing FM Department Culture

Often, when The Friday Group is assessing FM department problems, we find the root cause to be systemic to the department's culture. Although we know culture is never completely "pure" throughout an entire organization, we also know that the concept of core culture, similar to core competencies, forms the nucleus of how an FM department functions. We look at the elements necessary to form strong cultures in addition to analyzing the type of core culture the department exhibits.

From the experts who have focused on organization culture research, we find the work of William E. Schneider to provide the best analytical framework for assessing core culture. Schneider's research concluded that there are four core cultures organizations exhibit, and understanding these cultures allows managers to determine which intervention strategy is appropriate if the culture needs to be changed. The 4 core cultures—control, competence, cultivation, and collaboration—are described here:[8]

1. *Control*—In a control-centered organization, the focus of cultural activities is to ensure that the goals of the organization are protected and achieved. The integrity of the organization as an entity is the foundation for the culture, and all efforts are tar-

geted toward ensuring that the organization survives at all costs. Control organizations often are likened to the military in that the integrity of the institution must be preserved. Managers will initiate downsizing, rightsizing, and activity-based costing as measures to keep the nucleus of the organization intact.

2. *Competence*—The central theme of organization culture is the attainment of conceptual goals. Organizations exhibiting this type of culture are constantly striving to exhibit the best in class or superior status. Employers in this cultural environment are driven to demonstrate their uniqueness or superiority. Individuals within these organizations are seeking to satisfy their self-actualization needs and ensure that the operational processes and procedures support their lofty goals. These organizations pay close attention to benchmarking, best practices, performance-based compensation, and continuous improvement.

3. *Cultivation*—Kotter's views on values drive the cultivation culture. The emphasis in this environment is on guaranteeing that the norms and ideals of the group are executed through daily activities. Organizations high in cultivation culture subscribe to management practices such as open book, empowerment, and entrepreneurialism, key motivation factors we discussed in Chapter 2.

4. *Collaboration*—This organization culture builds on the diverse experiences of employees within the organization and those of its customers and external contacts. The organization strives for harmony between the experiences of its employees and the reality of the work environment. In a way, this core culture seeks synergy between the psychological contract and the organization. In a collaborative culture, the organization functions in such a way that there is intense commitment to achieving customer-oriented objectives. These organizations are prone to using self-directed teams, brainstorming techniques, and consensus-building efforts similar to those identified in Chapter 3.

Facility professionals are better able to suggest and participate in efforts to redirect an inappropriate culture or strengthen a highly effective one when they know the predominant core culture of the department. The responsibility of facility managers is to determine which culture is right for the delivery of FM services given the overall corporate culture and initiate change management strategies to correct a less than desirable environment.

How Do Facility Managers Direct Department Cultural Changes?

Spotting and assessing a faulty culture in an FM department is one thing; implementing a successful change process is another. Often facility managers find they have telltale indicators of the former, but have great difficulty structuring the latter. This situation is where planning and hard work enter into the picture.

Diagnosing Cultural Maladies

Sometimes it is easy to see why the culture of an FM department is in trouble. Often The Friday Group will see three or four glaring cultural problems after briefly observing department staff within the work environment. How and where staff congregate informally, how they greet each other in the corridors, how staff spend their day at work, and how they interact with supervisors and facility managers all provide valuable clues about the department's culture.

Other valuable information about a department's culture can be obtained by interviewing staff, reading correspondence and documentation, and talking with the department's customers. Conversations with staff about length of service, opportunities for advancement, organizational norms and rituals, teamwork, and customer orientation reveal a great deal about the department's culture. Such conversations provide insight into how employees view their work environment and the level of commitment they have to each other, the organization's well-being, themselves, and their customers. Random conversations with customers serve to balance the external and internal perspectives. Customer comments, or the lack thereof, speak volumes about the health of FM department culture.

Other means of obtaining feedback from employees about the culture of the department include anonymous surveys, focus groups, and facilitated staff retreats. These mechanisms, if designed well, give facility managers a snapshot of whether the culture is focused or fragmented, healthy or ill.

Intervening to Promote Cultural Change

The subject of interventionist strategies to promote change in culture has been a favorite topic for many experts on organization culture. For the most part, however, those experts seem to agree there is no magic formula to ensure a change in culture, only guidelines and techniques to make the road to change less bumpy, sort of the trial-and-error theory we talked about earlier in the chapter. Deal and Kennedy have provided some of the best guidance for promoting change, which I have adopted and labeled the do's of managing change in Figure 4-2.[9]

Evaluating Change

Once facility managers have implemented a strategy to correct or modify a department's culture, they should evaluate the impact the change has made. Judith Gordon has captured the essence of change by describing the four levels at which change can occur.[10] Evaluating change determines if the desired result has been achieved.

Behavior—Managers need to know if employee actions within the workplace have changed. It is important to determine if employees are interacting with one another and external customers and suppliers differently. It also is critical to assess how they are performing their job functions to see if new approaches related to cultural change have been implemented.

Attitude—The key is to assess how employees feel about the process used to initiate change and if they find the process effective.

Learning—When facility managers conduct training to effect a cultural change, they want to measure the effectiveness of the training. If staff participated in team-building exercises, customer service training, conflict management, or cultural sensitivity workshops, it is necessary to measure the extent of learning.

Performance—Finally, facility managers will want to know the effectiveness of change on staff performance. Depending on the types of interventionist strategies put into place to change compensation programs, entrepreneurial initiatives, or service delivery enhancement, it is critical to learn how much these practices stabilized or bolstered an FM department's culture.

Figure 4-2. Ten do's of managing changes.

DO'S OF MANAGING CHANGE

1. Do use consensus-building to gain support for change. ❐ Peer relationships are strong change agents.	6. Do use an inspired staff member to lead the effort. ❐ Remember heroes are an important element of culture.
2. Do establish an atmosphere of trust and confidence. ❐ A two-way trust environment stimulates positive communication.	7. Do be wary of subversive activities outside the department. ❐ Culture change threatens those who are outside.
3. Do provide training to enhance skills building. ❐ Change in culture can't occur unless staff are equipped to implement new ideas.	8. Do provide a transition period for staff to bury and mourn old ways. ❐ Long-standing rituals are hard to relinquish but new symbols and rituals need to be celebrated.
4. Do expect change to take place over a long period of time. ❐ Shortchanging the time required for staff to adapt by creating an overly ambitious schedule is a death knell for change. Be patient.	9. Do use an outside catalyst to intervene when necessary. ❐ Consultants often can jump start the process, infuse energy into a lagging process and measure outcomes. Then they leave!
5. Do less rather than more management of change. ❐ Staff need to make the culture change work in their own world without being constricted by management hovering over them.	10. Do keep the basic organization intact until change has been completed. ❐ Having staff worry about job security or hidden agendas will diminish acceptance of change.

Source: Terrence E. Deal, and Allan A. Kennedy, *Corporate Cultures* (Cambridge, Mass.: Perseus Publishing, 1982).

How Does Diversity Affect the Culture of an FM Department?

Diversity among FM employees can have a significant impact on the overall department culture and specifically that of work groups. Not only do these employee "sets" have different interests, norms, and values, but they also have different languages, customs, work ethics, and motivational factors. At times these differences have potential for conflict within FM departments, requiring facility managers to employ their diagnostic skills to determine the impact on the department's culture. More often, however, this workforce diversity has the potential to enrich department performance if facility managers understand how to mesh the differences appropriately.

Globally Integrated Staffs

As the global business environment becomes more fully integrated, so also do FM departments. It is not uncommon for FM departments in a headquarters location to have employees from multiple countries working side by side, in addition to having field locations in multiple countries around the world. We talk more about global FM department structures in Chapter 6.

For facility managers, cultural diversity may mean language differences as well as nuances in the meaning of FM-related terms. The Friday Group has witnessed examples of these subtle, yet often critical, differences in almost every term pertaining to FM. They range from the word *service* in the broadest sense to the word *bookshelf* in the most specific instance. In integrated multinational FM departments, it is important that facility managers establish common definitions for FM terms to ensure all staff are using the same terminology.

Another challenge associated with multinationally integrated FM departments is the way work is negotiated and structured. For some FM employees, the concept of formal written agreements with customers and providers may be one that is uncharacteristic of their native culture. For other employees, it may be the concept of time frames and sense of urgency, which may vary from one native culture to another. The role of the facility manager is to identify for all staff what the culture of the FM department is in terms of norms, values, ethics, and other business conduct.

Aging FM Staffs

There is no escaping the fact that the workforce in general is aging, which poses a whole new set of problems for the provision of FM services. We could have an elaborate discussion on the aging workforce and the implications for providing FM services, but that is not a discussion congruent with our emphasis on department culture. As the general workforce ages, so too are the employees of many established FM departments. This aging workforce poses several different issues for facility managers.

First, how facility managers handle aging workers plays an important part in the stability of the FM department culture. Remember, stability is an important ingredient for healthy culture. Facility managers need to ensure that older workers are respected and given the same opportunities and tools the younger workers have. As these workers age, not only can they provide development and guidance to younger workers on-site, but the technological advances in FM may allow them to make positive contributions to the department from remote locations such as their homes or regional centers far longer than we once might have envisioned. It will be incumbent upon facility managers to ensure that subgroups within the department remain age diverse to take advantage of the cross training and sharing that occur among the various age groups of the workforce.

At the same time, however, the aging FM department workforce presents another challenge for facility managers—the impact of the "brain drain" on the institutional memory of facilities. Many FM departments have older buildings in their portfolio that often do not have extensive as-built drawings or documentation about infrastructure, remodeling, and upgrade changes. FM staffs that have worked around these buildings have information about them that typically isn't found in documentation. They know how things work, what the idiosyncrasies are of particular equipment, and what the department has done over the years to correct specific problems. When these staffs retire or leave for other purposes, FM departments lose much of their valuable institutional knowledge.

Generations X and Y

Younger workers bring new and different sets of values, beliefs, and norms about work to FM departments than aging baby boomers. Their requirements and expectations about the workplace may pose challenges for facility managers with respect to motivation and individual and group activities.

What so many of these younger workers want out of the department is balance between work and personal time or a new twist on the psychological contract of expectations they have for their work experience. For some older FM staffs, this balance is a foreign concept, because they are accustomed to rigorous demands of FM in terms of time commitments. Sometimes the older workers find it difficult to understand and accept the generational work ethic difference and the impact it has on the culture of the department.

Tree-Huggers

For those of you unfamiliar with the term, it has nothing to do with being an environmentalist. A *tree-hugger* is a human resources term for someone who stays with one company longer than the norm for that particular industry. Although the FM profession has no formal statistics on what our industry norm is, over the years The Friday Group has conducted its own informal research. We find the norm for FM staff to be between 10 and 12 years, but it is not uncommon to find tree-huggers, or staff, who stay in one FM department way beyond 12 years.[11] Contrast this with staff in the high-tech professions who stay with one company on average 2 to 3 years and are considered tree-huggers if they stay longer than 3 years.

Tree-huggers pose challenges for facility managers because they may not be able to convince them they should either move to another position within the same corporation or seek new avenues outside the company. Sometimes there are no opportunities for tree-huggers to advance or diversify within a department, and this lack of opportunity causes employees to be disruptive to the department and its culture. I am not saying facility managers always should encourage their staffs to leave—it would be considered blasphemy by some facility managers who have suffered severe staff reductions due to downsizing, rightsizing, and corporate mergers. We have only discussed the relationship between workforce stability and organization culture, not advocated wholesale staff turnover.

Often, however, FM staffs need exposure to other corporate cultures and methods of service delivery in order to keep current and add value to the departments they serve. While the greater challenge for facility managers is to provide opportunities for staff growth and development within an existing department, there are instances where they need to consider a career move for employees outside the department. Employees who move into another corporate venue provide an expanded network for the FM department and opportunities for information and process sharing.

In summary, the culture of an organization is the fabric upon which the imprint of FM is stamped. As facility managers, it is imperative that you make certain you and your staff understand the corporate culture and how it affects the FM department. In addition, being on top of the culture within the department and having the skills to diagnose when the culture is not working and intervene to redirect culture in a positive direction is key to a department with strong DNA. To do this, facility professionals have to be able to analyze the impact that differences in language, native customs, age, and other factors have on the department's culture. We turn now to strategic planning, our next DNA link.

DNA Link: Culture

Company: Hertfordshire County Council UK (local government)

Background

Hertfordshire County Council is a major UK local government organization responsible for 15 million square feet of offices, schools, and community buildings. The responsibility for the work of the council rests with elected political representatives. A Senior Management Board under the direction of the CEO carries out the day-to-day governance and management of the organization in conjunction with a small cabinet of elected representatives. In 1997, the former Property Department was outsourced. The decision was driven by government legislation requiring public authorities to market-test their services. It was also driven by the staff's conviction that they needed to become more competitive if their business was to flourish and survive. The contract itself provided for a Total

Facility Management (TFM) service—with all property and facility services provided by a single supplier who took over the staff and business of the in-house department. A separate contract was negotiated with the County Council's customer service center to provide help-line support for the large number of end users who regularly used the Property Department's services. Each contract was let on a partnering basis that encouraged and rewarded innovation and continuous improvement.

A small Intelligent Client Function (ICF) was kept in-house following the externalization. Three functionally oriented teams provide oversight of the outsource provider. The first team interfaces with project and facility management services. The second specializes in asset and disposal strategy. The third provides contract management. All three teams work with the external provider on the planning and utilization of the county's facilities. Coordinating the needs of the County Council's service departments, such as schools, libraries, offices, and children's homes, is handled by a Property Board that meets four times a year. The board is responsible for preparing the Corporate Asset Management Plan that is presented to the cabinet each year. The organization chart is showed in Figure Hertfordshire 1.

Their Story

Core Competencies

The current Property Department of the Hertfordshire County Council has identified 4 core competencies:

1. *Facility Strategy*—This role links the business plans of service departments to an overall Corporate Asset Management Plan, which is renewed each year. The strategic role both facilitates and challenges the thinking of the service department's aim to promote innovation and enhanced benefits from corporate real estate resource management.

2. *Contract Management*—The success of the service depends on the performance of the TFM provider. Under-

Figure Hertfordshire 1.

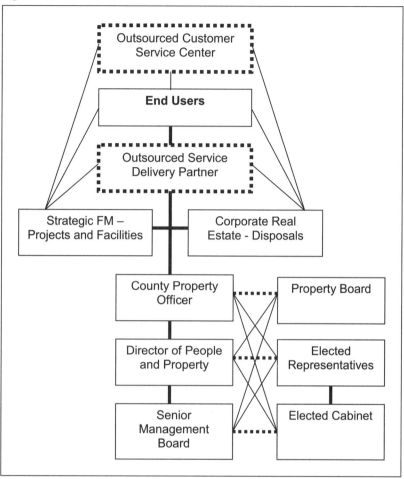

standing how to structure, monitor, and provide incentives for performance improvement is a key skill within the unit.

3. *Project Management*—Delivering facility change requires skillful project management, facilitation, and communication skills to identify business benefits and ensure that projects achieve the specified business outcomes.

4. *Organization Development*—A key role of the ICF is to develop the skills and competencies of managers at all levels and in all parts of the organization to contribute effectively to facility and project management.

Service Mix

The outsource provider is responsible for all Facility and Estate Management services, either directly or through their own supply chain, under the TFM contract. There are a number of exclusions, however, including:

❑ Catering, Cleaning, and Grounds Maintenance contracts that are let directly by the County Council

❑ Construction services that are let to contractors included on a government-supported national register of construction companies

❑ Specialized consultants, such as those advising on facility strategy and development Project Managers who work closely with end users and service departments

❑ Town Planning and Site Development Managers who are retained in-house because of the political sensitivity of many projects

Best Practices

The mission of the Property Department is to ensure that the supply of property and facility services supports the work of the council and the community. There are a number of areas in which it seeks to use best practices to meet this need.

❑ The preparation of the Corporate Asset Management Plan is now in its fifth year. The program aims to bring together the various needs of the organization and maximize facility resource utilization. The planning process is carefully co-ordinated with the preparation of annual service plans that define business needs for each part of the organization. The plan is supported by regular surveys of the condition, suitability, and sufficiency of each of the buildings in the estate. As a result of the planning process, the county has been able to sustain regular asset disposals that bring in an income large enough to support the ongoing capital investment program. Through the introduction of carefully selected targets, elected representatives have been able to help set a strategic direction for managing the county's facilities.

From the outset, both the county and the external provider were committed to a partnering approach. The CEOs of both organizations signed a mutual Partnering Agreement that committed both sides to an open and constructive relationship. This relationship has been sustained by regular partnering forums to allow for the exchange of ideas for improvement. Both sides recognize that partnering must be supported by tangible benefits. At the beginning of the contract term, a review of the areas where these benefits were likely to be most valuable was performed. The review included a prioritized action plan for a series of joint studies to test the business case for each change or improvement. The Council has achieved twice the benefit from this shared savings program as it did from the cost reductions achieved at the tender stage.

Finally, the county's view is that even though individuals manage facilities, facility management can be done only by the organization as a whole. The Property Department aims to provide a center of excellence in facility management skills. But, however expert it is, it still relies on an understanding and appreciation of the benefits and potential of the FM approach from managers throughout the organization. Consequently, the Hertfordshire County Council's Property Department has taken the lead in developing corporate facility competence through:

❏ General and specific training events for general managers involved in facilities management

❏ Sessions raising awareness of new developments or innovations

❏ Induction of incoming managers taking on facility responsibilities for the first time

❏ Developing general management competencies in collaboration with the corporate training department

---

Learning Points

❏ FM service team structure culture mirrors corporate culture

❏ Culture centered around people as most valuable asset to create center of excellence

❏ Partnership approach with outsource provider

❏ Strategic service link to corporate business plans

About the Author

Phil Roberts, CFM, is head of Strategic Facility Management at Hertfordshire County Council. Prior to that he was Facilities Advisor at the British Council, an international government agency. Phil is a past member of the International Facilities Management Association (IFMA) Board of Directors.

Endnotes

1. John P. Kotter and James L. Heskett, *Corporate Culture and Performance* (New York: The Free Press, 1992), p. 4.
2. *Random House Webster's College Dictionary* (New York: Random House, 1999), p. 323.
3. Heard by The Friday Group in corporate hallways.
4. Kotter and Heskett, op. cit., p. 11.
5. Ibid.
6. Adapted from Terrence E. Deal and Allan A. Kennedy, *Corporate Cultures: The Rites and Rituals of Corporate Life* (Cambridge: Perseus Publishing, 2000), pp. 13–84.
7. Adapted from Franklin C. Ashby, *Revitalize Your Corporate Culture* (Houston: Cashman Dudley, 1999), pp. 82–112.

8. Adapted from William E. Schneider, *Reengineering Alternative: A Plan for Making Your Culture Work* (New York: Mc-Graw-Hill/Irwin, 1994).
9. Deal and Kennedy, op. cit., pp. 164–177.
10. Judith R. Gordon, *Organizational Behavior: A Diagnostic Approach,* 6th ed. (Upper Saddle River, NJ: Prentice Hall, 1999), pp. 486–487.
11. The Friday Group research, 1995–2000.

CHAPTER FIVE

The Role of Strategic Planning and the FM Organization

DNA Link: Visioning and Strategic Planning

Where Do Visioning and Strategic Planning Fit into Our DNA Scheme?

In building our DNA for an FM department, we need to discuss visioning and strategic planning. Before we consider the OD skills that enable FM managers to structure and staff departments to deliver services, we need to focus on the relationship between visioning and strategic planning and FM organizations. In a sense, visioning and strategic planning are the linchpin between the elements we have been discussing thus far and our exploration of FM department structures, configurations, staffing, and benchmarking.[1]

This chapter is not intended to be an instructor's manual on the mechanics of visioning and strategic planning. Although we are going to review the major process components, we are not going to go through specific process steps. Our focus here is to fully understand how visioning and strategic planning serve as the glue that links individuals, teams, and corporate culture to organization design.

As you contemplate this DNA link, think about the following three questions and see if you can answer any of them. These questions are pertinent to our discussion. The means to obtaining the answers will be revealed as we proceed through this chapter.

1. How do FM departments know they are providing the right services?

2. How do FM departments avoid fire fighting and become more proactive?

3. What measures do FM departments use to determine if they are adding value to the enterprise they serve?

What Do We Mean by Visioning and Strategic Planning?

The terms *visioning* and *strategic planning* are part of our OD lexicon. Our definition of visioning is derived from the 1999 edition of *Random House Webster's Collegiate Dictionary* for the word *vision*.

> The power of anticipating that which may come to be; foresight.[1]

Strategic planning has a simple definition used by The Friday Group for many years. We believe our definition evolved over time, but we may have appropriated it from another source long ago. If this is not an original Friday Group definition, we apologize to the creator!

> Strategic planning is figuring out where you are headed *before* you start on a journey and then creating a plan to get there.[2]

Because these two terms have a hand-in-glove relationship similar to that of management and leadership that we talked about in Chapter 1, we are discussing them as a single focus area, even though they are slightly different concepts. The two need to be performed in concert with one another as part of FM organization development.

A famous Robert Frost poem, "The Road Not Taken,"[3] begins our visioning and strategic planning discussion. This poem seems to epitomize the situations FM professionals often face as they attempt to determine what direction to take.

Frost's poem starts with "Two roads diverged in a yellow wood, and sorry I could not travel both."[4] Through succeeding passages, the poet describes the plight of a traveler who is faced with making a decision about which path to follow when he approaches a fork in the road. He has to select a single path in order to continue his journey. The traveler studies both roads and agonizes over which one to select. At first blush the roads look to be the same, but as he assesses them further, he finds they are quite different. The first road has been used more often: It is well trampled and easy to traverse. The second road has seen little use and is not well worn: The grass is long and there isn't any path to ensure safe footing along the way. As he confronts his dilemma, the traveler concludes the well-worn road makes the journey easier, whereas the "road less taken"[5] requires major work to create a path fit for him to walk. Deciding which road to choose is the essence of the poem.

Is There a Payoff Associated with Strategic Planning?

If you haven't figured it out, Frost's traveler decided to take the second road, "the road less traveled by."[6] Although the road appears to be more difficult, the traveler concludes it is worth the effort to embark down an unknown path even though he doesn't know what lies ahead.

Our focus area, visioning and strategic planning in FM, is similar to the road less traveled. Often visioning and strategic planning are unknown entities in FM departments, and their values not well understood. In many instances, it is a road not traveled at all!

FM departments tend to concentrate on performing day-to-day activities without taking time to lay them out in advance. Frequently, they start their journey at the beginning of a fiscal or calendar year without a clear picture of what they want to accomplish or how they are going to get there. Sometimes their facility managers justify the lack of planning by saying it is a luxury they can ill afford. Confronted with the issue of taking time away from a hectic schedule of routine activities, they put off strategic planning, saying it is difficult and takes an inordinate amount of time: They haven't discovered the strong correlation between strategic planning, staff motivation, and positive service outcomes.

It is understandable why FM departments get bogged down. When the demand for services exceeds the ability of the staff to deliver them, the work gets out of control. As the pace becomes more frenetic, FM departments start operating in a crisis mode. Soon this mode of operation becomes the norm rather than the exception, and the department gets completely off track. When a real crisis takes place, staffs are ill prepared to handle an emergency. They have been operating in this mode for so long they can't think or act quickly enough to mobilize a true crisis plan of action. This situation is typical of FM departments and underscores the need for a road map to guide activities.

Taking time to look at the future and develop an action plan for services delivery has tremendous benefit for FM departments. Absent the development of a plan to cover a specific work cycle, such as a fiscal or calendar year, FM departments end up making critical decisions without a context or framework to guide them. The Friday Group characterizes this mode of operation as SOP: not Standard Operating Procedure—as you might think—but Seat-of-the-Pants facility management! This approach to FM often is the road most taken because it appears to be easy and less time-consuming. What facility managers don't understand is that time spent planning at the front end means less frenzy throughout the year.

FM departments that don't plan also can't answer the three questions I posed at the beginning of this chapter. They don't know if their departments are providing the right services, they can't figure out how to stop putting out fires, and they won't be able to ascertain how their departments add value to the overall enterprise. The visioning and strategic planning process creates the framework needed to answer these questions.

We talk about the process of strategic planning, a process that ultimately results in a plan or series of plans to guide FM actions. These plans serve as the foundation for all FM activities and can be used to analyze, evaluate, acquire, and dispense staff and financial resources methodically to satisfy customer requirements throughout the year. Through visioning and strategic planning, FM departments are able to forecast corporate and individual organization requirements.

The strategic planning process serves another pivotal role in determining FM department structures. Visioning and strategic planning guide facility managers in their decision making so they can configure their departments and create a service team with the right mix of skills to do the job. We discuss the relationship between strategic planning and organization structure in detail in Chapter 6.

The correlation between the Robert Frost traveler and strategic planning in FM should be clear. The traveler in "The Road Not Taken" blazes a trail by taking a less journeyed path. At the conclusion of the poem, the traveler feels he made a wise decision because "the road not taken has made all the difference."[7] While the traveler never tells us what the *difference* is, he leaves us with the feeling that his choice resulted in a very positive experience. FM departments can have the same experience through visioning and strategic planning.

What Do Visioning and Strategic Planning Involve?

The process of visioning and strategic planning for FM departments consists of several parts. The first part centers on figuring out where the company or enterprise is headed. The next part involves analyzing how FM relates to the enterprise direction, establishing an FM department vision and strategic goals and objectives, and creating a plan to assist the enterprise with achieving these goals and objectives. Once the department creates strategic goals, objectives, and a plan to accomplish them, decisions about the requirements for FM services and the most appropriate organizational configuration can be made. A graphic representation of the process is shown in Figure 5-1.

Finding Out Where the Enterprise Is Headed

FM departments should consider the first part of the process as an outreach to corporate and other department leaders to obtain perspective on future direction. Since FM visioning and strategic planning should not occur in a vacuum, determining strategic direction for FM has to be influenced by, and parallel to, the strategic direction established for the overall company. The FM planning process begins by ascertaining corporate and department vision for the future, as well as specific business goals and objectives established to attain that vision.

Although many FM departments think they understand their

Figure 5-1. The visioning and strategic planning process.

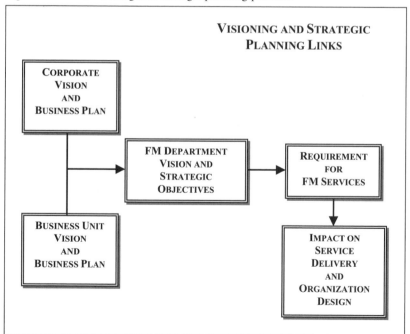

Source: The Friday Group.

company's vision, goals, and objectives, they often do not. The Friday Group has heard staffs say they believe they know what senior management has in mind for the company, only to learn they are way off the mark. Thinking your department is on top of what senior management is planning for the company isn't good enough because lack of clarity about corporate expectations makes it practically impossible to conduct FM strategic planning. Corporate thinking about where the company is headed and the path corporate leaders will take to get there influence the way in which vision, goals, and objectives for FM departments are crafted.

FM departments need to know about corporate business strategy to build an FM service strategy responsive to business priorities. FM departments need insight into issues such as targeted areas for growth and reduction; potential opportunities for mergers, acquisitions, or consolidations; new product development; global expansion; and marketing initiatives.

FM departments also need input from top management on other human resources issues. Much like exploring the needs of individuals within FM departments discussed in Chapter 2, FM departments need to have guidance from senior executives on issues such as employee health and safety, as well as an understanding of their commitment to provide services and amenities such as fitness areas, child care centers, and food services.

Another aspect of corporate thinking FM departments need to investigate is senior management's vision about facilities from a real estate perspective. Developing FM strategies associated with facilities issues such as owning versus leasing, centralization versus decentralization, and scattered site versus campus settings requires senior management to articulate how they envision the enterprise in the future. FM departments need this corporate viewpoint about facilities issues to target FM strategies responsive to corporate direction.

A client of The Friday Group provides an example of the need to have clear perspective on corporate facilities strategies. For years, the company leased the majority of its buildings, to the extent they were housed in twenty-two leased facilities. No one ever queried senior management on their views about facilities until the FM department initiated strategic planning for the first time. The department interviewed senior executives and talked with them about issues ranging from corporate image to building concepts and costs. With the information gleaned from senior management during these interviews, the FM department analyzed various building scenarios and provided a series of options for senior management to consider. Through this process, the department convinced top management to select a strategy based on owning its own facilities and creating a campus environment. The company adopted the FM department's recommendation, which ultimately led to consolidation of all employees from the twenty-two leased buildings to a campus setting with facilities owned by the company.

Another example from The Friday Group client files illustrates the importance of strategic facilities direction. This company inherited facilities around the world, and although they didn't have documented proof, the FM department felt many were inappropriate for future activities. Years of providing services to these existing buildings, however, had provided ample documentation on costs associated with maintaining the facilities. The department also was searching for guidance on the types of buildings that would be needed to accommodate future business streams of the company in every country.

In an effort to conceive more cost-effective ways to deliver FM services around the world, the department initiated a strategic planning process. Finding no statements about vision, goals, or objectives from the highest corporate echelons, the FM department held strategy sessions with the company's in-country representatives to gather valuable information. From these sessions, they learned about the plans for services to support activities in other countries over the next 10 years. Armed with this valuable information about long-term corporate service goals and objectives, the department crafted and recommended a facilities strategy for executive review. Their proposed strategy centered on more flexible, mobile facilities that could be transported easily throughout a country. Senior management adopted the strategy recommended by the department, and department staffs were praised for their leadership, foresight, and innovativeness.

One of the worst fears for FM departments is being the last to know about the plans of a *business unit*, our organization nomenclature for a corporate subunit. Business units have to reorganize, expand, or reduce space; add new staff or reduce staff; and reconfigure work areas due to new program mandates, changes in executive personnel, or shifts in budget priorities. Unfortunately, they frequently neglect to inform FM departments about these plans in the beginning or keep them in the loop as plans unfold. In all fairness, however, sometimes even the business units don't know about changes until the last minute, but this lack of information makes it difficult for FM departments to provide timely and responsive service.

When FM departments are the last to be informed, they don't have time to plan, and planning, as we know, is essential to figuring out the desired outcome and the best way to get there. Without advance information, FM departments function in the crisis mode we talked about earlier. When departments don't do their homework on business units, they can't come up with the most appropriate course of action to satisfy the requirement for FM services.

Herein lies the beauty of visioning and strategic planning. They provide the opportunity for FM departments to be proactive with customers, rather than being forced into the usual reactive mode. Instead of operating in the dark, FM departments contact customer organizations while they are developing plans for the upcoming year to uncover what the customer is planning. It is even more helpful when customers actually have plans providing details about how corporate objectives have been translated into strategic goals and objectives for their units. If FM departments are able to project customer business direction and strategic goals in advance, they can be much more responsive when they are called on for service.

Getting the Information

You might be wondering how FM practitioners get this information. There are a couple of very basic ways this information on corporate strategies can be obtained. The first way is through the corporate strategic plan, a document articulating executive vision for the company and outlining specific corporate goals and objectives. (Some of you probably are chuckling at the prospect of actually having such a document in your companies.) For the vast majority of companies, formal strategic plans of the type we are discussing usually do not exist. Like FM departments, many companies also fail to take the "road less traveled." Companies often don't take the time to go through the strategic planning process or create a document reflective of the corporate vision and strategic direction. Absent any documentation about corporate vision, goals, and objectives, however, FM departments do have another avenue to obtain this type of information—they can *ask* senior executives.

Asking senior executives their opinions about these issues is a smart idea, even when a fairly cogent corporate planning document exists. Engaging senior management in dialogue about corporate strategies affords FM departments the opportunity to interact with high-level decision makers and demonstrate their own capability to be strategic thinkers. By capturing the attention of senior management as they do their research, FM departments may become corporate trailblazers. Especially when corporate-wide visioning and strategic planning have not occurred, FM departments assert their leadership position by raising first-time questions about vision, goals, and objectives for the enterprise. Leadership, you will remember, is an important OD skill.

Sadly, most of you know business units don't plan any better than corporate executives, and when they do have plans, they generally lack substantive information. The Friday Group advises FM departments to create their own business unit database and has suggestions on the type of information that should be gathered. We encourage FM departments to create documents called Client Profiles.[8] (For those of you who have read *Quality Facility Management: A Customer Service and Marketing Perspective,* the book I coauthored with Dave Cotts, you might remember Client Profiles.) Client Profiles are introduced in the book as an excellent means of gaining access to customer organizations. Client Profiles provide the vehicle to have discussions about strategic direction and FM service issues.

Sometimes The Friday Group finds the research process involved in constructing Client Profiles to be painful for FM departments. Too many facility managers and their staffs feel they must be invited to business unit meetings to obtain critical data instead of making overtures themselves to have these discussions. If your department waits to be invited, it never will develop a strategic plan that is responsive to corporate and business unit needs. In other words, if you wait for an invitation to business unit strategy sessions, you'll probably miss the party.

The development of a Client Profile is a good entrée for FM staff to have discussions. Completing Client Profile information is an excellent means of getting the department's foot in the door with key individuals in business units to learn about business direction, validate existing information, and fill in information gaps. To be most effective for strategic planning purposes, we recommend that the Client Profile contain information similar to the following:

Demographic Data—Information is collected on the characteristics of the organization. This information should be updated periodically and may require FM staff to obtain information from human resources (with the sanction of the organization) as well as directly from the organization. When we refer to the demographics of the customer organization, we are talking about items such as organizational charts, numbers of employees by the various types of occupation codes they occupy (e.g., administrative, manager, executive), and any type of specialized personnel (which we call the *niche market*) such as scientists, lawyers, marketing, or technical staff who might have need for FM services that differ or are above and beyond what other employees of the organization might require. In this portion of the Client Profile, the FM department also can capture trend information: how frequently reorganizations occur, if they use temporary or seasonal personnel, if they have a cooperative program with local universities, for example. This data paints a picture of the organization's population and its statistics.

Facilities and Real Estate Demographics—Data captured is about the organization and its relationship to the physical facilities. This information helps establish the relationship between personnel demographics and the demographics of your buildings. For example, the information should cover the distribution of personnel within facilities in terms of the buildings they occupy (both owned and leased), where they are located in the buildings, the number of square feet they occupy, the categories of space they occupy in each facility (for example, R&D, computer, office, conference room), the space density, and churn rate. This information completes the demographics picture by relating the personnel in the organization to the space they occupy.

Expenditures on FM and Real Estate—Expenditure information is particularly critical to development of FM strategies because it establishes a mechanism to document trends on how a particular organization uses FM services. Regardless of whether FM departments have a charge-back system, they can develop a profile of FM and real estate-related expenditures. For every service the department covers, from rent to conference room scheduling, a profile should detail the amount of dollars expended on a particular business unit. If a charge-back system is in place, it is even easier to capture this data.

Sociological Data—In Chapter 4, we talked about culture as an important element of an organization's development. FM departments need to capture similar information about the culture, values, work styles, and habits of customer organizations, in addition to the type of work environment they prefer and the extent of external customer interaction they have. This information completes the picture of how individuals within the customer's organization relate to one another, what their tolerances are for certain activities, and what is important to them. If the FM department knows, for example, a business unit works almost exclusively in teams, this information defines the work environment they need so the department can serve them better. If the department learns they are an organization interacting with the external public a great deal, the department also will have an idea of how important the appearance and flow of their physical space are to them. The sociological data developed is as important as the demographic data.

Financial Information—A component of the Client Profile is information on the funding/revenue streams and approval authorities. This information helps to determine when organizations are more likely to undertake major projects and who needs to be involved in the decision-making process. If a particular business unit is dependent on seasonal, product-driven revenue streams, as an example, your department will know when the organization is likely to have the ability to initiate renovations or alterations.

Collecting and analyzing this data give FM departments the ability to tailor service offerings to particular components of the organization because the profile has information specific to that entity. Later in the chapter, we discuss how FM departments use the Client Profile to demonstrate the value they provide to customer organizations by helping them make sound business decisions.

Figuring Out Where the FM Department Is Headed

Armed with information about the enterprise as a whole, FM departments then conduct their own visioning as a prelude to developing a strategic plan of action. Assessing the vision, goals, and objectives for the corporation and business units and aligning those of the FM department with them is the first step in determining where the FM department is headed. Strategic alignment of FM and corporate vision, goals, and objectives helps FM departments address the question of providing appropriate services.

Often overlooked in the visioning and strategic planning process is the consideration of where the FM department wants to be from an OD perspective. Considerations about leadership, professional and personal development, entrepreneurism, team-building, and the culture of an organization should be factored into the discussions about the department's future. These OD issues are of equal importance to those regarding service strategies. To achieve a department's vision to become a world-class provider of FM services, for example, goals and objectives related to the vision have to be established. OD goals and objectives require their own set of actionable items to ensure that the FM department takes the appropriate path to achieve its goals. In order to become a world-class facilities management organization, the FM department must pursue a course of action designed to create strong DNA.

Creating an FM Action Plan

The end result of visioning and strategic planning is a deliverable. This deliverable is an action plan for FM that outlines the path the department will take over the established life of the plan. The action plan is of value to the department only when it is perceived as a living, breathing, working document—one that is reviewed, updated, and modified as corporate, business unit, and FM department needs change.

Too many strategic plans gather dust on FM department bookshelves. Facility managers and their staffs point to these documents as a "badge of courage" for having made it through the process. Beyond that, the documents never serve as true guidance for the department's operation, management, or service delivery. Strategic plans should be viewed as utilitarian tools containing specific and consistent types of information necessary to shape the FM department's activities. The information contained within the strategic plan serves as the structure against which the FM department's management gauges success in meeting their goals and objectives through routine monitoring of planned versus actual outcomes and actions. For our clients, The Friday Group suggests a strategic plan structure consisting of the following components:

Vision Statement—The statement reflecting the ideal of the FM department. It is a statement articulating where the department hopes to be in the future.

Mission Statement—The statement identifying the purpose of the FM department or how the department wants others to describe what it does.

Values Statement—The manner in which the department conducts its business.

Goals/Objectives—Statements that are specific, time-related, measurable, and feasible within the context of the overall corporate goals/objectives.

- *Strategies/Initiatives*—Action steps necessary to achieve goals and objectives.

Responsibility Matrix—Department subunits and specific individuals within the department who will have lead responsibility for overseeing the achievement of certain goals and objectives, in addition to individuals within the department who will be involved with each goal and objective.

Renewal Schedule—A process and schedule for reviewing the strategic plan to determine if changes, modifications, or deletions of goals and initiatives should take place.

Who Needs to Be Involved in FM Department Visioning and Strategic Planning?

The quick answer to this question is, everyone in the department should take part in visioning and strategic planning. In order for staff within the FM department to have a sense of ownership in the direction the department is headed and to understand the role they play as individuals toward the achievement of departmental goals, they have to be involved in the visioning and strategic planning process. Remember back in Chapter 2, we learned about a critical motivating factor for FM staff—the sense that their input was heard and valued. Involvement in visioning and strategic planning is one of the means to ensure that everyone in an FM department has a voice about the department's future and the path to get there.

The Friday Group suggests to our clients that visioning and strategic planning are both a top-down and a bottom-up process. We recommend commencing the process through the issuance of a strategic-planning white paper prepared by the facility manager that articulates his thoughts on the future of the department in terms of vision, goals, objectives, and initiatives that need to be considered. After this document is circulated throughout the department, managers of subunits then conduct brainstorming sessions with their staffs to prepare for a management team planning session. Subunit staffs provide their managers with thoughts on vision, goals, objectives, and initiatives that are shared by all managers on the FM department management team during the team's strategic planning retreat.

It is the goal of the management team, consisting of the facility manager and his leadership group, to map out the vision, goals, objectives, and initiatives that will serve as the department's overarching strategy. Once the department's plan has been developed, the management team members take the information back to their subunits and replicate the process. Each of the department's subunits will have specific departmental goals and objectives they have lead responsibility for and some for which they are team members.

In addition to overarching departmental goals and objectives, each subunit will have targeted goals and objectives specific to the function the subunit performs within the overall context of the department's service delivery strategy.

Can Strategic Planning Really Demonstrate How FM Departments Add Value to Companies?

Countless FM departments need to be applauded for their leadership role in the area of visioning and strategic planning. The Friday Group has watched FM departments take the first bold step in strategic planning by polling senior executives about strategic initiatives and creating business unit Client Profiles to find their intelligence is better than their customer's! Often FM departments became so skilled at conducting research as part of their strategic planning effort, their customer organizations ask them to customize their profiles further with additional information of particular interest to the customer group. FM departments find that their customers are so impressed with the data on their organizations, they invite FM staff to join them in strategic planning exercises. This becomes the means to demonstrate the value an FM department adds to a customer's business planning process. Then the department becomes a regular player in that process.

When FM departments realize they either have or can obtain valuable information to assist the company and individual business units in making strategic decisions, they are on their way to becoming key corporate players. One area in which FM departments can provide invaluable information is providing their own competitive analysis of the customer organization's market. Another way to assist customer business units is to perform an analysis of how the FM department might help the customer achieve a better business bottom line through use of your department's services.

In the first case, I am not suggesting that you become the business unit's market research component, but I am proposing that you have some knowledge of the unit's competitive market. Even if a business unit is not a product-based entity, you can develop some information in the Client Profile that might help the organization make more informed business decisions. Take, for example, a human resources department. The FM organization might include in its Client Profile a section on industry trends, some benchmarking data on recruiting strategies, or a section on trends with respect to motivating and keeping good employees. This added information demonstrates to your client that you are as committed to their business mission as they are and that you understand what it takes to keep them competitive within their industry or profession.

The second way the FM department can demonstrate interest in a client's organization would be your analysis of ways in which you can help the organization become more productive, spend less money, etc. You might make suggestions regarding cost savings associated with consolidation of their employees into one location, or reconfiguring their space, or reducing their churn rate. If they have a number of back-office operations, for example, you might identify potential cost savings if they move these components out of expensive downtown space into a suburban campus setting.

On the one hand, if you are on a charge-back system, you might show them how they could reduce their costs by having fewer alterations/renovations in their space or reducing their expenditures on housekeeping by moving to evening rather than daytime cleaning. On the other hand, if they feel they need services that are above and beyond the standard, you might provide suggestions for add-on services that would enhance or upgrade their operations.

The benefits to the FM organization are multiple: Not only have you demonstrated your organization's understanding of the customer's business and an ability to present options that will enhance business objectives but that you can be flexible in developing your own plan for providing service to this business organization.

Are Visioning and Strategic Planning a One-Time Effort?

If you think carefully about our discussion thus far, you should see that visioning and strategic planning for FM departments are a continuous process ultimately feeding back into the corporate business planning process. We know corporate and business unit visions and plans drive the decisions the FM organization makes regarding its own goals, objectives, and initiatives. Once the process becomes institutionalized, the department builds a database that can be used for service forecasting and trends analysis. The database provides input into the FM strategic plan and feedback to corporate and business unit management to complete a continuous planning loop. The continuum and interrelationships of FM visioning and strategic planning are shown in Figure 5-2.

What Type of Environment Has to Exist for Visioning and Strategic Planning to Work in an FM Department?

You remember from our discussion of culture in Chapter 4 that the corporate and FM department environments play a critical role in

Figure 5-2. The continuum and interrelationships of FM visioning and strategic planning.

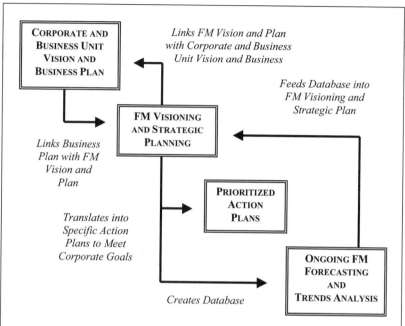

Source: The Friday Group.

shaping the FM department's DNA. One aspect of the influence of culture on FM organization development is seen in the relationship between culture and the ability of the department to perform visioning and strategic planning. We know that the department's planning process should reflect the strategic goals and objectives of the corporation and its organization subunits. There are certain aspects of culture for both the enterprise as a whole and the FM department in particular that need to be in place in order for the department to be successful in the visioning and strategic planning process.

The corporate and FM environment should have:

❑ An articulated corporate business vision and mission

❑ A strong commitment to creative thinking of senior executives

❐ A strong commitment to empowering the FM department to think outside the box, make critical decisions, and drive the process upward

❐ A strong corporate vision and strategy regarding facilities and asset management

❐ A corporate culture that embodies customers as the critical link between business and planning

❐ An analysis of current facility conditions and their link to corporate goals

❐ A forecast of future facility requirements based on organization and mission predictions

❐ A customer-driven internal organization structure and external support system designed to implement the mission-based FM requirements

❐ Provision of the tools to manage the FM function, which includes training, technology, financial management, networking, and benchmarking

❐ A time frame that outlines priorities and critical milestones

❐ Management commitment to an institutionalized visioning and strategic planning process

Have We Answered Our Three Questions?

How strategic planning answers our 3 questions should be crystallizing at this point. These answers provide the best summary of what we learned in this chapter and a bridge to lead us into our review of organization design.

1. How do FM departments know they are providing the right services? Because they have asked their customers what services they need to achieve their business and organization goals and objectives and formulated a service strategy accordingly.

2. How do FM departments avoid fire fighting and become more proactive? Through visioning and strategic planning, they are able to do trends analysis and forecast customer

needs. Because they have anticipated how customers will be operating during the course of an FM planning cycle, FM departments can develop a framework for providing their services, which removes the guesswork and the likelihood of operating in a crisis environment.

3. What measures do FM departments use to determine if they are adding value to the enterprise they serve? By providing valuable data on the usage and cost of FM services from various business units and the enterprise overall, they are able to guide decision makers in implementing FM business strategies that are cost-effective, yet achieve business goals.

DNA Link: Visioning and Strategic Planning

Company: Metavante (data services for banking industry)

Background

With more than 3,300 clients, including the 20 largest banks in the United States, Metavante Corporation is a leading financial services enabler, delivering virtually all of the supporting technology that an organization needs to provide financial services. Metavante offers technology solutions that drive key financial processes:

❐ Customer relationship management
❐ Electronic banking
❐ Electronic funds transfer
❐ Card solutions

❐ Electronic presentment and payment

❐ Financial technology services

❐ Private label banking

❐ Wealth management

Headquartered in Milwaukee, Wisconsin, Metavante (formerly known as M&I Data Services) was founded in the early 1960s and is now a wholly owned subsidiary of the Marshall & Ilsley Corporation.

From a fee income business of only $2 million in 1964, the services provided by Metavante grew to $270 million 32 years later. Although the original department had fewer than 50 employees, the data center grew so rapidly that in 1996 it employed more than 3,000 people. By 1997, it had become the fourth largest bank processing center in the country, with regional processing centers in Chicago, New York, Boston, Atlanta, Minneapolis, Des Moines, Kansas City, St. Louis, Phoenix, Madison, and Tampa, as well as the main processing center and satellites in the Milwaukee area.

Their Story

Prior to the mid-1990s, the trend in most information technology companies was to invest heavily in those areas that were part of their core competencies and to place Band-Aids on areas deemed "support functions" to the core competencies. Areas developing products for market received funding that allowed them to acquire the biggest and best technology tools for their areas, while internal support areas were left to make do with outdated equipment and software. Facilities teams, being internal support units, received funding for construction or leasing projects that would enable the core areas to grow, but were expected to manage those projects with pencil, paper, and bulky drawings. Although the employee growth within technology companies was in some cases growing at an average rate of 12 percent compounded annually, many Facilities units—including Metavante's—were expected to deal with the rapid growth in employees with no increase in Facilities staff.

By 1995, the majority of the Metavante staff was housed in over 600,000 square feet of both owned and leased facilities. The Facilities organization at that time was structured as in Figure Metavante 1.

The Building Maintenance unit performed housekeeping and custodial duties. The Building Engineering unit provided the support for all of the internal infrastructure elements within the two data centers operated by Metavante. The Project Planning unit, consisting of three full-time Facilities Project Planners, managed internal efforts to accommodate new employee hires as well as the moves and changes that occurred within the company.

By 2000, the number of Metavante staff required to support the new base of 600,000 customers had risen to over 4,000 people. This staff now manages over 1.3 million square feet of real estate around the country. The Facilities organization of the early 1990s was no longer able to manage the requirements of a rapidly growing technology company.

The original Facilities structure assigned staff responsibility by building. If a business unit was contained within a single building, then a single Facilities staff member supported that unit. But when a business unit was spread over several buildings, the responsibility for providing Facilities services to that business unit was likely shared by multiple Facilities personnel. It was time for the Facilities organization to become more customer-driven.

To this end, a new Facilities Coordination Center was created. All customer requests are now directed to a single point within the Facilities group. Once a request is received and logged, it is dispatched to the appropriate Facilities unit. This provides a record identifying the ticket number, the unit assigned to the request, and the estimated completion date. This system makes customer follow-up more efficient.

Other changes were also required. Due to the rapid growth that the company encountered, the need for a dedicated real estate person with experience in negotiating leases and managing landlords became apparent. A new Real Estate management position was created.

Figure Metavante 1.

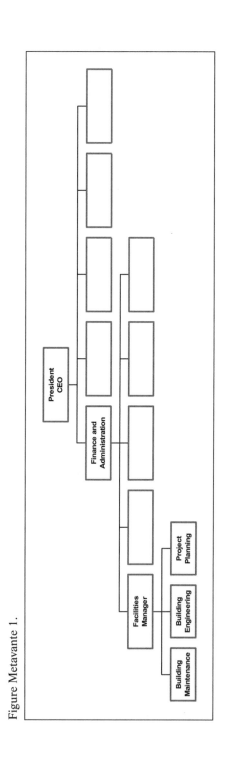

As additional office space was added to support Meta-vante's employee growth, the Facilities unit was also faced with the need to add contract services to areas in which creating internal staff positions was no longer economical. These services were primarily in the housekeeping area. The organization also grew to include responsibility for physical security and food services. By the end of the year 2000, the Building Engineering group had been transferred to the data center operations organization where the majority of engineering work was performed. The old organization structure had changed (Figure Metavante 2).

As the Facilities unit evolved in both function and form, it became important to keep the unit from bogging down in daily events, commonly referred to as the "crisis du jour," and also to begin to consider strategic planning initiatives that were more closely aligned with Metavante's corporate goals. To accommodate both needs, the unit initiated an annual Strategic Planning Session. The purpose of this session is to establish goals and objectives that the entire team can commit to working toward.

The Strategic Planning Session is held for 2 days at the end of each calendar year at an off-site location. The attendees include the individual unit managers within the Facilities organization and the Facilities Director. A third party moderates the session to ensure that the group stays focused on the process of developing goals, action steps, and performance measures.

Once the objectives are determined, the team creates a responsibility matrix that identifies who will take responsibility for ensuring that the action steps are implemented and who will provide support to the team. Each manager is assigned one or more of the goals, which become part of his or her personal performance measurement for the year.

The team establishes a time line for each action step and a completion date for achieving the overall goal. They also develop a schedule to meet as a group to review planned actions against actual accomplishments.

There are significant benefits associated with the strategic planning process. Strategic planning:

Figure Metavante 2.

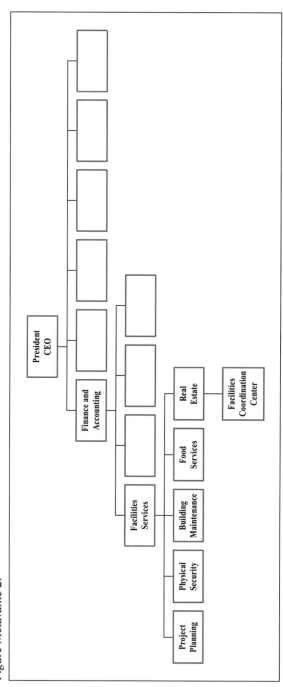

❐ Becomes a fluid activity that can be revised as corporate objectives change

❐ Helps to knit the individual managers into a management team

❐ Moves the unit forward in improving the way it does business

❐ Creates goals and action items that can be drilled down to every individual within the unit

❐ Establishes key performance measures that tie results to expectations

The main challenge of the strategic planning process is that staff changes during the year often require other team members to take responsibility for completing goals.

Learning Points

❐ Goals mapped to business objectives

❐ Acceptance of goals by management team as realistic, doable, and measurable

❐ Assignment of lead management responsibility for goals and objectives

❐ Institutionalization of planning process as annual activity

❐ Regularly scheduled plan versus actual progress sessions as component of planning process

---

About the Author

Ed Wimer is a vice president with the Metavante Corporation and is the director of Facilities Services. He is currently responsible for the management of over 1.5 million square feet of real estate and directs the efforts of Building Maintenance, Housekeeping, Real Estate Leasing, Physical Security, Project Planning, and Food Services. Prior to joining Metavante in 1993, Mr. Wimer served as a vice president and Data Center manager with Huntington Bank of West Virginia.

Endnotes

1. *Random House Webster's College Dictionary* (New York: Random House, 1991), p. 1457.
2. The Friday Group.
3. Robert Frost, *Mountain Interval* (New York: Henry Holt & Company, 1920).
4. Ibid.
5. Ibid.
6. Ibid.
7. Ibid.
8. Stormy Friday and David Cotts, *Quality Facility Management: A Marketing and Customer Service Approach* (New York: John Wiley & Sons, 1994), pp. 100–106.

CHAPTER SIX

Designing the FM Organization Structure

DNA Link: Structure

What Is the Difference Between Design and Structure?

We spent considerable time in our first five chapters focusing on elements of OD that prepare us for our discussion about organization structure. We learned how individuals play a key role in making FM departments work. They come to their jobs with certain needs and expectations, forming a psychological contract with their companies and, specifically, with their FM departments. These individuals also interact with one another in work groups and teams, establishing yet another set of expectations from each other and their facility managers. Companies and FM departments share distinctive cultures consisting of norms, values, and tolerances, all of which influence how individuals work alone and together. Finally, we learned corporate and departmental vision, goals, and objectives affect the way FM departments plan their service strategies. These DNA links are a prelude to determining the most effective way to design an organization structure.

Too often in the OD realm the terms *structure* and *design* are used interchangeably and incorrectly. Practitioners typically use the term *structure* when they are examining the way an organization functions, when they really should be using the term *design*. Authors Galbraith, Downey, and Kates have definitions for the two terms that provide the clear distinction we need for the rest of our discussion in this chapter.[1]

Organization design is the deliberate process of configuring structures, processes, reward systems, and people practices and policies to create an effective organization capable of achieving the business strategy.

Organization structure comprises the organization components, their relationships and hierarchy, as well as determining where formal power and authority are located.

Much of what we have already discussed is the process of *designing* an organization. You may remember in Chapter 1 how I described OD as a process of planned system change to make organizations achieve short-term and long-term goals. Organization design and development are inextricably linked together. In this chapter, we continue our discussion about organization design by first concentrating on organization structures. We cover basic configuration terms and organization prototypes and then examine the patterns and characteristics influencing FM department configurations. We explore factors influencing FM department structures, including the impact of FM functions and responsibilities, positioning of the department within the corporate hierarchy, and the impact of rightsizing and outsourcing.

We then move back to design issues such as how facility managers should approach staffing FM departments and the importance of organization benchmarking. Finally, we look at how Service Level Agreements (SLAs) serve as vehicles to ensure that the design of the department meets the service requirements of the company and individual business units.

Since we use them extensively in this chapter, we need to define other terms associated with organization configuration. These terms become part of our overall OD vocabulary.[2]

❏ *Functions* are the activities, roles, or specific jobs performed by the organization.

❏ *Organization chart* is the graphic presentation of the organization structure that depicts the way in which these functions are grouped or coordinated. It also demonstrates the reporting relationships.

❏ *Centralization* is a means of structuring an organization in such a way that the decision-making authority is vested in those who are at the top of the organization or close to the top. Centralization also may refer to decision-making authority between a headquarters organization and those in the field (regional and local offices) in such a way that only the headquarters organization may make decisions.

❏ *Decentralization* is a means of structuring an organization such that decision making is granted to those who are not clustered at the top of an organization. A decentralized organization structure may even extend decision-making authority to the bottom levels of the organization or to those who are closest to the customer. *Decentralization* also may refer to decision-making authority between a headquarters organization and those in the field (regional/local) in such a way that the field organizations may make decisions.

❏ *Chain of command* is the series of reporting relationships any one function has within an organization. For example, an engineer may report to a shift supervisor who, in turn, reports to a facility manager, who then reports to the chief financial officer. This is a single chain of command. In some organization structures (discussed later in this section), individuals have multiple reporting relationships in which the chain of command is not as clearly defined.

❏ *Span of control* refers to the number of people (or subordinates) individuals have reporting directly to them. There are no firm rules for managerial span of control because there are a number of factors contributing to the decision. The span of control will vary depending on the knowledge, skill, and ability (KSA) levels of subordinates, the degree of difficulty of the functions performed by subordinates, and the level of supervision required. Sound management practice, however, indicates a span of control extending beyond 15 individuals, regardless of the above factors, may be too large. Individuals reporting to a supervisor are called *direct reports*.

❏ *Differentiation* is the way in which the functions are grouped together or differentiated within the organization horizontally, vertically, personally, or spatially. This concept is hard to understand without some visual examples, so after each of the following definitions, a schematic representation of the concept has been provided.

❏ *Horizontal differentiation* is the number of groupings at the same level within the hierarchy of the organization. An organization with a high horizontal differentiation might look like Figure 6-1.

An organization with a low horizontal differentiation would have fewer groupings at the same level, as shown in Figure 6-2.

Figure 6-1. An organization with a high horizontal differentiation.

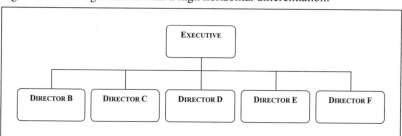

Source: The Friday Group.

Figure 6-2. An organization with a low horizontal differentiation.

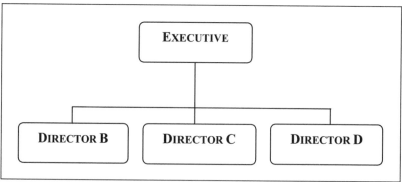

Source: The Friday Group.

❑ *Vertical differentiation* means jobs are grouped according to their level within the organization. These organizations are like the ones Max Weber described in his early assessment of manufacturing organizations. We say organizations with high vertical differentiation are more bureaucratic in that their structures are layered and more complex. The opposite structure, organizations that are flatter, has fewer groupings of jobs at multiple levels. Examples of organizations with high and low vertical differentiation would resemble Figures 6-3 and 6-4.

❑ *Personal differentiation* means that the organization is configured around areas of specialization that do not mix with one another. Another way of looking at personal differentiation is to say that the functions of the organization remain separate and there is no mixing of functions across organization lines.

All of the organizations represented in Figures 6-1 through 6-4 have high personal differentiation or functionalization since they are grouped by specialty. All of the directors and direct reports have the same area of specialization, and there is no crossover between the specialized staff in B and C (see Figure 6-4). We review

Figure 6-3. An organization with a high vertical differentiation.

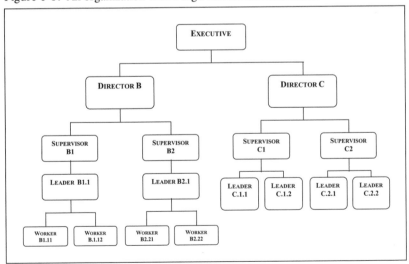

Source: The Friday Group.

Figure 6-4. An organization with a low vertical differentiation.

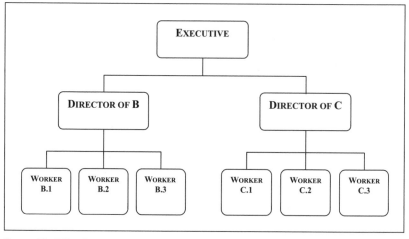

Source: The Friday Group.

the opposite organization design from personal differentiation, the *matrix organization*, in a later section.

❏ *Spatial differentiation* indicates the extent to which the organization design takes into account geographical locations. An organization might group the functions or jobs performed according to the geographical requirements. This differentiation takes into account the deployment of functions based on needs in specific areas.

An organization with a high spatial differentiation would look like Figure 6-5, whereas a low spatial differentiation design might look like Figure 6-6.

❏ Stovepipes and *silos* are terms used to describe vertical organization components such as those shown in Figures 6-3 and 6-9. Often when an organization has high vertical differentiation, the stovepipe or silo effect becomes a negative organizational factor because staffs get tunnel vision. They become so focused on their own organization unit and the work they are performing that they lose sight of the overall organization's goals. A high vertical differentiation organization also may suffer from excessive growth by virtue of the high degree of personal differentia-

Figure 6-5. An organization with a high spatial differentiation.

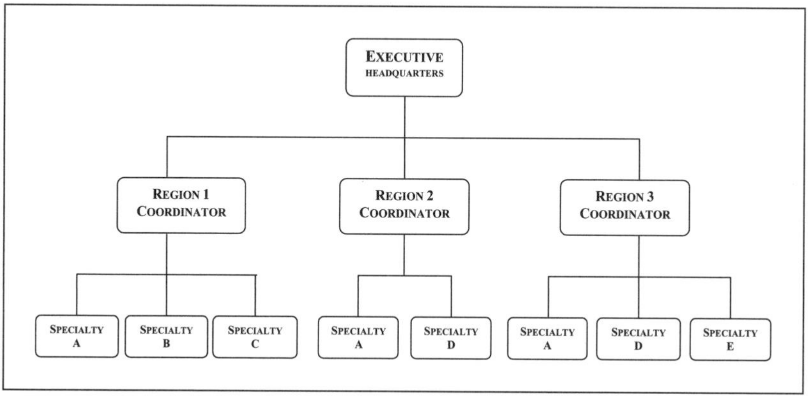

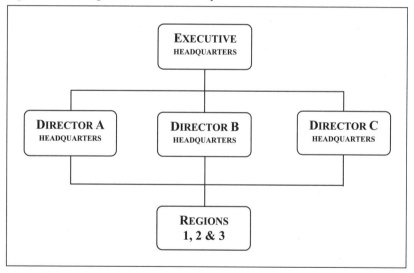

Source: The Friday Group.

Figure 6-6. An organization with a low spatial differentiation.

Source: The Friday Group.

tion or specialization within the various levels. Growth for growth's sake may be an outcome of organization structures with high vertical differentiation. When this happens, stovepipe/silo organizations often are unable to respond quickly and efficiently. They become the crisis mode organizations we talked about in Chapter 5.

What Would Generic FM Department Structures Look Like Using Variations of Functional Groupings or Differentiations?

Before we explore the factors influencing the multitude of department configurations actually found in FM practice, we should look at how departments are structured if they strictly follow the differentiation tenets just introduced. Applying these terms to actual FM department structures provides a frame of reference for our trends analysis in the following section. The schematics show simplistic representations of the differentiation concepts.

FM Department Differentiation

You recall differentiation is the way functions are grouped together: horizontally, vertically, personally, and spatially.

Remember, horizontal differentiation is the number of groupings at the same level within the hierarchy of the organization. In Figure 6-7, the FM department has high horizontal differentiation—there are five functional groupings at the same level. Figure 6-8 has fewer functional groupings at the same level, representing a low horizontal differentiation design for an FM department.

Vertical differentiation is another way of saying organizations are more bureaucratic; there are multiple layers with varying degrees of complexity. High vertical differentiation organizations have lots of complex layers, whereas low ones are flatter. Personal differentiation relates to the degree of specialization in the organi-

Figure 6-7. An organization with high FM department horizontal differentiation.

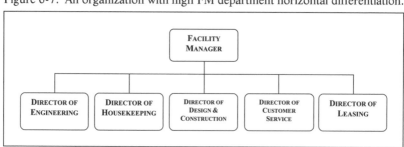

Source: The Friday Group.

Figure 6-8. An organization with low FM department horizontal differentiation.

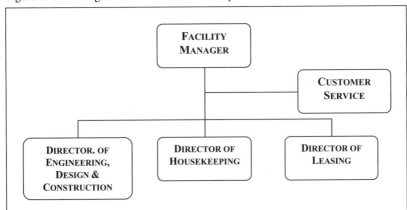

Source: The Friday Group.

zation design. When an organization has high personal differentiation, it is organized around specialized expertise. Typically, highly specialized organization design does not foster interaction across organization lines. Figures 6-9 and 6-10 depict FM departments that have high degrees of personal differentiation.

Figure 6-9. FM department with high vertical and high personal differentiation.

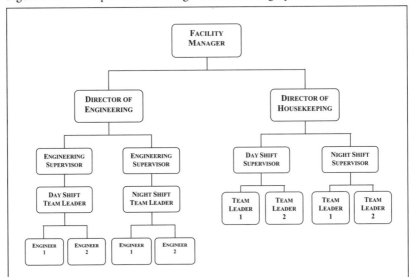

Source: The Friday Group.

Figure 6-10. FM department with low vertical and high personal differentiation.

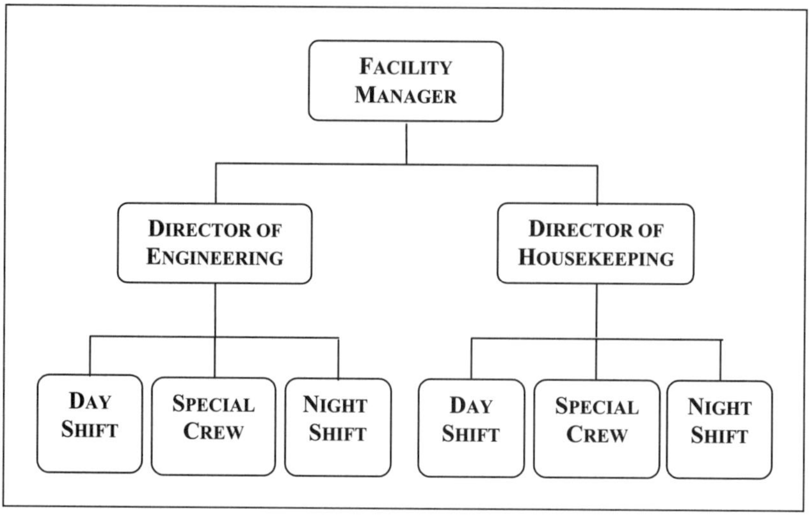

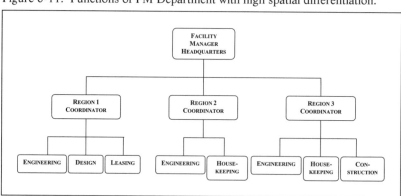

Source: The Friday Group.

Spatial differentiation looks at geographical considerations as a means of organizing. A high spatial differentiation FM department might be organized around regions, each of which provides specialized functions according to regional need. A low spatial differentiation FM department has all regions providing the same or similar functions through the functional entities at headquarters. Figure 6-11 shows an FM department with high spatial differentia-

Figure 6-11. Functions of FM Department with high spatial differentiation.

Source: The Friday Group.

tion, whereas Figure 6-12 depicts what a low spatial FM differentiation design might look like.

Figure 6-12. Functions of FM Department with low spatial differentiation.

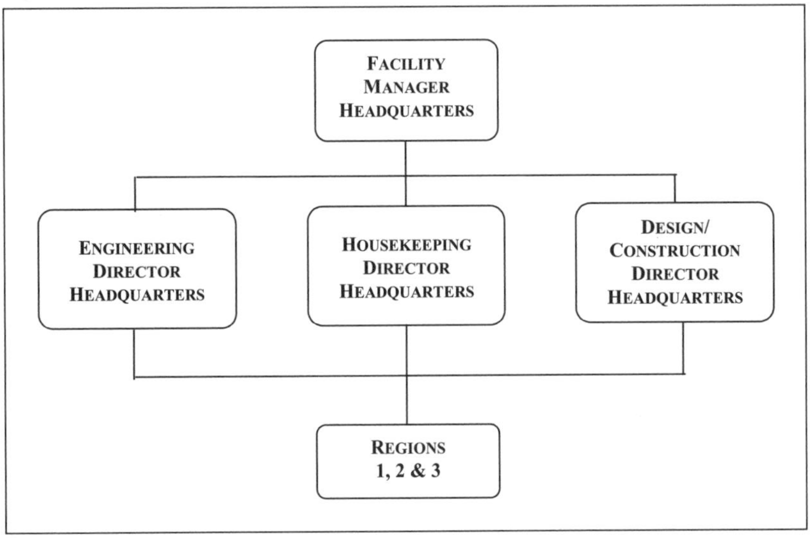

Source: The Friday Group.

How Do FM Functions and Responsibilities Influence Organization Design?

We just looked at the way functions are grouped together and how
they influence generic organization structures. We turn next to
functions associated with FM and how they impact department
configurations. Just as we traced the history of OD, we can trace
the development of FM department functions and their relationship
to organization structure.

Mapping FM department structures starts by looking at the
definition of FM to determine if it provides insight into the functions FM departments should perform. Our profession has a broad,
standard definition of FM adopted by the industry's association,
International Facility Management Association (IFMA), from its
predecessor, the Facility Management Institute.

Facility management is the practice of coordinating the physical workplace with the people and work of the organization by integrating the principles of business administration, architecture and the behavioral and engineering sciences.[3]

Many of you are familiar with the graphic interpretation in Figure 6-13 of the definition showing the intersecting of people, process, and place.[4]

While the definition can be viewed as broad guidance, it does not provide specifics on which functions should be performed in the "practice of coordinating the physical workplace with the people and work of the organization." I alluded earlier in the book to the fact we cannot find "typical" FM department functions, hence no consistent, single organization model for all departments. Our best source of formal and informal research on FM department patterns and trends on FM department structures comes from IFMA and other facility management consultants.

Figure 6-13. FM Venn diagram.

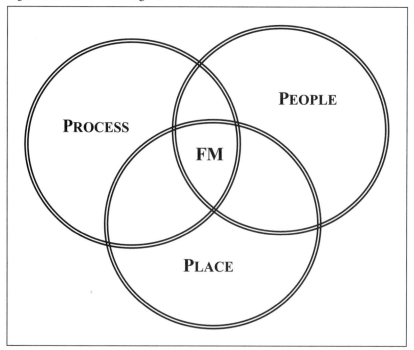

Very few people were studying FM organization structures until 1986. FM departments had a tendency to grow and restructure almost haphazardly as functions were acquired or dropped on FM departments during the boom in real estate during the 1980s. The earliest representation of functions associated with FM dates back to 1986 when IFMA first conducted research on organizations and published a report. From survey responses, researchers identified five factors that seem to have significant influence over the way in which companies organized their FM activities. They found that the 5 factors were driven by certain characteristics of the parent company and included the following:[5]

1. *The size of facilities*—The number of square feet managed by the FM department

2. *The number of employees*—The number of people employed by the company served by the FM department

3. *The types and diversity of space*—The complexity of space managed in terms of purpose and function; the mix between manufacturing, special-purpose, office, and other space

4. *Churn rate*—The number of times employees relocate from one office to another

5. *Status of space*—Whether the majority of space is owned or leased by the company

These factors also appeared to determine the basic functions for which the FM department became responsible and around which an organization structure was created. The functions were somewhat common regardless of whether the parent company was public or private. Researchers discovered that most FM departments were configured according to one of the responsibilities, which served as the department's primary core.[6] They categorized the basic functions or responsibilities into 4 macro groups.

1. Strategic—*Short-term planning* within a 1–3 year time frame, emergency planning, energy conservation, environmental planning; *long-range planning* for a 3–10 year and 10-plus year time frame; *real estate planning* for building, leasing, site selection and acquisition, purchasing, disposal, and appraisals; and *fi-

nancial and budgetary planning for capital, operations, furniture, and other activities

2. Planning and Design—*Architectural and engineering*; *construction* for code compliance, facility systems management and design; *interior planning* for furniture specifications, purchase, and disposal; *interior installations* for moves, furniture moves, and inventory; and *space management* for inventorying, development of standards, allocation, and forecasting of space

3. Maintenance and Operations—*Preventive maintenance, housekeeping, exterior maintenance, trash removal, energy management, landscaping,* and *computer equipment maintenance*

4. Administrative—*Security, mail, telecommunications, copying and printing, records management, purchasing, shipping and receiving, concierge services,* and *special services* such as cafeteria, health, day care, and conference facilities

Researchers also looked at the combinations of responsibilities plus any other factors that influenced organization structures and discovered additional patterns they deemed FM organization models. Although they could group responsibilities and factors together, like The Friday Group, they could not identify a particular model that worked for all FM departments. From the patterns identified, they constructed three models. I use their model names but have added my own description to each model.

❒ *Administrative Service Model*—The core of the FM department is administrative service delivery based on the above description.

❒ *Maintenance and Operations Model*—The core of the FM department is to provide support for the building infrastructure and other services based on the above description.

❒ *Planning Model*—The core of the FM department is planning and design based on the above description.

In addition to the three basic patterns driving the configuration of FM departments, the researchers found some other conditions that seemed to be prevalent with each of their models.[7]

Figure 6-14 represents the conditions under which Administrative Service Model FM departments operate:

Figure 6-14. Administrative Service Model.

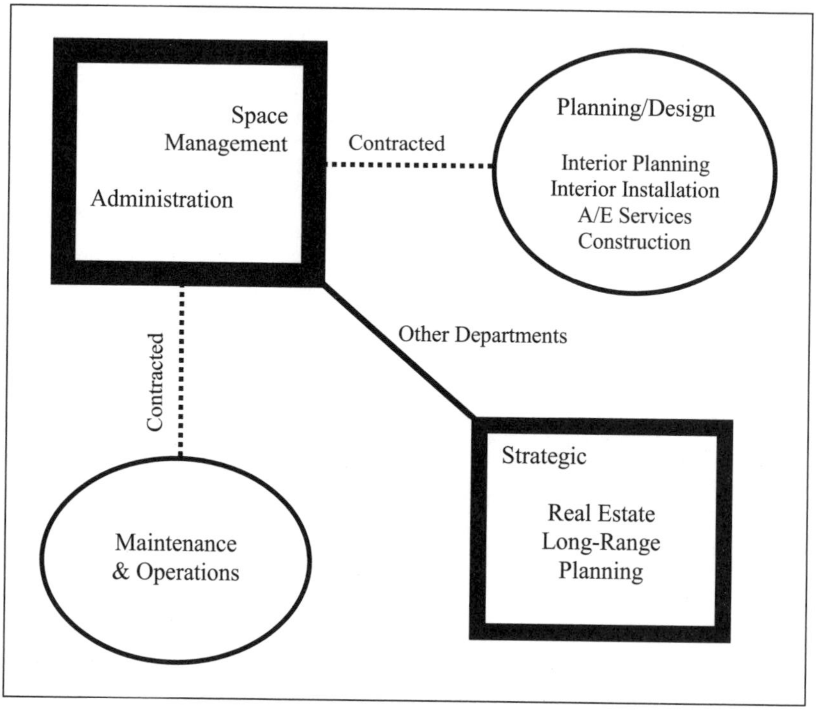

Source: IFMA Research Report #2, 1986.

❐ Space is mostly office space.

❐ Churn rate is low (under 30%).

❐ Facilities are mostly leased.

❐ Facilities are smaller (although small wasn't defined).

❐ Strategic direction is provided by upper management.

❐ In-house staff is small (size not determined).

❐ Planning is contracted out.

❐ Maintenance and operations are responsibilities of building owner.

❐ FM emphasis is on day-to-day administrative operations and implementation, not planning.

The conditions under which Maintenance and Operations Model FM departments operate, as shown in Figure 6-15, include:

Figure 6-15. Maintenance and Operations Model.

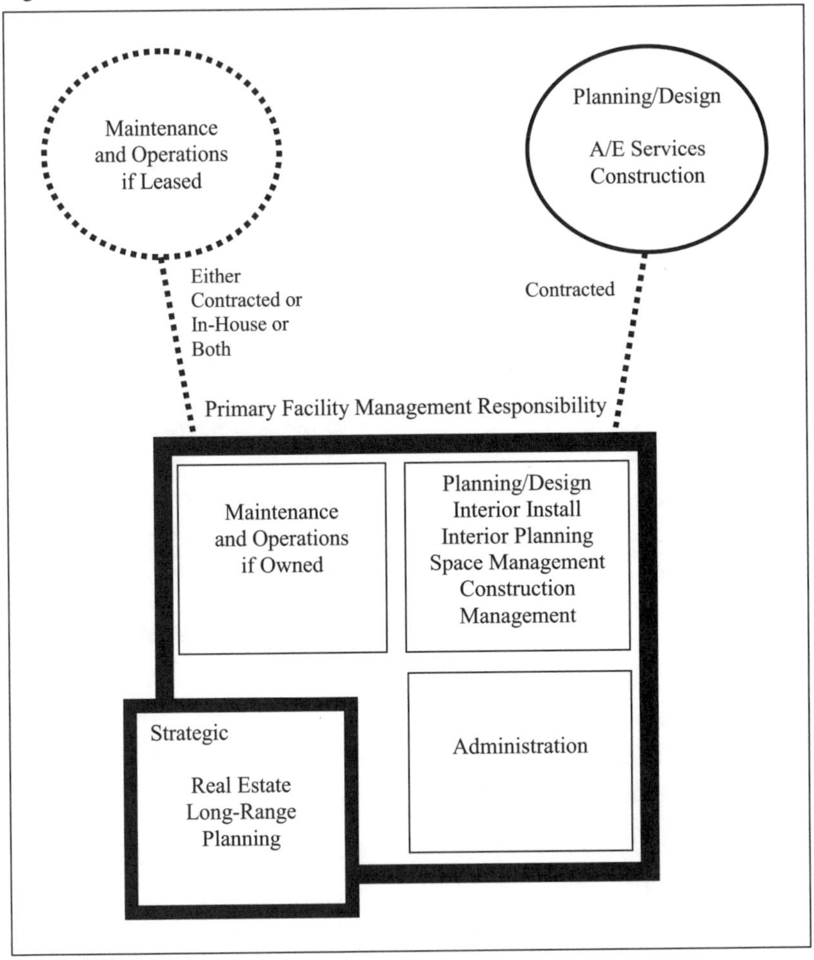

Source: IFMA Research Report #2, 1986.

❐ Space is mostly office space but there is some special-purpose space such as laboratories, eating facilities, warehouses, and computer rooms.

❐ Churn rate is higher (30% to 60%).

❐ Facilities are a mix of owned and leased.

❐ Strategic direction is provided by upper management with some input from FM department.

❐ In-house staff is larger and more specialized.

❒ In-house staff performs planning and manages architectural/ engineering (A/E) services and construction.

❒ Maintenance and operations are responsibilities of in-house staff in owned facilities.

❒ FM emphasis is more than day-to-day and has a more significant role in planning.

Figure 6-16 shows the conditions under which Planning Model FM departments operate including:

❒ Space is mostly office space but there are larger amounts of special-purpose space.

❒ Churn rate is high (60% to 100% plus).

❒ Most facilities are owned.

❒ FM staff have more input into strategic direction.

❒ In-house staff is large to manage specialized space.

❒ In-house staff performs A/E services and construction management services.

Figure 6-16. Planning Model.

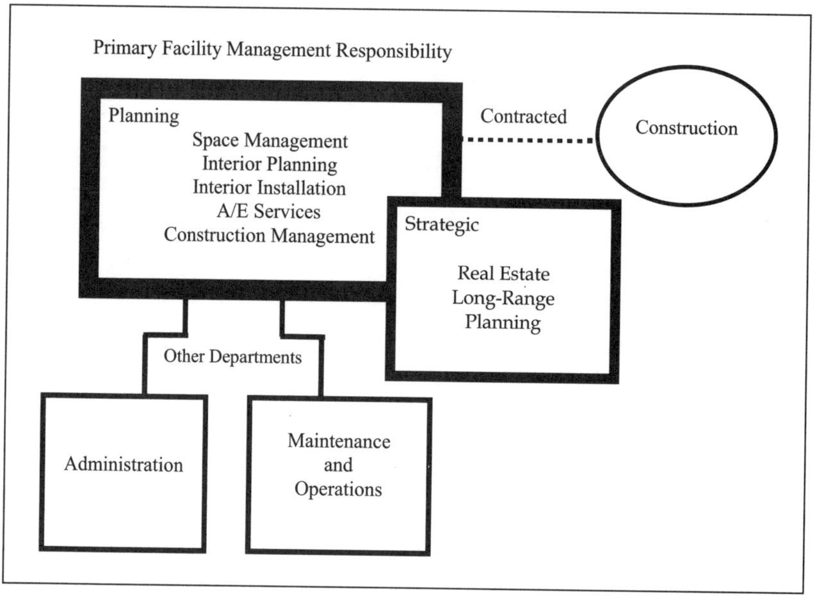

Source: IFMA Research Report #2, 1986.

❐ Functions are decentralized and under direction of several in-house subunits.

This first assessment of FM department structures contains a wealth of information, much of which still is relevant today. From this early research, the core functionality concept seems to be the most sustaining as a guide for FM practitioners who are developing FM department structures. The Friday Group looks routinely at core functionality when we perform organization assessments for FM departments. We talk more about core functionality, or core competencies, later in the chapter.

We have recent information on other factors that also contribute to FM department structures. The latest IFMA Foundation research provides empirical evidence to support what The Friday Group has learned over the years through informal research. We now know that several other factors have dramatic effect on organization configuration in FM. These factors are reviewed after we visit one other perspective on FM functions and organization structures.

As mentioned previously, David G. Cotts is a leading authority on FM. After the 1986 report on FM organizations, Dave wrote about FM functions in his 1992 book, *The Facility Management Handbook,* later revised in 1999. In addition to the universal functions he attributes to managers in general, Dave presents a comprehensive list of functions he considers to be common among FM departments. His list covers a wide breadth and scope of FM. These functions are described in much more detail in Dave's book, and I encourage you to read it. A summary of the macro categories of functions Dave attributes to FM departments follows:[8]

Facility Planning and Forecasting

Lease Administration

Space Planning, Allocation, and Management

Architectural/Engineering Planning and Design

Workplace Planning, Allocation, and Management

Budgeting, Accounting, and Economic Justification

Real Estate Acquisition and Disposal

Construction Project Management

Alteration, Renovation, and Workplace Installation

Operations, Maintenance, and Repair

Telecommunications, Data Communications, Wire and Network Management

Security and Life Safety Management

General Administrative Services

Before he talks about the various organization models he sees for FM, Dave also looks at certain factors he feels influence the FM department structure. I have developed a list of his factors, using a combination of Dave's terminology and my own.[9]

Size of the department

Single or multiple locations of facilities

Company preference for standard versus user-driven services

Facility manager's place in the corporate hierarchy

Contracting out

Owned versus leased facilities

Line (management) versus staff view of FM functions

Dave's perspective adds several new factors to those previously detected by FM organization researchers. His factor about standard versus user-driven services is another way to look at the issue of tailoring service delivery through organization structure to meet business unit needs that we discussed in Chapter 5. We spend a great deal more time on this factor in an upcoming section in this chapter.

The facility manager's place means how he is perceived within the company as well as the reporting relationship within the corporate hierarchy. It has to do with titles for facility managers as well as organizational placement within the company. The factor of line (management) versus staff view of the FM function is an interesting one. Dave equates line versus staff with the size of a department, for he believes what would typically be a staff function in a smaller organization becomes a line, or management, function in a larger one. We spend more time on reporting relationships, hierarchy and staff, and line functions later in the chapter.

The final factor Dave talks about as having tremendous influence on FM department structures is contracting out. Dave talks about contracting out as the result of the rightsizing effort accompanied by increased outsourcing. You remember we discussed the impact of outsourcing on FM staff from a need and motivational standpoint in Chapter 2 and we talk about the impact of the outsourcing or contracting out on FM department structures shortly.

From his discussion of factors, Dave proceeds to describe five organization models he feels are sufficient to cover any functions of FM. I debated whether or not I should spend time in this book reviewing each of Dave's models and providing his schematic for each. Since this is an opportunity for FM practitioners to review OD thinking as it applies to FM in one place, I opted for overkill and have incorporated Dave's five models into our discussion. His models go beyond the conceptualization framework for an FM department demonstrated in the IFMA Report #2. His models show actual organization charts for each model.[10]

Office Manager Model

This first FM department model is constructed for a single-site company that is in a leased facility. This model essentially has an Office Manager in the role of the senior FM executive who is responsible for managing a series of service contracts covering service areas ranging from food service to security; leases covering items such as the building, vehicles, and equipment; and consulting contracts for such things as architecture and engineering. As Dave describes it, this organization primarily works for a company that doesn't want to make an investment in human resources to staff FM functions. The model is depicted graphically in Figure 6-17.

One Location, One-Site Model

Dave's next model, Figure 6-18, is a straightforward approach to providing FM services for a company with one site and one location. For this model, Dave shows the company having an FM department and indicates the department serves a building that is primarily owned. In the model, in-house FM staff perform the majority of the work, although consultants and contractors are used to augment staff efforts during peak loads or when there is need for a particular technical skill.

Figure 6-17. Office Manager Model.

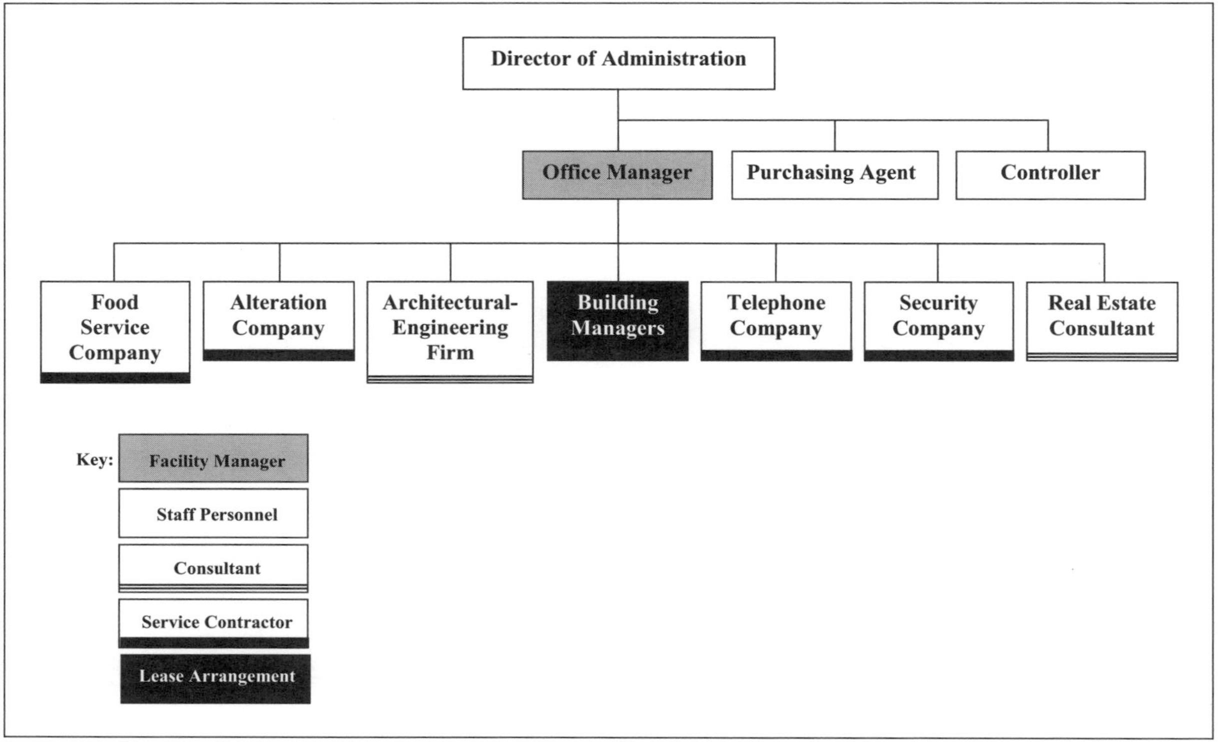

Adapted from: David G. Cotts, *The Facility Management Handbook, 2nd ed.* (New York: AMACOM, 1999).

Figure 6-18. One Location, One-Site Model.

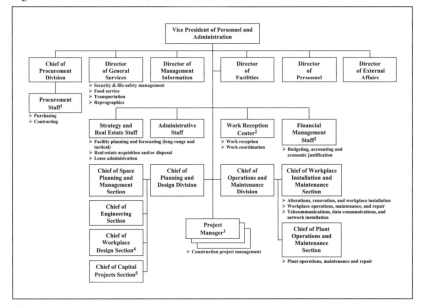

Notes:
1. Procurement and financial management staffs collocated with facilities staff but operate under central-
   ized policies of Chief of Purchasing Division and Controller, respectively.
2. Work reception center staff has limited tasking authority of design and shop assets for service order
   execution.
3. If desired, matrix formed project teams (designers, engineer construction manager, phone/datacom
   specialist, etc.) may be formed to concentrate on a building or group of staff customers. The PM is
   then the sole customer contact for projects. Otherwise the Workplace Designer functions as the PM.
4. If Project Managers are not used, the Workplace Design Sections designers are the principal user
   contacts (project managers) for workplace alterations.
5. Architectural services provided from this section.

Adapted from: David G. Cotts, *The Facility Management Handbook, 2nd ed.* (New York: AMACOM,
1999).

One Location, Multiple-Sites Model

For this model, the premise is the company has a headquarters
facility with other components such as manufacturing plants, laboratories, or branch facilities located in the same geographical area.
This model, Figure 6-19, introduces the concept of centralization
of policy, oversight budget control, and other headquarters functions as well as the decentralization of operational responsibility for
facilities to the other components. Dave indicates that the component facilities are more likely to operate as in the office manager or
one location/one-site model. He also feels that many combinations
of consultants, contractors, and leases will be used to execute ser-

Figure 6-19. One Location, Multiple-Sites Model.

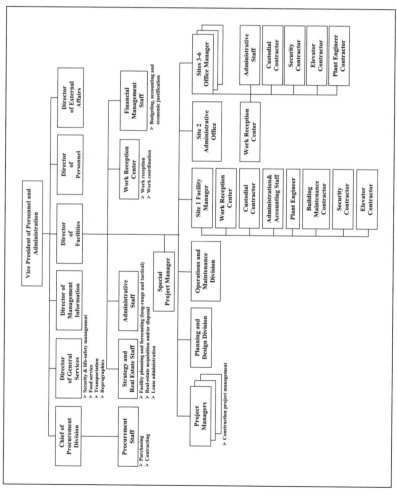

vices, although only responsibility for operations and maintenance activities is delegated to the component locations.

Multiple Locations, Strong Regional/Divisional/Headquarters Model

In this model, the concept of a nationally based company with multiple locations is introduced. Each of the regional or divisional sites has its own FM department patterned after the one location/one site or one location/multiple sites models. Dave describes the functions of FM to be allocating resources, tactical and strategic planning, real estate acquisition and disposal, policy and standards setting, technical assistance, macrolevel space planning and management, and oversight. This model, shown in Figure 6-20, has most of the FM department as staff, with consultants and others used extensively, particularly those operating on a broad geographical base. You will note that there are numerous functions outside of FM (procurement, legal counsel, human resources) that may not reside within the FM department but perform the function for the department.

Fully International Model

The final model, Figure 6-21, Dave indicates could be interchangeable with Figure 6-20. He indicates that in this model as well, headquarters functions primarily in an oversight and policy-making role. His view is that the FM subcomponents either could have a direct reporting relationship to individual business units or report to the headquarters FM department.

What Is the Latest Research on FM Department Functions and Structures?

As cited earlier, recent statistics on FM departments come from the 2001 IFMA Foundation research report, *Designing the Facility Management Organization*. The foundation funded a study to look at FM departments using both a survey format and two on-line focus groups. Findings from the study are quoted extensively in this section, because the research provides excellent documentation on the current status of 905 FM departments.

Figure 6-20. Multiple Location—Strong Regional or Divisional Headquarters Model.

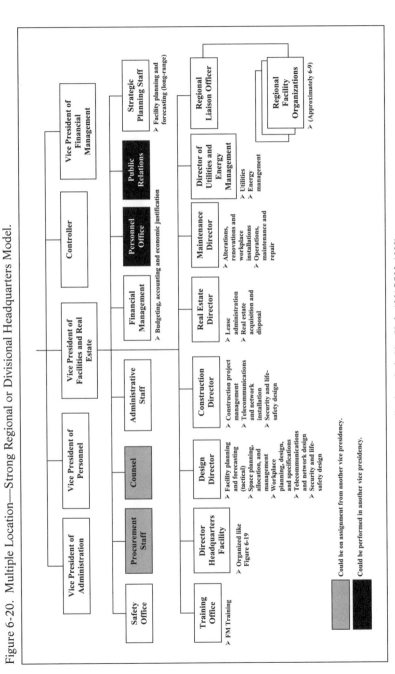

Adapted from: David G. Cotts, *The Facility Management Handbook, 2nd ed.* (New York: AMACOM, 1999).

Figure 6-21. Fully International Model.

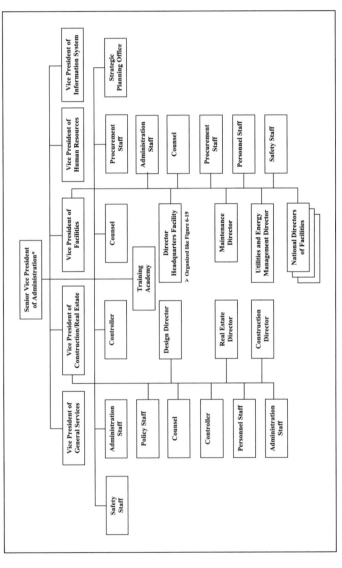

Notes:
This model is completely interchangeable with the one in Figure 6-20; two ways of organizing for the same mission.
* = Facility Manager

Adapted from: David G. Cotts, *The Facility Management Handbook, 2nd ed.* (New York: AMACOM, 1999).

FM Functions

This research report treats the issue of FM functions in a way that is slightly different from earlier studies. The foundation survey asked respondents to identify the functions reporting to their department. The following are the functions respondents indicated report to their FM departments.[11]

Maintenance and operations (91%)

Facility planning (88%)

Space management and planning (86%)

Project design and construction management (84%)

Energy management (75%)

Environmental health and safety (58%)

Real estate management (56%)

Administrative services (52%)

Factors Used to Decide Formalization of FM Functions

The most interesting patterns reported by respondents are with respect to what *should* and what actually *does* influence a company's decision to establish a formal FM department. Think carefully about the wording of the last sentence. We are talking about factors influencing the formalization of the FM function, not factors governing the FM department structure. You will see some crossover, however, between these factors and those identified in the 1986 study in which researchers identified patterns appearing to influence how companies *structured* their FM departments. The IFMA Foundation study shows the top three factors mentioned most frequently as the number one factor to influence the creation of a formal FM department (from highest to lowest percentage) are: (1) size of facility, (2) number of facilities, and (3) rapid growth/churn. Construction projects received second mention as the number four factor.[12]

The report indicates that size of facilities was consistently important across industries and market segments. Rapid growth was critical to FM departments representing financial services, telecommunications, and the hardware/software industries. Considering the study was conducted in 2000 and companies in these industries were in a growth mode, the response of rapid growth as a factor is understandable. The outcome of the study in terms of the rapid growth portion of the factor might be rated slightly lower if the study were conducted today, given the change in the economy after 2001. Both churn and size of facilities were factors present in the 1986 findings.

The IFMA research also found the top three reasons why companies establish a formal FM function (from highest to lowest percentage) also are: (1) size of facility, (2) rapid growth/churn, and (3) number of facilities. Respondents indicated that while the number of facilities is an important reason to establish a formal department, construction projects are the second most important reason why companies actually create the formal FM department.[13]

Importance of Factors Influencing FM Department Structures

The IFMA Foundation survey again posed a slightly different question to obtain data on the structure of FM departments. The questionnaire asked respondents about the importance of factors that influence an FM department's organization. The top four factors rated as very important include:[14]

Ability to meet customer needs (74%)

Total number of facilities (51%)

Rapid growth (50%)

Total number of employees (34%)

The finding about the most important factor influencing the structure of a department is the most significant for our OD discussion. Through the foundation study, we have empirical evidence to support the shift in thinking about what is important to FM. We now have proof that more FM departments consider the customer as key to the design of FM departments. Having the customer rated as the most important factor also adds credence to our discussion in Chapter 5 about the need for FM departments to obtain business unit and corporate input into the visioning and strategic planning process. We have validation that facility managers must have information about customer requirements if they are going to structure their departments to be responsive to customer needs. This data also confirms The Friday Group's findings from years of providing OD assistance to FM departments and supports Dave Cotts's view about corporate preference for standard versus user-oriented FM services as a driver for department structures. We talk about how this most important factor is used by facility managers in designing their FM structures.

Is the Positioning or Reporting Relationship of the FM Department Within the Corporate Structure Consistent?

We have another factor to address with respect to FM department designs: the positioning or reporting relationship of FM within the corporate structure. We know from previous sections there are numerous corporate factors influencing decisions to establish a formal FM function, in addition to factors influencing the structure of the function. We also know corporations have different perspectives on positioning the department within the corporate hierarchy, whether FM departments should be stand-alone entities or reside within another organization unit, and the reporting relationship.

Again we find inconsistency in both the reporting relationship and positioning within the corporate hierarchy. Some of this inconsistency stems from corporate uncertainty about the interrelationship between FM and other corporate components. We know not every company views FM as having a strategic and operational relationship with other service organizations such as human resources, information technology, procurement, and purchasing. They often don't see a strategic relationship between FM, finance, or, often, even real estate. The inconsistency of reporting relationship also emanates from the diversity of responsibilities included within the purview of FM. We see this in tracing the history of FM department development and finding that the functions associated with FM departments have evolved over time.

We have comparison data regarding FM department reporting and positioning relationships from two different IFMA research reports. From the 1996 *Facility Management Practices: IFMA Research Report #16*, we have data on the reporting relationship of approximately 2,000 FM organizations.[15] We also have data from the 2001 *Designing the Facility Management Organization* IFMA Foundation research report on approximately 905 organizations.[16] Figure 6-22 compares findings from the two studies on the reporting relationship of FM departments. It shows the number of FM departments, in percentage terms, reporting to various corporate entities.

Although the sample size is smaller in 2001, there has been an impressive increase in the percentage of FM departments reporting to senior management since 1996. There also has been a drop in the percentage of FM departments reporting to administration, operations, and finance during the past 5 years. The most dramatic of these changes is in the percentage of departments reporting to finance entities.

This recent sample appears to be representative of the organizational positioning and reporting relationships of FM that The Friday Group has observed in practice. We have seen that when FM departments focus more on strategic planning and less on operational issues, their reporting relationship and positioning within the corporate hierarchy typically are at a more senior level.

The Friday Group has had serious discussions with FM practitioners about what constitutes the most successful reporting rela-

Figure 6-22. Percentage of FM departments reporting to various corporate entities.

REPORTING RELATIONSHIP	PERCENT 1996	PERCENT 2001
Administration	34	12
Operations	23	13
Senior Management/Other	19	45
Finance	16	8
Human Resources	8	9
Real Estate	N/A	5

tionship, and we have no empirical data to support our informal findings. Although we know there are many elements comprising a successful reporting relationship, such as corporate culture, the management and leadership style of the reporting official, and his level of background and understanding of FM, The Friday Group has identified patterns associated with reporting.

We found, through focus group discussions and individual interviews, facility managers and staff who report directly to a senior executive within the corporation, particularly to a chief executive officer (CEO), a chief operating officer (COO), or the chief administrative officer (CAO), have relationships that are more likely to be successful from several perspectives. Individuals in these positions seem to have a better understanding of FM and the relationship between FM and the business of the corporation. We also find senior executives in these roles better able to serve as an FM advocate and champion. We hear that the reporting relationships providing the greatest challenges for FM are those in which an FM department reports to a human resources department or officer. In these relationships, facility practitioners indicate the human resources organization focuses more on the people aspect of FM and less on ways in which FM contributes to the bottom line. Often, they report, human resources executives want solutions to FM situations that are not necessarily cost-effective, realistic, or in the best interest of the overall enterprise. As long as the people are satisfied, human resources executives feel the FM department is successful.

Is One FM Department Configuration More Common Than Others?

Through years of working with FM departments to conceptualize and restructure the functions they perform, The Friday Group has consistently identified a predominant organization configuration for the practice of FM. We find most FM departments to be highly vertical and personally differentiated. This finding means most FM departments we encounter tend to have numerous vertical layers, or a bureaucratic configuration, consisting of highly specialized functions, or stovepipes and silos, similar to the configurations shown in Figures 6-3 and 6-9.

Often these are more mature FM departments, structured before the Total Quality Management (TQM) movement, which was accompanied by an increased emphasis on the importance of the customer to FM service delivery. It wasn't until after this movement that FM departments began to think about the impact of customer requirements we talked about in Chapter 5. The traditional approach to organization structure also is referred to as the *functional/structural* approach, since it takes the basic functions provided and structures the organization around them. We have found that facility managers feel comfortable with functional/structural design because it groups individuals by very traditional degrees of specialization. We find this type of FM organization structure within corporate environments having conditions similar to those described in the 1986 IFMA research report:

When corporate requirements are for highly specialized staff

When corporate organization design is a traditional function-based structure

When the corporation overall has a small span of control such that managers communicate uniformly on a regular basis

When the nature of FM service requirements is fairly stable and repetitive

When the FM department is reactive rather than strategic

When the FM department is not highly involved in corporate business planning

When the corporate chain of command is hierarchical and bureaucratic

When decision making is not highly decentralized

We also have a body of research from the 2001 IFMA Foundation study to support the findings of The Friday Group. The foundation study shows 64 percent of the survey population has an FM department structure structured along what the report refers to as "service" lines, or what we refer to as functional/structural lines.[17]

There are clear advantages and disadvantages of a design that is highly vertical and personally differentiated. Figure 6-23 lists both.

Figure 6-23. Advantages and disadvantages of a highly vertical and personally differentiated design.

ADVANTAGES	DISADVANTAGES
■ Clear lines of authority and reporting	■ Lack of staff interaction
■ Single source for establishing goals, priorities, and expectations	■ Overspecialization
■ Clear channels for communication through the vertical hierarchy	■ Development of functional cliques
■ Clear career path through a vertical channel	■ No formal mechanism for communication across functions

What Is a Matrix Model Organization?

In the first section of this chapter, "What Is the Difference Between Design and Structure?" we identified generic organization configuration concepts around which some organizations, including FM departments, are structured. We talked about personal differentiation as a design concept in which a high degree of specialization occurs and the organization design encourages these specialized functions to operate independently of one another. In other words, there is little interaction among the highly specialized organization components. I said at the time we would review the opposite structure in which interaction among organization units is the focus of the design. This model is called a *matrix organization.*

Organization development trends analysis indicates that during the 1970s and early 1980s, companies were seeking new organization designs that would combine the functional/structural approach with the capability to integrate product and service lines. During this period, many companies began to use a structure that integrated both of these features. This organization model became known as the *matrix model.* The matrix model provides a means for staffs from functional disciplines to come together as a team for special assignments, task forces, and projects. Staffs continue to report to their respective functional supervisors, but they also report to the special assignment, task force, or project manager.

The matrix model for an FM department works well when the corporate environment has the following characteristics:

When corporate requirements call for multiple FM projects occurring simultaneously

When there is a corporate organization scheme integrating function with service and product delivery

When the corporate business environment is changing rapidly

When the corporate span of control is large and managers have a need to communicate frequently on a formal and informal basis

When the managerial staff is small and must oversee multiple projects

When the FM department is highly involved in corporate business planning and must respond rapidly through project vehicles

When FM staff is limited and must work on multiple projects

When decision making is decentralized

When external service providers are integrated throughout the company

When a headquarters organization is responsible for multiple field projects

Most matrix FM departments are only two-dimensional as Figure 6-24 shows. FM staff report on an ongoing basis to a primary functional supervisor and to a project manager when part of a team. The Friday Group also has configured FM departments with multiple dimensions where the department has need to manage multiple projects in addition to having staff participate in ongoing task force activities.

Figure 6-25 lists advantages and disadvantages of matrix model organization structure.

Figure 6-24. Two-dimensional matrix model.

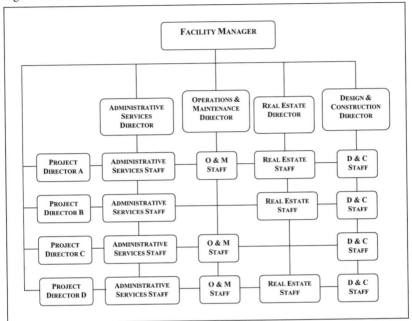

Source: The Friday Group.

Figure 6-25. Advantages and disadvantages of a matrix model organization structure.

ADVANTAGES	DISADVANTAGES
■ Opportunity for cross training/ learning	■ Confusion about reporting relationships
■ Maintenance of functional identity	■ Conflicting priorities standards and expectations
■ Opportunity for project economics	■ Competition for talent
■ Flexibility to respond	■ Lack of clear-cut career paths

How Is a Customer-Driven FM Department Structured?

We reviewed a tremendous amount of historical information on the factors contributing to the design or structure of FM departments.

We know some FM functions are common among departments, but a universally accepted set of functions isn't applicable for all FM departments in all industries or market segments. The way in which a company views FM has tremendous influence on the set of functions performed, how they are structured, and how they report within the corporate hierarchy. We also know when certain functions are predominant; departments sometimes structure their service delivery around those functions.

Recent research supports findings of The Friday Group on the role of the customer in contemporary FM department design. According to the 2001 IFMA Foundation survey, the top factor influencing FM department structures (as reported by 74 percent of respondents) is the need of the customer, and 22 percent of respondents say they have a customer-driven organization design.[18] From an OD perspective, customer-driven organization design means the structure meets the following criteria:

More responsive to the customer population

Built-in flexibility to shift services and service delivery as corporate business changes dictate

Capability of tying staff performance to specific service delivery objectives established by the customer

If the goal of facility managers is to build organization structures to meet the above criteria, the design must place the customer entity at the center of the service delivery structure. As discussed in Chapter 5, customer organizations have different names in different companies. A customer organization may be labeled a department, staff office, task force, or business unit of something else, depending on the corporate nomenclature. For our discussion, the customer organization entity is the same as the one we used in Chapter 5, the business unit.

For the past 10 years, The Friday Group has assisted FM departments in designing client-focused organization structures. As a result, we have developed our own model, which we call the Business Unit Model©. The model, discussed in detail below, focuses on a service team structure consisting of staff who provide the services required by the business units that are their clients. In order for this model to work, FM staff must have detailed information about mission, vision, goals, and objectives of business units and their specific FM service needs (see Figure 6-26).

We talked in Chapter 5 about FM departments having an understanding and ongoing interaction with business units and reviewed the importance of creating Client Profiles for each business unit. This Client Profile information is used to determine the FM service requirements for the business unit, which, in turn, establishes the menu of FM services provided and guides the design of the business unit's service team. A graphic representation of the Business Unit Model© in Figure 6-27 shows the relationship between business unit goals and objectives (articulated in Client Profiles), their FM service requirements, and FM organization design.

The heart of the Business Unit Service Team Model© is service teams configured around the services necessary to support the business unit. Each service team has a team leader who functions as the primary client representative or contact and team members

Figure 6-26. Business unit dictates service mix requested.

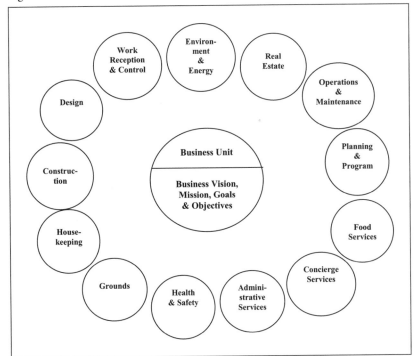

Source: The Friday Group.

Figure 6-27. Business Unit Model©.

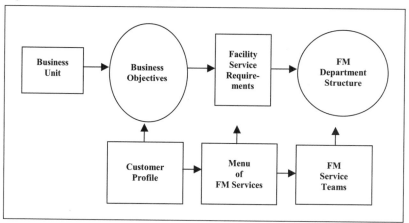

who represent the core services provided to the business unit. Team members can either reside permanently on a team or float among teams, depending on the size of the staff and business unit demands. The number of service teams is determined by several factors: the number of business units served by the FM department, the size and diversity of business units, and the complexity and frequency of service required from the FM department. A single service team would be responsible for a large business unit or one with high service needs. Conversely, a single service team might be responsible for multiple business units that are small or need fewer or less complex services. A graphic representation of the Business Unit Service Team Model© appears in Figure 6-28. This version of the model shows one service team with multiple business unit clients and two teams each serving separate business units.

There is an appealing aspect to this FM organization design. Using this model, service teams have direct responsibility for tailoring their service delivery strategy directly to targeted requirements of individual business units. The model is based on the ability of FM staff to develop a close business relationship with clients. Because they are intimately involved with their customers, they can predict and anticipate business changes and their impact on the need for FM services. The service team can expand or contract in staff size and function depending on the mix of services required. It also affords them the opportunity to track business unit needs so they can retool the mix of services as needs change. Another benefit

Figure 6-28. Business Unit Service Team Model©.

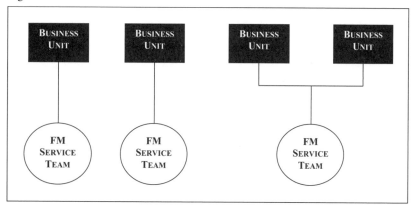

Copyright © The Friday Group.

of the model is that it reduces the potential for duplication and conflict by having a single team dedicated to one or multiple client groups. Think back to our discussion in Chapters 2 and 3 about what motivates individuals and teams. They want to be empowered to make decisions affecting their clients, have their opinions heard and respected, and be able to measure their success and that of the overall department. What better way to create the entrepreneurial spirit we talked about than by establishing self-directed service teams?

Another attractive feature of the model is that it provides facility managers with flexibility in terms of staffing service teams. They can create teams comprised wholly of in-house staff or establish teams that are a mix of in-house personnel, external provider staff who are on site, or provider staff who are on call. The Friday Group also has constructed service teams consisting entirely of external service provider personnel. Figure 6-29 is a graphic representation of the staffing flexibility associated with service teams.

Not only do service teams provide facility managers with tremendous flexibility in terms of staffing individual teams, they also add flexibility for configuring the total FM department. With the Business Unit Model©, facility managers have options for structuring their total department. It can be the total department structure in which all service is delivered through service teams, or the teams can be part of functional or matrix organization designs. I show the Business Unit Model© as a component of three different organization schemes next.

Figure 6-29. Service team consisting entirely of external service provider personnel.

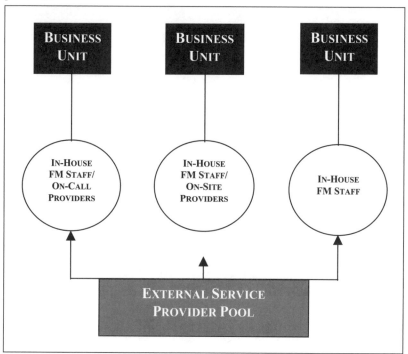

Source: The Friday Group.

Stand-Alone Service Teams

In Figure 6-30, the entire FM department is structured around service teams. For this company, business units are departments, and service teams have direct responsibility for one or more customer departments. Team leaders receive requests for service directly from their department contacts and with their core team members determine how service will be delivered using in-house or service provider staff. Occasionally, staff from one team also may assist another team if a project warrants particular in-house staff expertise.

Service Teams and Functional Components

Figure 6-31 shows service teams as part of an FM department with a basic structure organized along traditional functional/structural

Figure 6-30. Stand-alone service team organization scheme.

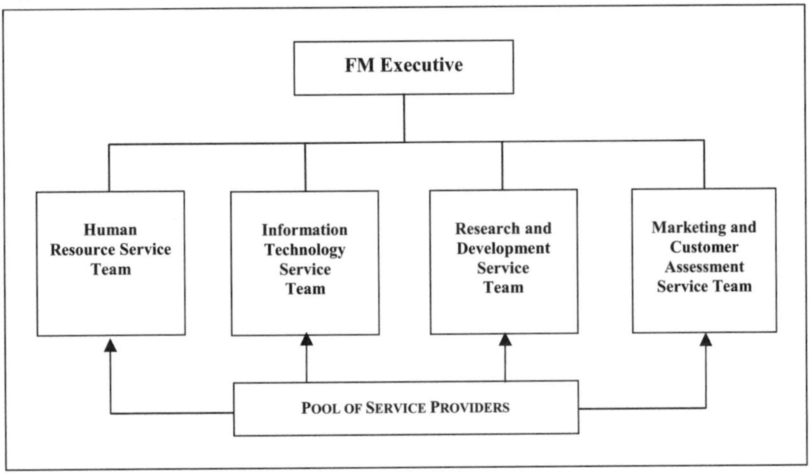

```
                        ┌─────────────────┐
                        │  FM Executive   │
                        └────────┬────────┘
         ┌──────────────┬────────┴────────┬──────────────┐
┌────────────────┐ ┌────────────┐ ┌────────────┐ ┌────────────────┐
│     Human      │ │ Information│ │Research and│ │ Marketing and  │
│Resource Service│ │ Technology │ │Development │ │    Customer    │
│      Team      │ │  Service   │ │  Service   │ │   Assessment   │
│                │ │    Team    │ │    Team    │ │  Service Team  │
└────────────────┘ └────────────┘ └────────────┘ └────────────────┘
         ▲              ▲                ▲                 ▲
         └──────────────┴────────────────┴─────────────────┘
                  ┌──────────────────────────────┐
                  │  POOL OF SERVICE PROVIDERS    │
                  └──────────────────────────────┘
```

Source: The Friday Group.

Figure 6-31. Service teams as part of an FM department.

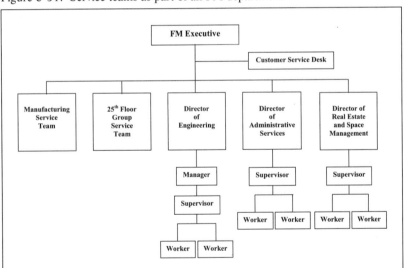

Source: The Friday Group.

lines. Two service teams are dedicated to two specific clients. The first team is responsible for providing service to the manufacturing business unit, a large organization with a high demand for complex FM services. The second team is dedicated to the senior executive group, or "25th Floor Group" as it is characterized. (Since twenty senior executives and their staff reside on a floor together, along with the staff who serve a board of directors, the facility manager decided to dedicate a team to these groups.) They require an extensive array of services and rapid service delivery. The rest of the department is structured along more traditional lines, with separate organization units for specialized FM functions. The department also has a customer service/help desk that receives requests for service from customers and channels them to the appropriate organization component.

Service Teams as Matrix Component

This FM department, Figure 6-32, is a matrix organization that is multidimensional. Service teams are used on an ongoing basis to

Figure 6-32. Example of a multidimensional matrix organization.

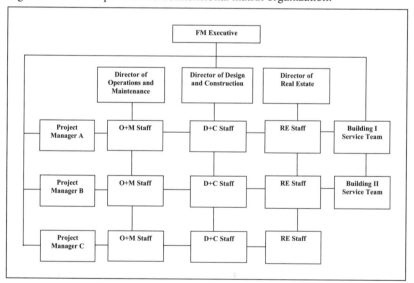

Source: The Friday Group.

provide basic services to several company organizations housed in separate buildings, so teams are building-oriented rather than organizationally structured. This means the service teams have to be knowledgeable about multiple business units in terms of their requirements for FM services. In addition to building service teams, the department also uses teams for specific projects such that a building team member may also be assigned to a project that is not being done in his service team building. Finally, there are functional directors who have responsibility for establishing department policy and who also have staff reporting to them. These staff may be on a building team or assigned to a specific project from time to time.

There are advantages and a few disadvantages of the Business Unit Model, which are shown in Figure 6-33.

As we discuss later, organizations have a distinct life cycle, and many FM departments start out as traditional functional/structural entities and evolve to the Business Unit Model in which there is a blending of in-house and contractor-provided staff. It is important for facility managers to know about each of the various configuration models in order to assess which model or components of models work best within particular companies.

Regardless of the actual configuration association with the Business Unit Model, the associated features have long-term effects on departmental DNA.

☐ Fewer subunits and staffs—FM department charts have fewer boxes and can function with staff as long as they have appro-

Figure 6-33. Business Unit Model© advantages and disadvantages.

ADVANTAGES	DISADVANTAGES
■ FM staff have deep understanding and close relationship with customer groups	■ Potential for limited exposure to other business units
■ FM staff modify services to meet changes in requirements	■ Potential for limited cross-team interaction unless fostered by FM department environment
■ FM staff develop sense of ownership for service delivery	
■ FM staff have decentralized decision-making authority	

priate KSA. The model provides the ability to flatten and decentralize decision making to lower levels in the department. Using well-trained teams, staffs are more empowered to make decisions, thus requiring fewer levels of management and supervision.

❏ Flexibility for business plan change—The beauty of this approach is that it has built-in flexibility for business plan changes. Standard service menus are eliminated in favor of those customized to meet customer need.

❏ Customer-friendly and streamlined business process—This physical structure provides each customer with a single point of contact and the capability to streamline processes since teams have ownership for developing and implementing them with their customers.

❏ Elasticity of service—The FM services envelope can be stretched as far as necessary to provide the scope and level of services required. Business units are involved in the decision making, and depending on their ability to support a higher or different level of service (through charge-back or fee arrangement), service teams can expand staffing by using external providers.

What Is the Impact of Rightsizing, Downsizing, and Outsourcing on FM Organizations?

No discussion of FM department design would be complete without discussing the impact of rightsizing, downsizing, and outsourcing. For many facility managers during the 10-year period commencing in the late 1980s, these terms were synonymous with the end of FM as it had been known since its inception. For facility managers who are students of OD and know organization diagnosis is an essential component in the process, however, the onslaught of outsourcing followed by downsizing and rightsizing was expected and predictable as part of the development cycle. From my perspective, the timing of the wave of outsourcing, downsizing, and rightsizing can be found by looking at the evolution of FM departments.

Most FM departments, like others, have an organization life

cycle. As we know from our discussion thus far, departments evolve and change much the way individuals do, and the trends and patterns of the life cycle can be used to guide facility managers in making organization decisions. The developmental stages of an organization's evolution have tremendous bearing on the impact of outsourcing, downsizing, and rightsizing.

At the time a company determines the need to formalize FM functions under an organization structure, the FM department is in what is known as the *entrepreneur state*[19] of its life cycle. As a parallel to the start-up of a new business, the FM department during its infancy is most interested in getting established and surviving. For the overall practice of FM, this first life cycle occurred during the 1970s and 1980s when corporations were growing and expanding and the real estate market was booming. Companies were looking for expansion space and determined they also needed an organizational entity to manage the expansion and maintenance of the space after its completion.

The goals and objectives for most FM departments were to deliver space and services in the most expedient manner; hence, many FM departments were structured around the Planning model identified by IFMA research in 1986 that we reviewed earlier. During this stage, to ensure target dates were met, FM departments were often not as concerned with cost implications, since time was more important than cost consciousness. To meet challenging deadlines, FM staffs were added as projects required, and FM departments were in a tremendous growth mode. While some traditional service providers such as architectural, engineering, and construction firms worked with FM departments in a supporting role, in-house staff performed many FM functions. These early structures tended to be quite large by the middle of the 1980s as accelerated growth during this period to meet demand took precedence over the development of policies and procedures, process review, careful budget scrutiny, or assessment of structure, size, and staff skills mix.

Continuing in the growth mode, FM departments moved to the next stage, known as *collectivity*,[20] in which an attempt is made to bring order and routine to rapid growth and development. From a historical perspective, in the late 1970s and early 1980s most FM departments became a fixture in companies, having achieved a high degree of success and visibility as the organization continued to meet the demands of corporate expansion. In retrospect, many staffs involved with FM during this period who talk with The Friday Group about organizational issues characterize it as the best of times. While they were working long hours and meeting unrealistic schedules, they were invigorated and had a sense of purpose and importance. It was during this time period, senior FM professionals developed a sense of commitment to the profession, position within the company, and prominence as a corporate contributor. The FM departments themselves were still largely amorphous in configuration in many ways, even when there was a formal structure. Staffs were pulled together on an as needed basis for projects and ongoing work.

Somewhere during the middle 1980s, FM departments entered the *formalization stage*[21] of their evolution. At this juncture, departments were feeling very much in control, largely stemming from their success in meeting corporate demands for growth in terms of space acquisition and build-out. The departments viewed themselves as experts in all aspects of FM and began to issue directives to customers in the form of FM standards—for size of office and cubicles, parking, environmental management, energy conservation, and a host of other categories. For the first time, "how quickly" was not the corporate byword, and FM departments had time to reflect on the lack of structure that led to more formal organization schemes with hierarchical structures. This is called *routinization* by Max Weber as part of his theory on bureaucratic organization structures. During this stage, many FM departments were structured along the Maintenance and Operations or Administrative Service model lines.

Policies and procedures manuals were developed, and for the first time FM departments began to consider strategic planning in the form of FM master plans that were based on a bricks-and-mortar approach to planning for the future. FM departments, to overstate the position, were somewhat expensive, overstaffed, and highly visible to customers in an almost dictatorial, rather than customer-friendly, way. In the evolution of organizations, FM departments were not prepared for what happened next.

Many FM departments were poised to enter into the fourth stage of evolution, the *elaboration stage,*[22] but took a slight detour. An organization at the end of the formalization stage typically begins to process information and feedback from upper management and customers about service delivery, but FM departments were not, for the most part, gathering or processing this information.

They were not acutely aware of the warning signs for organizational change that were taking place in corporations as the need for reengineering of processes, management of product and service quality, staff retooling, and cost containment became necessary to maintain competitiveness in the marketplace.

FM departments were ill prepared for corporate initiatives related to downsizing and rightsizing, and facility managers in particular were surprised when top management informed them that external providers could make assurances to manage FM operations more efficiently and effectively, at less cost, with fewer staff, and at a service level that yielded higher quality and customer satisfaction.

These departments were struggling to counter the claims by external providers because they did not have sufficient data on customer satisfaction, benchmarking, or cost-effectiveness. As highly visible entities within their companies, FM departments were considered to be high overhead and were not prepared to take a proactive approach to the claims made by external providers. They were not in a position to demonstrate customer support and best practices techniques and, as a result, were in a reactive or defensive mode about their own capabilities. Outsourcing became an adversarial term.

Outsourcing Shock Wave

The initial impetus for outsourcing in corporations and institutions was driven by senior corporate management rather than senior facility management. The aftermath of the rush to outsource left many FM departments decimated in terms of numbers, skills, and morale. While much of what happened to FM departments in the early days of "total outsourcing," or turn-over-the-keys-to-the-buildings-and-walk-away, was shortsighted on the part of corporate senior management, there were several residual benefits from this devastating exercise.

First, due to the sheer volume of outsourcing taking place, FM departments often were involuntarily downsized without much forethought about whether or not the resultant organization was appropriately rightsized. This situation forced facility managers to take a look at their departments and make adjustments to requirements for staff with skills to include contract management, customer service, and business-oriented skills that were long overdue.

Second, in the wake of outsourcing, facility managers found the need to focus on determining the department's core functionalities or competencies I described earlier. In other words, it forced FM departments to look at what functions their companies expected them to provide as a basic core. Once facility managers had a grasp of their department's core or "sacred" functions, they knew which functions should reside in-house. Then they could determine which functions were candidates for further outsourcing. As other components of companies were coming to terms with the need to focus on core competencies, FM also had to assess what functions could be provided only by in-house staff and those that potentially could be provided by external service companies.

The aftermath of the initial round of outsourcing and the resultant downsizing forced FM departments to become introspective with respect to functions and service delivery mechanisms while, at the same time, to become more proactive with respect to their customer base. Being catapulted into the spotlight and suffering from close examination under the corporate microscope forced FM departments to enter the *elaboration* stage of their organization life cycle. As we discussed in Chapter 2, although outsourcing posed more than a veiled threat to the survival of FM departments for almost 10 years, a stronger, more business-oriented department emerged with the potential to become the standard-bearer for organization design within the enterprise.

How Do You Decide What Is the Right Structure for Your Own FM Department?

Facility managers may be suffering from information overload on organization design at this point in the chapter. We have looked at so many factors influencing the design and structure of FM departments, your head is spinning just thinking about the thought process to determine the right structure for your own department. It should be clear why facility managers' skills to diagnose their own situation are so important. Facility managers need to consider all the potential factors and evaluate which ones apply to them, given the corporate culture, corporate philosophy about FM, demographics of buildings and their occupants, goals and objectives of customer entities, and individuals within the FM department.

To help facility managers with this assessment, The Friday Group has developed a process we use with our clients. I have provided a graphic illustration in Figure 6-34 showing the process first, and then I describe each component of the process.

Step 1: Gather Corporate Intelligence

This first step essentially involves collecting all the information we discussed in Chapters 4 and 5. In order for facility managers to make smart decisions about their department structure, they must be informed about the corporate environment within which they are operating. They have to have intelligence on the direction the company and individual corporate entities are headed, know what the essential business drivers are for success and how these impact the need for FM services, and understand the overall corporate culture.

Step 2: Consider and Target Factors Influencing Organization Structures

The second step focuses on evaluating all the factors found to influence FM organization design that we identified in this chapter and determining which of these have the most bearing on the FM department. Each of these factors needs to be assessed in the context of the corporate intelligence gathered in Step 1. Some of the factors will be more important than others in companies, and a few will emerge as the driving factors for FM service delivery.

Step 3: Evaluate Organization Structure Options

At this stage, facility managers are able to review structure options for the FM department. The priority factors from Step 2 will guide facility managers in their selection of one option over another. If, for example, there is a high customer orientation and a high churn rate, the Business Unit Model may be the most appropriate structure, because it allows FM staff to be highly interactive with customer entities.

Step 4: Determine Staff Knowledge, Skills, and Abilities Required for Organization Structure Selection

This last step leads us directly to our discussion in the next section about matching staff skills to organization needs. In the final phase, facility managers need to evaluate the KSA they need to make the structure work, as well as the KSA of existing staff.

Figure 6-34. Process for FM managers to use to assess appropriate department structure.

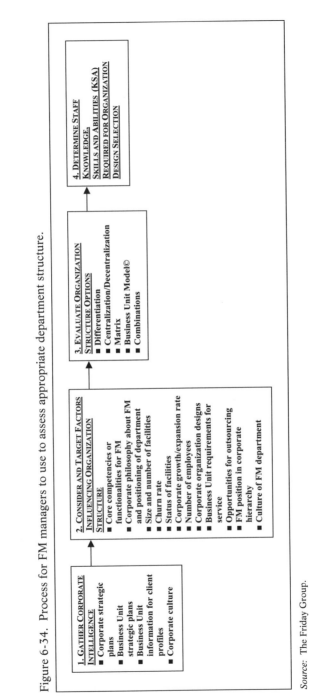

1. GATHER CORPORATE INTELLIGENCE
- Corporate strategic plans
- Business Unit strategic plans
- Business Unit information for client profiles
- Corporate culture

2. CONSIDER AND TARGET FACTORS INFLUENCING ORGANIZATION STRUCTURE
- Core competencies or functionalities for FM
- Corporate philosophy about FM and positioning of department
- Size and number of facilities
- Churn rate
- Status of facilities
- Corporate growth/expansion rate
- Number of employees
- Corporate organization designs
- Business Unit requirements for service
- Opportunities for outsourcing
- FM position in corporate hierarchy
- Culture of FM department

3. EVALUATE ORGANIZATION STRUCTURE OPTIONS
- Differentiation
- Centralization/Decentralization
- Matrix
- Business Unit Model©
- Combinations

4. DETERMINE STAFF KNOWLEDGE, SKILLS AND ABILITIES (KSA) REQUIRED FOR ORGANIZATION DESIGN SELECTION

Source: The Friday Group.

How Do You Determine Staffing Needs and Skills Mix for the FM Department?

Having discussed the characteristics of the various approaches to designing an FM department structure, we turn to the topic of determining how to staff the department with FM professionals who have the most appropriate mix of skills. This section focuses on staff capabilities only and doesn't address salaries or salary structures. We could spend a lot of our time on the money aspect and still not get to the critical issue of the right mix of staff. Remember from Chapter 2, *money isn't the most important motivator*. No matter how carefully the organization structure has been crafted, if it doesn't have the "right" people performing the "right" functions, it will not achieve its goals. Yet, even the most poorly designed organizations sometimes can operate effectively and efficiently if they have the right blend of professional, technical, and interpersonal skills among staff.

Often facility managers focus on the number of staff they should have in their departments before they figure out the core KSA needed to provide the department's core functions. This determination of KSA should occur before the number of staff for the department is even considered.

Developing the KSA Base for the Department

We are adding another dimension to facility managers' diagnostic capability to determine the appropriate staff mix for departments, rather than specifying the type of staff necessary for every FM organization. It is the role of facility managers to assess what core skills are needed, both when the organization is being staffed for the first time and at various junctures during the department's evolution as new functions are added or deleted, personnel changes occur, and as corporate business initiatives and priorities fluctuate.

As described in the previous section, the first step in staffing the FM department is to determine what responsibilities or functions the department will perform. As we know, there is a wide range of functions and responsibilities around which FM departments can be structured. These functions and responsibilities are determined by corporate strategic directives, facilities strategic directives, and specific business unit requirements development.

Once facility managers have identified the organization's functions or scope of services, the next step is to answer the following 3 questions about the personnel required for each function. The answers establish the KSA staff will need within the department.

1. What *knowledge* is necessary to perform the function? To answer this question, it is important to know what body of knowledge an individual must possess in order to perform the job. Does an individual need to have a formal educational or informal experiential background in FM, business management engineering, architecture, space planning, design, finance, contracts, etc., in order to perform the work?

2. What *skill* is necessary to perform the function? To answer this question, it is important to know what specific skills an individual must possess in order to perform the function. Does an individual need to be proficient in Computer-Aided Facility Management (CAFM) systems design and development, reading blueprints, graphics, drafting, mechanical/electrical repair, equipment diagnostics, etc., to perform this job?

3. What *ability* is necessary to perform the function? To answer this question, it is important to know what specific abilities an individual must possess in order to perform the function. Does an individual need to have the ability to work in teams, work independently, make presentations, develop reports, lead discussion groups, perform analyses, and make recommendations, etc., to successfully perform this job?

Using these questions as a framework, facility managers perform job mapping to obtain a clear picture of how functions and responsibilities are translated into specific jobs and positions. This job mapping consists of developing a functional statement about the job based on the KSA required.

This same mapping technique also is relevant when facility

managers are trying to determine where there are gaps in the organization's skills mix. Using job mapping and gap analysis, facility managers can determine where the organization has KSA holes by functional components. Facility managers perform KSA job mapping analysis for each position and the individual occupying the position. Where there is synergy between the KSA required for the position and the KSA of the individual, a good match has been made. Where there is a gap between the KSA required for the position and that of the individual either being considered for or occupying the position, some corrective action is required. This KSA analysis is shown in Figure 6-35.

Figure 6-35. KSA analysis form.

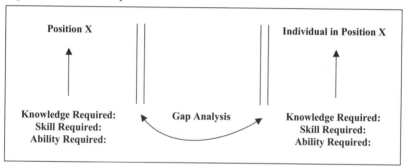

Source: The Friday Group.

What Intelligence Do We Have on FM Department Staff Skills?

To date there has been no scientific research on the types of KSA required to perform specific FM functions within organizations or on the KSA makeup of any sample of FM personnel currently performing these functions. The information currently available contains data on the professional/educational disciplines represented among FM professionals.

The International Facilities Management Association (IFMA) has been profiling its members since 1989. Since the first profile, the members who have responded to the IFMA survey questions regarding professional discipline have reported their major fields of concentration as seen in Figure 6-36.

The numbers have fluctuated and even declined in a couple of

Figure 6-36. Percentage of degree concentration of IFMA members.

DEGREE CONCENTRATION	1989% (N = 1.784)	1994% (N = 3.815)	1998% (N = 3.953)
Business	43	41	34
Engineering	18	18	15
Liberal Arts	13	12	10
Architecture	12	9	9
Interior Design	8	7	8
Sciences	4	5	3
Facility Management	2	3	7
Other			14

the categories, but there is some consistency among individuals in FM who have backgrounds in business, engineering, liberal arts, architecture, interior design, and the sciences. The important statistical trend we find over the 9-year period is the increase in those who report their field of study as FM.

Number of Staff Within FM Organizations

The Friday Group frequently is asked how facility managers determine the number of staff they should have in their FM department. It is a valid question and one for which there is no standard answer. Determining an appropriate staff size is an area in which a facility manager's diagnostic skills really pay off.

Our profession does not have a wealth of data on staffing counts for FM organizations. Unlike some other professions that have been able to quantify head counts for certain functions, it is difficult to do this in FM. Most FM departments The Friday Group works with have relied heavily on reported practices using ratios between square footage managed and number of occupants, coupled with facility usage. The International Facilities Management Association's *Facility Management Practices Research Report #16* presents the most recent compilation of data on staffing profiles from a sample of 2,200 questionnaire respondents. I encourage you to review the staffing section of Research Report #16, for it serves as a source of information on reported staffing profiles by various industry segments and facility uses, but I caution you, as the report does, not to use the data as an absolute benchmark for comparison.

> Comparing the size of your FM staff directly to a single industry average is risky at best. The factors determining staff size [of employed, internal resources] are as varied as the facilities themselves. There are many factors determining staffing in addition to facility use and size. Examples include outsourcing, number of amenities, unionization, number of responsibilities assigned (scope), number and formality of policies, extent of office spaces and density.[23]

The Friday Group concurs with the research report and routinely advises our clients not to limit themselves to square footage, occupancy, and facility use as the sole means of assessing and determining staffing components. After we identify the core competencies of the department, we look at many of the same factors identified in the research report as well as corporate culture, number of customer organizations, and workforce diversity (age and culture). Our list of factors facility managers should consider in determining the number of FM department staff includes:

Core functions

Size of facilities managed

Corporate culture

Workforce diversity (age and culture)

Diversity of facility usage

Number of occupants

Number of business units

Variety of noncore services

Unionization

Density and churn

Outsourcing philosophy

In summary, research on size of staff serves to strengthen the argument for developing the diagnostic skills of facility managers. If we think back to our discussion about potential organization models for FM, the use of the Business Unit Model provides one option for resolving the problem of staff size. If customer organizations dictate the level of service required then determine the type of service team structure necessary to support these requirements, the number of staff required on the team also can be determined by customer need rather than structure or function of the department. This form of FM department design provides the greatest flexibility for facility managers to expand and contract the team size as customer need fluctuates.

We spent considerable time discussing various types of organization structures in this chapter. We looked at the trend in structuring FM departments to parallel overall corporate movement away from functional silos that tend to feed on themselves at the expense of the customer toward a more business unit-driven structure that is flexible enough to respond to changing customer requirements. We know from this discussion that functional FM department structures are hampered by the fact that when functionality spawns organizational growth, the service delivery capability becomes slower due to the shear size and complexity of the organization and its processes. Those who are closest to the customer are hampered by their inability to push decisions and resolution of problems through the organization hierarchy.

A Business Unit Model or similar organization structure eliminates the problems associated with functional hierarchy by positioning a service team directly in front of the customer. It provides them with the capability to make their own decisions regarding requests for service and service challenges as they happen. This approach streamlines the number of processes required by FM staff to deliver services to customers and allows customers to access FM staff directly. FM staffs no longer are isolated from their customers, but interact with them on a regular basis. To better serve their customers, these service teams also need to have resources to draw on when customer requirements necessitate additional staff or expertise. The concept of a focused service team lends itself to the creation of a resource pool that can be available not only from within the FM department but also from external providers on an as needed basis.

What About Outsourcing in Relationship to Structure?

As we discussed earlier in this chapter, a positive by-product of the initial corporate push for outsourcing in FM is an awareness by facility managers of the importance core functions or competencies play in making organization decisions. When outsourcing was imposed on facility managers, it made a dramatic point about the need to assess core competencies central to FM service delivery and, therefore, performed by FM employees and those that are non-value-adding or -supporting and can be provided by contract providers. If facility managers do not address core competencies themselves, others within a company who are less knowledgeable about FM will perform it for them.

Outsourcing can be a positive restructuring tool when it is used to initiate internal dialogue about an FM department. Prior to initiating any organization transformation, the issue of outsourcing has to be considered within the context of core and noncore functions, which sparks internal debate and discussion about issues such as customer relationships, compatibility with corporate culture, service delivery responsiveness, institutional knowledge, and cost/benefit value. Making the decision to move departments from a functional structure to one that is more customer-friendly signals the need for facility managers and FM staff to assess which functions should reside in-house and which ones could be outsourced. This assessment of core functions or competencies is a critical precursor to any organization transformation.

How Do You Determine the Need for In-House Staff, Outsource Providers, or Process Reengineering?

To guide an FM department through the process of determining the appropriate mix of in-house and external service providers for noncore functions, we can turn to a decision-making technique called *intuitive prioritization*. An FM consulting colleague, Fred

Klammt, wrote a piece in the August 1998 issue of *The Outsource Report*[24] about applying this concept to FM through the creation of a numerical scorecard and prioritization matrix. I found it to be such a good tool, I wanted to share it with more FM practitioners.

The matrix permits FM departments to compare various service delivery options against critical business drivers and service attributes. The service delivery attributes are developed by each FM department based on what the organization feels is important. The FM department might consider attributes such as:

Flexibility

Cost reduction

Availability

Experience

Industry knowledge

Skill

Use of technology

Customer orientation

Best practices

Benchmarking

Monitoring/tracking

These service attributes are applied to internal FM staff and external service providers as well as process improvement. The relative weight of each service attribute is determined by the FM department, depending on its importance or priority to FM and the company.

This technique is valuable to FM facility managers as a tool to help them make tough decisions about organization improvement. It provides a quick assessment based on an intuitive thought process. While it is just one such tool for facility managers to use, it seems to provide rapid insight into the importance of in-house staff, external providers, and process reengineering on the transformation of an organization.

Using an example is helpful to understand the assessment process (see Figure 6-37). Taking housekeeping as one noncore function a facility manager is considering as part of an organization design exercise, he wants to determine if he should use internal or external personnel. He would use the prioritization matrix as follows:

Step 1: List all the appropriate service attributes.

Step 2: List the service delivery options being considered.

Step 3: Determine an appropriate numerical scale for each attribute (in this case 1–10).

Step 4: Score each service delivery option and tally the numbers.

In this instance, using an external service provider has an edge over the internal FM staff, but the analysis involves not only the total score but also the details of each attribute. If the FM organization places a high importance on the use of technology as a factor, then the three-point advantage of the external provider is significantly greater. If, however, the FM organization highly values customer service orientation, then perhaps the internal staff advantage of six points over both external providers and improving the process takes precedence.

Figure 6-37. Example of prioritizing a noncore function using a matrix model.

SERVICE ATTRIBUTE	IN-HOUSE STAFF	EXTERNAL PROVIDER	IMPROVE PROCESS
Flexibility	5	8	2
Cost	8	4	4
Availability	10	9	1
Experience	5	6	4
Industry knowledge	2	8	3
Skill	9	5	7
Use of technology	4	7	3
Customer orientation	9	3	3
Best practices	3	5	4
Benchmarking	3	4	3
Monitoring/tracking	4	7	9
TOTAL	62	66	43

In summary, it is necessary for an FM department to determine its core competencies as a prelude to discussions about the mix of in-house and external staff. For every FM organization, there are some functions and services that only should be provided by internal staff, while others can be easily transferred to outside experts.

The impact of this assessment process is directly related to the FM department structure. In a transformational organization, or one that is both moving toward a customer-driven structure and a service visioning consisting of a balance between in-house and external sources, assessing core competencies is an important first step.

Should You Benchmark Your FM Department Design?

We all know benchmarking means gathering data about how well we do in FM in comparison with other excellent or best-in-class FM departments. Typically, when we talk about benchmarking in FM, though, we forget to include the assessment of the FM organization and service delivery structure. We forget to look at benchmarking from an OD perspective.

Continuing our theme of strengthening FM diagnostic skills in order to conduct OD, it is important to determine how facility managers use benchmarking data and analysis to strengthen their FM departments. If facility managers are going to use benchmarking information as an organization diagnostic tool, they should consider the following as potential benchmark areas:

❏ Categorization of functions and services—what types of services/functions are collected under the umbrella of FM (or a larger umbrella)

❏ Structure of functions—how functions are grouped together

❏ Relationship of service delivery structure to client organizations—to what extent the FM department structure is driven by the customer/business units

❏ Staff numbers—number of staff departments have to perform the services and the factors used to determine the size of the FM staff

❏ Staff KSA—the mix of KSA among staff of other FM departments

❏ Processes—the impact of FM processes on the delivery of services and service structure

One source for the above benchmarking data may reside within the FM department's own corporate structure. It is an excellent idea for FM departments to identify other service organizations within the company with an outstanding reputation for service and gather data on the above components. Too often, FM departments feel benchmarking is only appropriate with external sources, whereas there may be good best-practices organizations within the parent company.

At the same time facility managers are considering other internal organization units for comparison, it also is important to consider the above components as they relate to organizations outside of FM. Not only should the FM department perform benchmarking studies of best-in-class FM departments within other companies, but the FM department should also turn to other service organizations and their delivery structures in general. Again, the point in moving beyond the FM realm is to step outside the box and obtain different perspectives on the best service organizations then design, staffing, and processes, regardless of their discipline.

Throughout the book, references have been made about the limited benchmarking data on FM organizations. While pertinent research has been conducted, it is largely a profile of what currently exists as reported by FM practitioners. Clearly, we have a need to continue to look at the impact of DNA links on effective FM departments.

My suggestion to facility managers is to establish an organization benchmarking group of colleagues in the service business from within your own company, other FM departments in similar business segments, and FM departments outside your own industry. As a group, you should discuss and develop data and analyze the findings with respect to the benchmark areas we have talked about thus far. Using your collective diagnostic skills to evaluate the components of successful and effective FM departments is the best approach to benchmarking your own department.

How Do You Link the FM Department Structure to Service Delivery Commitments with Customers?

Now that we have covered the considerations that go into decisions about FM department structures, we turn to an FM business tool that links FM department structures to customer requirements for service. This business tool is used to close the loop between the essential task of identifying customer organization needs for FM services and our organization commitment to delivering these services. The business tool I am referring to is Service Level Agreements (SLAs).

A recent example from The Friday Group illustrates the value of SLAs for FM departments. A project we worked on involved focus groups with administrative and support customers of FM departments. Throughout our interviews, focus group participants kept steering the discussion back to the pressure they all felt within the company to perform faster, better, and smarter. They recognized and were empathetic about the sometimes unreasonable requests they made to the staff of the FM department, but they repeatedly said that they had to depend on the facilities group to help them meet the constant demands of their organization's executives who also were under pressure to achieve corporate goals and objectives for their departments. They talked about senior executives who relentlessly told them to "get it now" from facilities and who were unwilling to hear even valid reasons why last minute requests couldn't be filled.

The tie to our discussion about SLAs is: FM departments need to be able to provide customers in the workplace with the tools necessary to perform their jobs as pressure mounts for both entities. One job of FM departments is to provide customers with a lifeline that helps them avoid second-guessing the actions of departments and gives them the information they need about doing business with them. Service Level Agreements are lifelines to make that happen.

FM customers also want to know that if they have to pay for something, there will be consistency and value associated with the effort. Even if they don't have to pay for FM services, customers want some means to track the accountability of the money we are spending on their behalf. Service Level Agreements provide the framework to document expenditures for FM services by individual business unit.

What Is a Service Level Agreement (SLA)?

For those of you who are not familiar with SLAs, I want to make certain we have a common definition. The key words to describe SLAs are *formal, contract,* and *guarantees.* The essence of an SLA is to ensure that FM departments are providing their customers with a critical lifeline to their services.

An SLA is a formal contract between the FM department (as the provider) and an internal key customer that outlines and guarantees specific performance levels and, in certain instances, consistency of service cost. In other words, the SLA becomes the standard by which the FM department conducts business with the customer. The customer can be another department, a specific business unit, a tenant of the FM department, an individual, or a project team. The definition of a key client is one that needs to be determined by the FM department within the corporate setting.

In the body of an SLA, FM departments establish firm levels to guide customer expectations for service responsiveness, availability, and consistency. In addition, for those FM service environments in which there is a charge for space in the form of rent and/ or services, these charges can be identified, negotiated, and confirmed as part of the agreement. The agreement becomes the infrastructure within which both the FM department and the client understand their respective roles, responsibilities, and expectations. As one client described the SLA process, it guarantees end-to-end quality for the customer with respect to the availability and performance of service.

What Should a Service Level Agreement (SLA) Look Like?

From the experience of The Friday Group developing SLAs and having them adopted by FM departments, we find there are several recurring components to an SLA regardless of the type of client the FM department has determined to be a key client configuration. The Friday Group finds the most effective SLAs follow a consistent format for the majority of the document and contain certain types of information.[25]

- ❐ Table of Contents
- ❐ Definition of SLA (specific to customer)
- ❐ Identification of Roles and Responsibilities of Facility Department and Customer—This is one of the most critical aspects of the SLA because it determines how the customer will work with the FM department. If the customer is to become a true collaborator, then the customer must also assume some responsibility for the relationship specified in the SLA.
- ❐ Commitment of Facility Department to Customer Strategic Planning Activities
- ❐ Agreed-Upon Services and Service Level Commitments— This section of the SLA defines the service commitment in terms of the type of service that will be provided, the standards for service delivery, and how the customer will evaluate the FM department. The menu of services that is specific and tailored for the client should be articulated here even if the services are the same for each and every client.
- ❐ SLA Performance Monitoring—The critical performance indicators for this SLA also need to be covered. The FM department needs to know how customers will be evaluating them.
- ❐ Corrective Action Steps—If this component isn't included, departments are asking for trouble. Both parties need to spell out exactly how problems will be identified and re-

solved. If it involves a series of meetings to resolve the problem, then specific steps need to be spelled out. This process is designed to avoid having the customer escalate problems to higher levels without first trying to resolve them with the appropriate service providers. When these steps are identified in the SLA, the opportunity for customers to go automatically to the next higher level is reduced.

❐ Lease Agreement (where applicable)—For those FM departments that charge their internal customers for the space they occupy, the lease agreement portion of the SLA is a significant section. In this section, it is important to incorporate all the information that is necessary for the customer to understand how rent is determined and what is included in the rent.

❐ Products and Services Offered by the FM—Include a description of all services provided by the department even if they are not covered in this agreement. Additional services not covered by the original agreement may be added at a later date.

❐ Rate Structure Governing the Agreement Period (where applicable)—Some FM departments provide basic services (mail, security, housekeeping, photocopying, cafeteria, conference room scheduling, etc.) for all customers at no charge so there wouldn't be a section like this in the SLA. Other departments charge for these services, and the rate structure needs to be articulated. In addition, more and more FM departments are making provisions for discretionary services that the customer may or may not want, such as graphic support, transportation, demand work orders, printing, etc., and they have a different rate structure for these services. They should be spelled out in the SLA. Finally, even in organizations in which the FM department provides all basic and discretionary services at no charge to the customer, there is a movement toward charging for project work such as space planning, design, construction, moves, etc. The project structure needs to be covered in the SLA.

❐ Signatures of Appropriate Parties

I also need to mention that the most effective SLAs contain information that is tailored to individual customers. You may remember our discussion in Chapter 4 about asking customers about their strategic and operational initiatives. It has been our experience that the best way to identify what additional information should go in a specific client SLA is to ask customers what types of information would be beneficial. In addition to the above documentation, we also have seen SLAs that contain:

❐ Process Improvement Commitments—I noted earlier the growing need for an SLA lifeline with customers to include components that demonstrate the collaborative nature of your relationship with them. Among the add-on components to SLAs we have used is one called process improvement commitments. This is the section where an FM department would commit to improving an internal department process to streamline or enhance service to the customer organization. As an example, FM department customers often say they don't feel they are sufficiently involved in the design and layout process. If that is the case, the department might want to consider including a specific item in the SLA to cover how it will improve the process with the customer. If the customer wants more meetings and additional reviews of layouts, for example, this is the place where they would be included.

❐ Client Satisfaction Ratings—This section would include the department's overall client satisfaction ratings and any pertinent information about satisfaction feedback from the customer organization.

❐ Business Unit Profile Data—We identified the components of a Client Profile in Chapter 4 and these would be incorporated in this section.

What Are the Benefits to the FM Department and the Customer of Using Service Level Agreements (SLAs)?

There are direct benefits from having SLAs, both for the FM department and for the customer organization. For the department, the SLA is a way to differentiate services and products from those that might be available to customers through a different venue such as an outsource provider. It makes the statement that this is what departments offer and how they offer it.

More importantly, the SLA allows FM departments to manage customer expectations such that they are not constantly calling or E-mailing the department with service questions. FM departments spell out the service levels and customers agree to them in the SLA.

An SLA also allows FM departments to articulate the service guidelines that generically cover the way in which the department does business. Where there are corporate standards appropriate for every customer organization, the SLA provides the means to advertise them.

For customers, SLAs ensure that departments are willing to put their money behind their service. In other words, FM departments are able to guarantee that this is the level and quality of service the customer will ensure. SLAs also establish a process for creating an audit trail so that there is never any question from the customer about the service or, where appropriate, what they were charged. The rate structure is spelled out in advance and can be audited.

How Do We Know When We Have Designed the Right FM Department Structure?

We leave this chapter with some essential building blocks as we near the completion of our journey through OD. The DNA links we discussed in previous chapters prepared us for the pinnacle of OD activities, designing the department structure.

Many facility managers will couple the generic principles of organization configuration with components of FM department structures that have demonstrated success. Having done this, however, they will question if the organization design is producing the desired result. Authors Michael Goold and Andrew Campbell share my approach to an analytical framework for OD and have created nine tests for organization design that provide an excellent means for assessing its fitness for FM departments.[26] I have adapted their concepts to the practice of FM OD.

Market Advantage Test—Does the design allocate sufficient management attention to the operating arteries and intended sources of advantage in each product/market area? For our purposes, the test means looking at the organization design to see if there is sufficient responsibility, authority, and attention given to those service areas that are priorities. If, for example, customer-focused service is a priority, then the organization must be structured around customer needs and requirements.

Parenting Advantage Test—Does the design allocate sufficient attention to the sources of added value and strategic initiatives of the corporate parent? For facility managers, this test involves assessing how the department adds value to the overall enterprise. We talked about this at great length in Chapter 5.

People Test—Does the design adequately reflect the motivations, strengths, and weaknesses of the available people? This one should be abundantly clear by now. Facility managers need to perform their assessment of KSA and fully understand staff capabilities and how they impact the organization design.

Feasibility Test—Does the design take into account constraints that may make it unworkable? In FM, we need to consider things such as corporate culture and how/if our design will fit in, enterprise hierarchy and politics, government and regulatory issues the enterprise is facing, and any legal or other business constraints. In other words, what are the circumstances that will prevent the FM department design from being effective?

Specialist Culture Test—Does any specialist culture or units with cultures that need to be different have sufficient protection from the influence of the dominant culture? As we discussed earlier in this chapter, FM department components or work groups (teams) need protection of their own culture in terms of critical success factors, operating styles and norms, and work processes and procedures so they aren't dominated by those of other work groups (teams).

Difficult Links Test—Does the design have any coordination benefits that will be hard to achieve, and if so, have solutions been included in the design? Our Chapter 3 topic on creating an environment to foster group process needs to be linked to considerations about the department structure to ensure opportunities for information sharing, integration of processes, and strategy development to take place.

Redundant Hierarchy Test—Are all levels in the hierarchy and all responsibilities retained by higher levels based on knowledge and competency advantage? Facility managers need to look at the KSA associated with core competencies for hierarchical units within the department and perform a skills assessment to ensure they are appropriately filled. This test also involves a human resources analysis to determine if the staffing complement in terms of numbers of staff is right for the responsibilities assigned.

Accountability Test—Does the design facilitate creation of a control process for each unit appropriate for responsibilities given, economy of implementation, and motivation of managers? In order for the FM department design to work, all subgroups must have delegated accountability for taking risks, implementing actions, and creating rewarding work.

Flexibility Test—Will the design keep the development of new strategies and be flexible enough to adapt to future changes? Turn to Chapter 7 to find out how to conduct this test.

▌DNA Link: Structure

Company: DFW International Airport Board (transportation)

Background

The DFW International Airport, which first opened to traffic a few minutes past midnight on January 13, 1974, is jointly owned by the cities of Dallas and Fort Worth and is governed by the DFW Airport Board. Today, DFW is the world's third busiest airport, serving over 60 million passengers a year. Airlines at DFW operate nearly 2,300 daily flights to over 150 nonstop destinations in 15 countries. DFW is also one of the world's largest airports, covering 18,076 acres (7,318 hectares) and with an extensive physical infrastructure. In fiscal year 2001, the Airport Board had 1,844 full-time employees organized into five divisions (see Figure DFW 1).

The Airport Maintenance (AM) department manages the airport board's multibillion dollar facility and infrastructure asset portfolio (estimated current replacement value in excess of $6 billion). The 458 members of this department provide a variety of services including energy management, thermal energy production and distribution, potable water and sewer system operation, transit system operation, facility management, fleet management, and infrastructure repair and renewal (planning, programming, designing, building). Airport Maintenance's fiscal year operating budget was $34 million. The department has undergone a significant structural and process transformation over the past 4 years in response to broader corporate changes and competitive pressures. Our story, which follows, summarizes the transformation and highlights key origins, features, and results.

Figure DFW 1. DFW Airport Board Organizational Structure (2001).

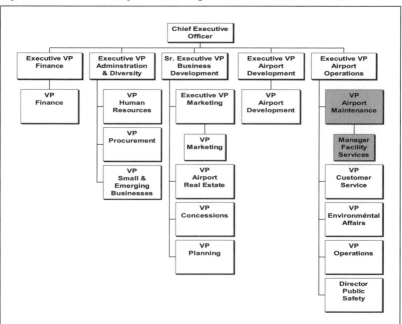

Their Story

Airport Maintenance Organizational Evolution

The original (circa 1974) Airport Maintenance department organization structure and business processes were largely modeled on the U.S. Air Force Civil Engineering (AFCE) organization. Key members of the initial department management team were career AFCE officers and senior noncommissioned officers who established structures and processes consistent with their previous experiences. The organization structure was purely functional in design (see Figure DFW 2), and business processes were dominated by a task orientation. Little change occurred within the department over the next 20 years.

In the early 1990s, the entire commercial aviation industry experienced severe financial losses that put pressure on airports to reduce operating costs. In 1993, a new executive director was appointed to the airport board. He championed the vision of "running the airport like a business." Over the next several years, he directed a corporate-level reorganization, implemented an aggressive program of diversifying airport revenues, and maintained a continued focus on cost

Figure DFW 2. Airport Maintenance Department Organizational Structure (pre-1998).

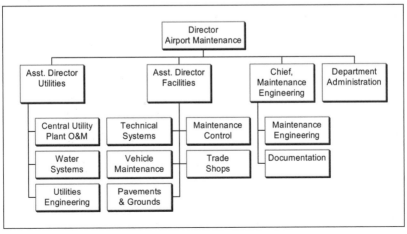

containment. The primary corporate metric became cost per enplaned passenger

The AM department was slow to respond to these changes in the internal and external environments. Consequently, the department came to be viewed by senior management as resource intensive, inflexible, dominated by a focus on internal department goals, and out of alignment with the evolving corporate culture. A new director selected in 1994 produced limited improvement but was replaced in 1997 by a member of the department's management team. Under this new leadership, a comprehensive performance improvement program was implemented, resulting in a near total revision of the department's structure and business processes. The new AM department and FM organization structures are depicted in Figures DFW 3 and DFW 4.

In May 2000, both the AM department and its FM organization were further rationalized to current organization structures as depicted in Figures DFW 5 and DFW 6. This was done to incorporate additional business functions and service areas as well as to improve service delivery.

Factors Influencing Organization Design

The AM department's performance improvement plan is guided by two fundamental principles designed to support board (corporate) business objectives:

DFW will be the airport of choice—To the AM department, this translates to *Best-in-Class Performance* (integrating best practices).

DFW will be operated like a business—To the AM department, this translates to *Value-Centered Asset Management* (understanding our competitive position, integrating board business goals, and listening to our customers).

The organization structure implemented in 1998 was developed from the perspective that structure influences delivery of services. The previous structure (organized around functions) had been a key factor in producing the narrow, vertical,

Figure DFW 3. Airport Maintenance Department Organizational Structure (10/98–5/00).

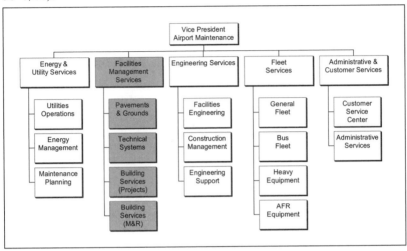

Figure DFW 4. Facilities Management Services Organizational Structure (10/98–5/00).

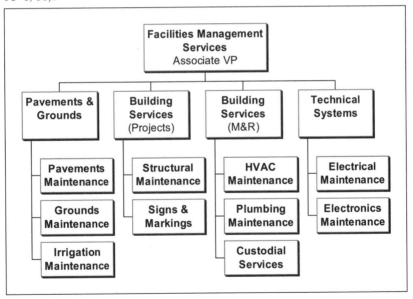

Figure DFW 5. Airport Maintenance Department Organizational Structure (2001).

Figure DFW 6. Facility Services Organizational Structure (2001).

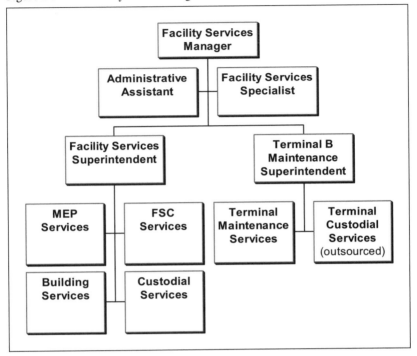

and heavily task-oriented perspective of the department's people and processes. The principal drivers in developing our new structure were the need to:

Integrate activities horizontally across multiple functions in order to facilitate a customer focus

Align business units with customers and/or core services

Promote a holistic perspective throughout the organization

Emphasize accountability for business results

Core Competencies

The nature of the AM business philosophy and structure dictates that its business units collaborate for services that are not feasibly provided within their own resource base. For example, the department's FM unit, Facility Services, provides overall FM business management but is also responsible to the customer for delivering various services such as landscape maintenance (provided by Public Services), energy management (provided by Energy & Utility Services) and project planning, programming, design, and construction management (provided by Engineering Services) via other department business units.

Consequently, the core competencies presented here are as viewed on a department-wide basis:

Technical maintenance and repair skills

Project execution (planning, programming, design, construction management)

Infrastructure asset management (condition assessment, reinvestment strategic development, planning, programming)

Energy management

Business management (strategic and business planning, financial analysis and management, process improvement, execution, metrics)

Insource vs. Outsource Mix

A macroindication of the amount of work insourced versus outsourced may be discerned from the total department operating budget. In fiscal year 2001, salaries, wages, and benefits constituted approximately 64 percent of the department's operating budget, while contract services comprised 14 percent. Most routine operations, maintenance, and repair functions (OM&R includes operating costs for energy, utilities, fuel, labor, etc., associated with operating transit and utility systems in addition to typical infrastructure maintenance and repair costs) are insourced including:

Landscape maintenance and general groundskeeping (augmented by contract labor)

Facility maintenance and repair

Custodial services for board-occupied facilities and certain public facilities

Fire alarm, security, and communication systems

Elevator, escalator, baggage conveyor, and jetbridge maintenance and repair

Condition assessments, facility audits, furniture asset management

Roof management, pavement management, energy management

Business planning

Outsourced functions include:

Custodial services in passenger terminal B

Window washing

Roof repairs/replacement

Asbestos abatement

Major renovations

Specialized services with infrequent or low-volume requirements such as machine shop work, insulation, motor rewinds, and glass replacement

Some functions may be provided by either insourced or outsourced resources depending on factors such as current work volume or shifting business priorities. These functions include:

Project design and construction management

Major repair, refurbishment, renewal, or redevelopment

Best Practices

Best practices adopted or developed by the AM department include:

❐ *Management by "Mission Orders"*—Business unit managers are given broad objectives to accomplish and the flexibility to deploy resources and utilize processes as they see fit to achieve them rather than having the means and methods dictated in a command-and-control manner.

❏ *Activity-Based Cost Management*—AM utilizes its Computerized Maintenance Management System (CMMS) to allocate, track, and report costs on an activity basis in order to give visibility to the full cost of providing various services.

❏ *Airport Infrastructure Maintenance (AIM) Program*—The AIM program establishes a standardized system of physical asset classification, inventory, and condition assessment. This program facilitates a long-term perspective on asset management, produces a 5-year reinvestment plan, and has increased the visibility of the asset management function and its value to the corporate enterprise.

❏ *The Airport Board Strategic Plan*—The plan validates the asset management function by establishing strategic corporate objectives for facility function and appearance, and level of reinvestment in facility and infrastructure assets.

❏ *Integrated Business Planning and Management*—Business planning, financial management, and performance measurement are integrated and continuous. These processes and standards have been adopted as a corporate-wide best practice.

❏ *Workforce Spirit of Adaptability and Ownership*—Department members have historically demonstrated great pride in their role and contributions to the success of one of the world's most well-known and respected airports. This spirit facilitates adaptability, innovation, and customer focus.

Airport Maintenance is also in the process of developing a Facility & Infrastructure Master Plan, which will establish airportwide standards for total physical asset management.

Learning Points

❏ Customer focus drives service delivery structure
❏ Flexible structure designed to adapt to changing requirements

❐ Matrix management approach of horizontally integrated functions

❐ Performance tied to achievement of business results

About the Author

Rusty Hodapp has over 20 years of diversified experience in facility, energy, and infrastructure asset management. He has held engineering and management positions with Texas Instruments, Mobil Oil, and for the past 15 years, the Dallas/ Fort Worth (DFW) International Airport Board. Mr. Hodapp currently is the vice president of Airport Maintenance for DFW where he leads a department of 458 people engaged in the maintenance, repair, and renewal of the airport's $6 billion infrastructure asset portfolio including public works, energy systems, utilities, facilities, transit system, and fleet vehicles.

Endnotes

1. Jay Galbraith, Diane Downey, and Amy Kates, *Designing Dynamic Organizations: A Hands-on Guide for Leaders at All Levels* (New York: AMACOM, 2002), p. 2.
2. Judith R. Gordon, *Organizational Behavior: A Diagnostic Approach,* 6th ed. (Upper Saddle River, NJ: Prentice Hall, 1999), pp. 365–372.
3. Facility Management Institute.
4. Ibid.
5. *The IFMA Report #2: Demographics and Trends* (Houston: International Facility Management Association, 1986), p. 36.
6. Ibid., p. 36.
7. Ibid., pp. 37–39.
8. David G. Cotts, *The Facility Management Handbook,* 2nd ed. (New York: AMACOM, 1999), pp. 5–7.
9. Ibid., pp. 23–24.

10. Ibid., pp. 25–33.
11. *Designing the Facility Management Organization* (Houston: IMA Foundation, 2001), p. 13.
12. Ibid., p. 21.
13. Ibid., p. 23.
14. Ibid., p. 25.
15. *Facility Management Practices: Research Report #16* (Houston: International Facility Management Association, 1996), p. 11.
16. *Designing the Facility Management Organization*, op. cit., p. 8.
17. Ibid., p. 4.
18. Ibid.
19. Gordon, op. cit., p. 415.
20. Ibid., p. 416.
21. Ibid.
22. Ibid., p. 417.
23. *Facility Management Practices: Research Report #16*, op. cit., p. 30.
24. Fred Klammt, "What Does Your Gut Tell You? Let's Check the Scorecard," *The Outsource Report* (August 1998), p. 6.
25. The Friday Group Presentation on Service Level Agreements, 2000.
26. Adapted from Michael Goold and Andrew Campbell, *Designing Effective Organizations: How to Create Structured Networks* (San Francisco: Jossey-Bass, 2002), pp. 249–291.

CHAPTER SEVEN

Linking FM Organizations to the Future of Facility Management

DNA Link: Future

How Has the New Workplace Affected FM Departments?

Although facility professionals don't have crystal balls allowing them to predict what will happen to the practice of FM (although often senior executives in corporations think they do), they should pay close attention to business trends and activities that might have potential impact on their departments in the future. Our last DNA link explores some of the issues FM practitioners should be tracking.

Working in the Technology Workplace

We are fortunate to be FM professionals during a time of rapid technological development, allowing us to perform functions better and faster. Since the early 1980s, when nearly every FM function was supported by manual systems that were tedious and labor-intensive, FM departments have witnessed fairly rapid developments in technology tools to aid their ability to serve customers in a better way.

Facility professionals now have the ability to perform routine and diagnostic work on building infrastructure systems from computers that are remotely operated, integrate facility information databases with CAD drawings, perform real-time space planning with customers on-site using laptops, create inventory systems for customers to track information on their own, generate management information at a moment's notice to answer queries from bosses, and a host of other technology-driven FM applications.

Facility managers also can communicate with personnel who are performing their duties within close geographical proximity as well as from globally dispersed sites via cellular and powerful two-way radio communications, personal digital assistants (PDAs), e-mail, and the Internet. These same capabilities give FM departments the ability to provide customers with timely information about services through FM Web sites, respond instantaneously to customer requests for service via automated work order and dispatch systems, and obtain timely feedback on customer satisfaction through electronic survey instruments.

In short, facility practitioners have a wealth of tools to assist them, but there also may be some pitfalls for FM departments associated with the growing dependence on technology. While wholeheartedly supporting and endorsing the use of technology tools and the advantages they present for the rapid deployment of service and information, I also believe there are some organization development (OD) implications associated with technology we need to consider.

I worry sometimes that the growing dependency on technology may become a crutch and ultimately a substitute for personal interaction with colleagues and customers. As FM departments become more and more dependent on technology tools as primary means of communication, they need to make certain that interpersonal skills remain the cornerstone of quality FM performance. As an example, I am reminded of an intern we had working for The Friday Group who was researching some FM benchmarking information for a client. She became quite concerned when she couldn't find the information she needed by searching the Internet. It never occurred to her that she might have to go to a library or pick up the phone and actually talk with some facility professionals to obtain the information. Her whole frame of reference revolved around the Internet, which led her to believe if she couldn't find it there, it probably didn't exist.

Technology tools often are only as good as the information given to them, which means we still need to use outside resources and old-fashioned interpersonal communication as supplemental sources for data gathering and dissemination. Facility managers do not want technology to cannibalize their FM staff's interpersonal skills in such a way that it becomes a substitute for thinking. These tools are just that and do not negate the basic underlying principles of independent thinking and judgment.

It also is important to realize all the electronic aids we have available do not negate the need for "face time" with customers. All too often it is easier for FM professionals to communicate with their customers through an electronic medium without ever having to leave the office and be visible to customers. While technology tools are critical to cutting-edge service, a close, personal service relationship with customers is paramount to the long-term success of FM departments.

Alternative Work Environments

There was a time in the early 1990s when futurists who were making predictions about the workplace environment were certain everyone would be working in some type of alternative workplace. These workplace futurists were convinced that hoteling, hot desking, geographical work centers, and other alternative office concepts would replace the more traditional office environment in the majority of companies.

What they failed to factor into their equation for the future, however, was the fact that alternative offices are not appropriate for every organizational function performed by most corporations and institutions. While it may make good sense for a marketing staff, for example, to spend the majority of their time out of an office in a feet-on-the-street approach to job performance, it doesn't necessarily mean that the R&D staff can work effectively and productively in locations other than their laboratories. While the use of alternative offices and work environments has seen steady growth over the past few years, it is still not standard practice for all organizations in most companies.

Where alternative workplaces are being implemented, however, they present both opportunities and challenges for providers of FM services. On the one hand, they afford an opportunity for you to think innovatively about providing FM services in an environment other than traditional bricks-and-mortar, while on the other hand, they present a challenge with respect to liability and responsibility issues such as safety, ergonomics, and air quality.

There is yet another challenge that changes in the workplace habitat present that is being explored and debated by organization behaviorists. For organization components whose entire staffs have been redirected to alternative forms of "officing," organization behaviorists fear that an absence in what has become known as the watercooler effect has potentially negative sociological implications. The watercooler effect in essence means that employees typically learn a lot about an organization's norms, values, culture, and philosophy from meeting and talking to one another around the office watercooler. The watercooler effect is similar to the concepts set forth in Chapter 4 on corporate culture. When employees no longer come into an office on a regular basis to interact with one another, it becomes more and more important to develop alternative mechanisms to ensure that the organization's norms, values, etc., are reinforced and communicated on a frequent basis. It is important to reinforce how the organization conducts its business in order to ensure consistency in behavior. The absence of employee interaction and group dynamics makes it even more difficult for new employees to assimilate the organization's standards unless managers make a concerted effort to provide alternative opportunities for the group to come together.

As technology enhances the FM department's ability to provide nontraditional office hours for staff, it is important to be aware of the sociological implications described above. If service technicians are spending time working on infrastructure systems from remote locations through a network of laptops, it is essential to convey the department's values and standards to them such that when they actually interact with a customer, they follow established protocols and customer service attributes.

Projecting even further into the future, you need to think about how you work with customer populations that are finding it increasingly easy to work from off-site locations. If more and more of your customer business units are participating in alternative work environments, how will your FM department continue to have "face time" with your customers? If the majority of your customers do not come into an office every day, how will you demonstrate superior customer service and receive feedback on the services you perform?

Is Your Organization Ready to Assume Nontraditional FM Roles?

In their book *Excellence by Design: Transforming Workplace and Work Practice,* authors Horgen, Jaroff, Porter, and Schön offer a nontraditional approach to the world of work in the future by conceiving of the workplace as a strategic component of corporations in which four interrelated dimensions coexist. From the perspective of these MIT scholars, the workplace is at the core of four dimensions: space, organization, technology, and finance, which are interrelated.[1] For them, one of the challenges for corporations in the future is to achieve cohesion between these four dimensions and the practice of work, which also is dynamic.

Basically, what they are saying is that we have an opportunity in FM to position ourselves strategically within our companies because the workplace and the practices associated with work are going to become more and more important to business decision making. In order for this to happen, however, there has to be a synergistic relationship among the four dimensions they identify. I think you will have a better understanding if you look at my adaptation in Figure 7-1 of the graphic they present in their book.[2]

The reason for bringing their ideas to your attention is that they are on the right track in their thinking about the nontraditional roles for FM in the future. Consider them to be a confirmation of the need for FM professionals to expand their horizons about what FM will be in the future.

Figure 7-1. Nontraditional approach to the world of work.

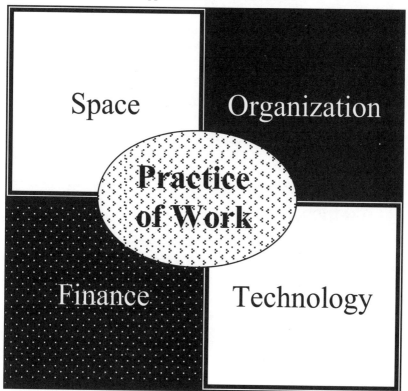

No Service Boundaries

This statement constitutes the message facility practitioners need to contemplate as they consider the future of FM. If they are to be in the forefront of their company's development efforts to capture more market share, increase the bottom line for returns to shareholders, expand globally, create strategic partnerships with complementary providers, and become an invigorating workplace for the best and brightest of workers, they will have to consider opportunities for providing services that may not have been previously considered as traditional FM functions.

The Friday Group has heard facility managers say there are some functions they would not perform because they weren't, in their minds, the types of services that an FM department should be providing. Because they weren't considered forward thinkers, some of these same facility managers are no longer gainfully employed by their companies and are having difficulty finding employment. Do I make my point?

My proposal is to have facility professionals expand their horizons by letting both corporate and individual business unit activities, in other words, customers, drive the functions performed by FM departments. In the same manner in which we discussed the need to have FM department structures dictated by customer groups, we also need to have customers determine the services departments should be performing. As an example, the facility manager for a company that is a client of The Friday Group has said over the years he would never take on the responsibility for travel management because he didn't feel it was an FM function. After much coaching, we finally convinced him to become more customer-focused, and in so doing he learned one of the most serious corporate problems was the management of travel services. Taking a huge step forward, he developed a proposal for corporate management to study and make recommendations on how to improve travel services. Not only was his report applauded as an excellent piece of business analysis, but also his FM department inherited the job of managing corporate travel. The story does not end there, however. His organization was so successful in managing corporate travel (some of which was outsourced and some provided in-house), the FM department went outside its own company to offer these services and became an independent business entity, offering travel management to other companies.

While some of you might be saying that travel management clearly falls within the purview of FM, the point of this story is to stretch your thinking with respect to what business areas might be potential candidates for inclusion in the FM menu of services.

Develop the Business Case to Invest in Technology

Most of you probably don't need a reminder about the value of technology in the business world of the future. As mentioned previously, the technological advances available to FM and business customers afford a workplace environment that would not have been contemplated or available when FM first became a recognized profession.

The key for facility managers is to provide a convincing argument to senior management that in order to be considered an integral business player, FM departments also must implement advancements in technology tools. Not only do they need to keep more traditional FM technology, such as CAD and CIFM systems, up to speed with industry standards, they must also have exceptional capabilities with respect to graphics software packages for presentations, statistical software packages for analysis, and communications software, such as Web sites and e-mail, to stay in touch with customers.

The only way to make this convincing argument is to provide a business case to senior management. Business case justification is the language of the boardroom, and so it is incumbent upon an FM department to develop a business case for expenditures on technology and present these to senior management.

Become a Corporate Standard-Bearer

As we discussed in Chapter 4 on strategic planning, a nontraditional role for FM is to be viewed as the standard-bearer within the corporation for initiating organizational change. Whether it is to initiate strategic planning if the corporation currently does not follow the practice, conduct customer feedback sessions using focus groups and surveys, transform the department into a customer-driven service delivery model, keep the facilities operating in a zero downtime tolerance mode, or perform benchmarking with best-in-class service providers, the FM department should strive to be known as a leader within the business circles of the company.

FM professional development does not naturally compel facility professionals to assume this role, for traditionally they have acted as a response agent to customers. Given the business climate of the future, facility professionals need to be proactive as corporate role models.

How Do Corporate Mergers and Acquisitions (M&As) Affect FM Organizations?

The year 1998 served as a bellwether for what would lie ahead with respect to corporate mergers and acquisitions (M&A) by the parent companies of FM departments.[3] From an OD perspective, these corporate M&As may well be one of the most challenging issues for facility departments in the future.

During 1998, unprecedented M&As totaling over $2.4 trillion stunned the financial world. These business changes did not reflect the hostile takeovers of the 1970s, 1980s, and early 1990s, but rather were geared toward the growing business strategies of increased market share through globalization, diversification, and expansion of services through alliances with complementary "families of services," pricing power and economies of scale, and increased population base through purchase of established customer markets. Companies were settling on growth strategies through M&As rather than the more traditional organic growth that takes time and requires an inward business focus.

In 2002, the M&A market was not making front-page headlines on a daily basis, and in fact, the first half of 2002 showed transactions down 39 percent from the previous year. Yet, when we look at M&A activity more closely, smaller deals are in the works, and consummation of mega-acquisitions, such as the Hewlett-Packard $19 billion purchase of Compaq, took place. The *Wall Street Journal* also announced that the $200 billion pharmaceutical company Pfizer planned to buy Pharmacia Corp. for $60 billion in stock.

An interesting study conducted by PriceWaterhouseCoopers in 2000 produced findings from 125 senior executives from companies around the world that have completed M&As. Their insights into the M&A world bring valuable lessons for FM.[4]

Companies acquire to obtain management and technical talent, build revenue. and market position.

Fewer than 40 percent of respondents involved in M&As met their cost-cutting targets, while revenue goals were achieved.

Problems integrating information systems caused delays, lost revenue, and missed opportunities in three out of four company M&As.

To avoid quick-deal depreciation, it is essential to resolve philosophical and operating systems differences up front.

Successful deals involve speed.

Transition teams early in the process build morale, focus initiatives and decision making, and reduce absenteeism, turnover, and internal strife.

The Implications for FM Departments

Many of the previous findings play into the hands of FM departments, which can help make an M&A deal go more smoothly. When companies are trying to determine if a merger or acquisition makes sense, they perform due diligence on potential company candidates to determine what the added value will be in terms of return on investment and financial potential, business and cultural orientation of the prospective company, business philosophy and practices, and a host of other important decision-making elements.

What often is overlooked in the due diligence process is the need to investigate significant real estate and facility issues of a candidate company and their impact on existing FM practices. In many instances, candidate companies have a real estate portfolio that may include owned and leased properties both within the United States and in locations around the world. It is important for the due diligence team to review and consider the implications of acquiring and managing these properties once they are part of the new company's portfolio. These properties must be analyzed in terms of how they will support the existing delivery system in the future and what the impact will be on the business equation if there is a need to update, reconfigure, acquire, or dispose of facilities.

Likewise, critical FM issues affecting the current and potential company employees also need to be assessed to determine if the policies and philosophies of the two companies are complementary. Issues such as the environment, ergonomics, indoor air quality, health and safety, space standards, and alternative workplace attitudes must be reviewed.

Finally, in the due diligence process, the host company should explore whether or not there will be redundant real estate and facility management functions and services once a merger or acquisition takes place. It is important to resolve the process that will be used to integrate the FM functions of the respective companies and who will be responsible for ensuring that the integration process is performed in the least disruptive manner to daily operations of the companies while taking into consideration the impact on the staff of the two FM departments.

In order to ensure that the corporate real estate/FM philosophy and service delivery issues are taken into consideration during the due diligence process, the lead company's facility department needs to establish a presence as a key player in the overall process. It is critical for the facility manager to address the business implications with senior executives and propose technical assistance for the FM department in the due diligence process. At a minimum, the department should suggest that the due diligence process incorporate the following:

Real Estate Issues

Location of candidate company facilities (domestic and global)

Status of facilities (owned versus leased)

Mix of facility use (office buildings, storefronts, R&D, special-purpose space, etc.)

Value of owned facilities

Financing arrangements

Lease configurations (triple net, fully serviced)

Lease management responsibilities

Use of third-party providers

Special issues such as code restrictions, zoning restrictions, use agreements, etc.

Country-specific provisions

Real estate acquisition and disposal

Facility Management Issues

Policy reviews

Environmental issues

Health/safety issues

Space planning and allocation guidelines

Design/construction standards

Furniture guidelines

Project management

Sourcing philosophy

Alteration and renovation guidelines

Operations, maintenance, and repair guidelines

Security policies

Administrative service guidelines

Real Estate and Facility Management Organization

Location of functions within corporate structure

Reporting relationship

Services provided

Structure of corporate real estate (CRE) and FM organizations

Staff knowledge, skills, and abilities (KSA)

Customer service orientation

Strategic planning capability

Customer satisfaction information

Mix of in-house versus outsourced service provision

Best practice/benchmarking activities

Master plan information

What Is the Impact of the Global Business Environment on FM Departments?

Several years ago at a World Workplace Conference, I gave a presentation on gearing up to do business in a global FM environment and no one came. I don't mean literally no one came, but the 30 or so people in the audience were not facility professionals from the United States, but rather professionals in our business from around the world. I might not have considered both the size of the group and the makeup to be unusual except that typically these sessions attract a crowd of significant size and balanced representation across the globe.[5]

Of particular concern, however, were the comments received while talking to participants during the remainder of the conference. FM professionals made a point of saying they were sorry that they didn't attend but just didn't consider themselves to be working in a global environment. They couldn't see the value in attending this type of discussion. I was shocked.

If we advance to the present, it still doesn't seem that the FM mind-set has expanded to the fullest extent. FM professionals still say that their companies are not working in the global arena and that they don't need to learn about the impact of the global workplace on FM organizations. Yet, if you read what any respected futurist has to say about business for the next 10 to 15 years, they say there is no such thing as a domestically based company, because even if your current company is not doing business overseas, there is the possibility that a foreign competitor could enter your domestic market. Even companies providing goods and services exclusively to a domestic market (whether it is in the United States or another country) are using foreign materials from foreign manufacturing plants with foreign local labor and technology.

We also have not been encouraging the profession to broaden its horizons through writings and publications on the subject. If you look at what has appeared in any of the FM-related journals or periodicals, you will be hard-pressed to find substantive information about globalization except as it relates to bricks-and-mortar issues such as design, virtual architecture, using business centers instead of direct-leased space, and understanding cultural nuances of doing business. There has been little, if any, information about the impact of globalization on FM departments and the provision of service from the cultural OD perspective we discussed in Chapters 5 and 6.

Taking on a New Role

Several years ago The Friday Group was working with an FM department that needed to consider the implications of corporate

272 ORGANIZATION DEVELOPMENT FOR FACILITY MANAGERS

expansion overseas on the delivery of FM services. The company was struggling to find an appropriate context for the FM role. We were doing a fair amount of reading in the futures realm and stumbled upon the term *cultural integrator* in an older issue of the publication *Business Horizons*. The term was designed to cover a function that many companies were establishing as they began to operate on a multinational level and found some unanticipated problems arising from intercultural differences that resulted in business costs that were hidden from the analysis during the due diligence exercises. The cultural integrator's job was to understand how and why the business processes were different due to intercultural differences and to recommend to senior executives how to overcome them through adaptations in operating methodologies.

As we studied the function of the cultural integrator, it was apparent that with some modification, the role was an appropriate one for FM in a multinational workplace environment. As a takeoff, we coined the term *workplace cultural integrator*, which appears to describe the facility professional's role in international FM. The role of the FM professional is neither to force the company to adhere strictly to the practices of a host country, nor to demand that the host country company accept business practices that are foreign to its culture. Instead, the role of the FM organization is to analyze the host country's norms and values, determine the impact on FM requirements and current operating procedures, and introduce workplace practices that are innovative and compatible with both cultures. As global companies shift to their own production and service delivery through the use of virtual organizations, it will be the role of the workplace cultural integrator (i.e., the FM department) to assess the best means of providing support services to accomplish the business missions.

To do this, professionals within FM departments have to add a whole repertoire of new talents including an understanding of divergent languages, personalities, work habits, interpersonal orientations, time perspectives, etc. In the situation in which the host country's culture is significantly different from that of the foreign company, the FM organization should have the ability to understand the nuances of how people within the country do business in order to serve as a valuable resource to the corporation overall.

Developing a Global Mind-Set

One of the thinkers in the arena of globalization and its impact on management issues who has provided some excellent insight into the approach we should be taking with respect to our organizations of the future is a fellow named Stephen H. Rhinesmith. Rhinesmith wrote a book entitled *A Manager's Guide to Globalization: Six Keys to Success in a Changing World* in which he talks about the need for managers to stop thinking domestically and grow into a global mind-set. Although others have written on the topic of global business since then, this work applies the principles of globalization to organizations, their people, and their structures. Rhinesmith's thoughts serve as a framework for my own thinking about the differences in a domestically oriented facility professional versus one that has made the transition to a global orientation. Here is my interpretation of the two mind-sets.

Mind-Set of a Domestically Oriented Facility Professional

Feels comfortable with traditional functional expertise and relies on what has worked in years past. This professional uses traditional skills and expertise to stay within a narrowly defined functional box.

Attempts to resolve all conflicts between facility priorities and those of the customer base. The attitude of the professional is that there is only one way to handle conflict and that is to resolve it. The historical experience of this professional within the corporation has proven that either the customer gets his way and the FM organization loses, or the FM organization poses rules and regulations to avoid conflict with the customer.

Has implicit trust in a structured approach to achieving success. In the mind of this professional, survival for the FM organization is to have a strategic plan and stay on course, analyze potential situations, and then present senior management with facts and figures to support decision making.

Accepts responsibility as an individual regardless of how much teamwork is involved. With this type of mind-set, the FM professional feels that if he is a leader, the buck stops with him, and ultimately he is accountable for all decisions.

Works to maintain the no-surprise element. From every customer survey and dialogue with senior executives, the facility professional has learned that his job is to make certain that there are no surprises. Keeping senior management apprised about the potential for a new roof, the need to replace chillers, or letting customers know in advance that a construction crew will be coming to their area has been standard practice for domestically thinking facility professionals.

Mind-Set of a Globally Oriented Facility Professional

Seeks out more than the obvious for the contextual picture. Because they play the cultural workplace integrator role, these professionals understand that the host country's history, government, and economy shape the way in which the employees will view the workplace. These facility professionals are constantly performing "global scanning" to identify workplace issues and place them in the context of the country within which they originate.

Accepts conflict management as a strategy that works globally. Conflict is regarded as healthy in many cultures, and compromise becomes the global mode of operation in certain workplace environments

Relies on process rather than structure to create workplace environments. Facility processionals who have embraced the concepts of quality management and process reengineering have an easier time transitioning to the global mind-set because in many countries the process required to reach a decision is more important than the outcome itself. In many countries, how the cultural workplace integrator handles the discussions with tenants, negotiates with subcontractors, and establishes time frames will set the tone for the success or failure of a project.

Promotes multicultural teamwork. It goes without saying that in a more global environment, the successful facility professional needs to rely heavily on the diversity of a team to heighten awareness and create strategies to accommodate differences in terminology, standards, and FM practices. The task then of the FM organization is to stimulate the idea stream through the use of creative processes to provide the framework within which teams can function.

Looks at surprise as a challenge associated with the new workplace environment. Of all the concepts related to the mind-set for a globally oriented facility department, I think this is the paradigm shift that is the most difficult for FM professionals. As the future thinkers tell us, the global business environment is unpredictable in the best of times, and those facility professionals who have international experience have learned to adapt to changing situations as they occur. In keeping with our diagnostic approach to developing effective FM departments, the role of the FM professional in a global company is to have the skills necessary to assess a problem and develop the appropriate contingency response.

Creating a Global FM Enterprise

We have a final issue regarding the concept of globalization and its impact on FM service delivery: We also need to consider how we construct an FM department in the global business environment. Again referring to the work of Stephen Rhinesmith, he has turned the pure business definition of globalization into one that is more appropriate for those pursuing managerial applications. Rhinesmith prefers to use what he calls a more technical definition of globalization: a state of development in international organization strategy, structure, and culture.[6] I wholeheartedly support his position that globalization as viewed earlier is quite different from simply conducting business internationally. It represents a way of organizing corporate entities around three critical factors— strategy, structure, and culture—that have dramatic impact on the workplace environment.

Facility managers need to translate what they know about global business objectives into FM terms. Global business strategy depends on the ability to reach and penetrate certain marketplaces before other local or multinational competitors do. For facility professionals that means speed, flexibility, and a resiliency to deliver FM services. To do this, we need to consider an organization structure that is entrepreneurial, highly networked in terms of people to take advantage of cross-cultural expertise and experience, highly developed in terms of technology transfer to share information resources, process driven, and decentralized to centers of excellence located in multiple countries. The end result is a global FM organization structure, similar to the one that appears in Figure 7-2, in which highly adaptable FM professionals operate in an environ-

Figure 7-2. Global FM organization structure.

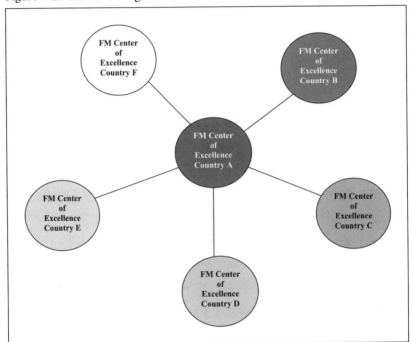

ment where the interconnectivity of strategy, structure, and culture drive service delivery.

Have You Positioned Your Organization for the Continuous Learning Process?

As we come to the end of our discussion on achieving organizational effectiveness for FM departments, there is an additional concept we need to cover. Facility professionals need to know how important it is for an organization to have a commitment to continuous learning. In the same way that an FM professional's journey for growth and development is one long continuum, so, too, is the learning cycle for the FM department.

As those who practice the art of "future-think" tell us, the survival and success of companies in the future rest in their ability to attract and develop workers who have an appreciation and thirst for knowledge. For our own profession, these knowledge workers will become the backbone of FM departments, but they also will be pushing facility managers constantly to strive for continuous improvement through the application of innovative and best-practice technologies.

We also know, however, that learning organizations filled with knowledge workers are not created quickly because it takes time to develop an organization climate that fosters continuous learning. All too frequently, organizations lose sight of their vision to become a learning organization and forget to assess whether or not the organization and the individuals within it are headed in the right direction and have the right tools to make it happen. Sometimes organizations become so engrossed in day-to-day activities that they fail to reflect on their strategic direction. It takes time to focus on efforts that ensure the organization is not stagnating with respect to its own growth and development.

You will remember from our discussions in Chapters 1 and 2, that an FM manager can become a superleader by planting the seeds of empowerment and entrepreneurism in FM employees and then cultivating them until they reach maturity. If you follow our agricultural analogy here, one of the problems we often see in FM departments is that once these seeds reach maturity and are harvested, facility managers forget that the soil needs to be tilled and fertilized before they plant again. In other words, we find that FM departments have taken so much from employees that they become barren in the area of growth and development. When FM staff are pushed so hard that they do not have time for reflection and regeneration, the organization as a whole suffers because the learning environment withers away.

A skillful facility manager understands that new ideas have to be generated throughout the organization if learning is to take place. Just as we saw in the discussions of leadership development for employees, the facility manager also must assume responsibility for creating an organizational environment that allows the building blocks for learning to occur.

Identifying the Building Blocks

I want to take a few minutes and explore these building blocks for a learning organization with you. The building blocks described below are derived from a number of different sources. Some are adaptations of the concepts Dave Cotts and I developed for our quality FM book. Others stem from ideas put forth in management articles such as the one David Garvin wrote for the *Harvard Business Review*.[7] Still others come from the experiences of The Friday Group while working on OD issues for specific clients. The result of this information synthesis is the following six elements that I think serve as guiding principles for the successful continuous learning organization.

Base decision making on facts—An important cornerstone in the development of knowledge workers within an FM department is an emphasis on the value of reaching decisions on the basis of fact rather than assumption and speculation. In order for your employees to develop good learning habits, you need to underscore their need to become disciplined thinkers, which means they have to provide facts to substantiate their decisions and recommendations. Fact-based decision making requires both individual and team activities to start with a basic hypothesis and then develop statistically valid data to either support or refute the hypothesis.

Over the years, I have found this to be a hard building block for FM departments to implement because fact-based decision making requires the use of tools that often make FM staff uncomfortable. Statistical tools, such as cause-and-effect diagrams, Pareto charts, histograms, and scatter diagrams, may appear daunting to FM staff until they have been given sufficient exposure and training on how to use them. Both Dave Cotts and I feel so strongly about the use of these tools in FM departments that we devoted a chapter in our book to them.

To ease staff into the idea of using these tools, we sometimes suggest to our clients that they begin every individual and team problem-solving or research exercise with a directive. The directive would be that before they bring a solution or recommendation forward for management to consider, they have to be able to answer the questions, "How have we arrived at this decision?" and "What documentation do we have to support our decision?" Once staff become accustomed to thinking in a fact-based framework, they will want to have the tools to make their analysis easier.

Instilling a systematic approach to problem solving and decision making throughout the FM department also ensures that staff have the requisite analytical skills for participation in the corporate business process. As we saw from our discussion regarding strategic planning, our FM departments need to focus on ways to add value to both corporate and business unit efforts. To do this, they have to be able to analyze and present data and engage in dialogue with corporate business leaders in a way that demonstrates knowledge of sound business practices. In the corporate environment, a fact-based business process is the universal language.

Learn from experience—A learning FM department benefits from the successes and failures it has had in the past and builds on those to become smarter for the future. In order to do this, however, mistakes must be treated as learning rather than punitive exercises in which staff assess what transpired to gain insight into alternative approaches. Another element of the building block is the sharing of success as a learning exercise such that all staff are able to recognize the conditions for success. As you also may recall, sharing success and failure is a condition for creating an entrepreneurial spirit among FM staff.

Learn from others—FM departments in search of continuous improvement recognize that valuable information is gleaned from customers, fellow employees, colleagues in other corporate entities, and external sources. In other words, the learning organization promotes the exploration of information and feedback from a variety of sources that bring different perspectives on the same issue. The learning FM organization appreciates that benchmarking with best-in-class service providers that often are outside the FM profession expands the knowledge base of how to deliver quality, customer-focused service.

Disseminate knowledge — The knowledge that is developed among the various components within an FM department needs to be disseminated throughout the department in order for the entire department to grow proportionately. If the perception of staff is that withholding knowledge is a sign of individual power, then the transformation into a learning organization will never take place. Transference and sharing of knowledge among staff have to be underpinnings for the organization to grow.

Take risk and experiment—Staff of the FM department need to know that management encourages and supports the idea of taking risks and experimenting with new techniques. This building block of the learning organization can be implemented both through individual and team assignments to ensure that there is a continual flow of fresh, new ideas. Demonstration projects in which teams conduct experiments with the use of new technology, streamline processes, or apply a best-practice concept allows the staff to showcase their talent and innovation both internally and throughout the corporation.

Measure learning—Those who study the development of learning organizations are quick to point out that unless the organization has a methodology for measuring the impact of its learning, it makes little sense to invest the time and effort in the building block approach. The typical excuse is the difficulty of applying a yardstick to the effectiveness of organization growth and development, but it must be done. For a facility manager, there are some very obvious signs that the organization is moving into a new realm with respect to its learning capability. The first is that when employees are exposed to different ideas, they begin to use the knowledge and think differently. This is called *cognitive learning*. The second indication that a learning environment has been established is that modifications to employee behavior begin to take place. As employees gain new insight and perspective, they begin to internalize the ideas and apply them to their own pattern of behavior. Finally, in a learning organization environment, measurable results in performance become evident. As staff become more systematic in their thinking, share in risk-taking and knowledge transference, and experiment with new tools and techniques, noticeable improvement in individual and group performance occurs.

Tomorrow

If I had a crystal ball, I would take this opportunity to tell you all what will happen to FM departments tomorrow and in the days ahead. Unfortunately, I don't have an inside track on what is happening to FM, but I am certain there is one constant all of us in FM can be sure of—change. It is why I feel so confident the OD skills we covered here will withstand whatever lies ahead. For those of you who have made it this far, I truly believe the key to unlocking the door and stepping into a future filled with promise and challenge for facilities management rests in the hands of professionals like you who have the power to make a difference. Use this power wisely to achieve an FM department that has the vision, goals, and values that serve our profession well.

DNA Link: Future

Company: Pharmacia (pharmaceuticals)

Background

The Genesis of a New Organization

On December 19, 1999, Pharmacia & Upjohn and Monsanto/Searle announced plans to merge the two organizations. This merger was considered to be synergistic and supported by strong business basics. Both regulatory agencies and shareholders ultimately approved it. The transaction closed on April 3, 2000, and a new global entity named Pharmacia was created.

The focus during the initial months following the announcement was on ensuring that the deal would close. By mid-March 2000, it was clear that the merger would launch, and the focus shifted to the process of integrating the two organizations.

Merger Impact on the Real Estate and FM Organization

For the Real Estate and Facilities Management groups of the two companies, there was not only the requirement to develop a merged organization model, but there was also the need to provide information to the business units on the portfolio of real estate assets around the world. This information was critical to determining which sites and properties would be retained and which would be targeted for consolidation or disposal. In order to support this effort, a dedicated task force (Site Consolidation Program Office) was created and staffed with seasoned facilities and project management resources. This team managed over 30 consolidation projects around the world.

The work of designing and developing a single organization structure was initiated in March 2000. Merger integration teams were formed for each business area and staff group. These teams were made up of representatives from both companies and given specific directions and targets for savings and head count reductions. A highly skilled team was assembled to address the business area—since renamed Corporate Services—that includes both Real Estate and Facilities Management operations and services.

The merger integration design phase included extensive data gathering and analysis and the development of proposed new organization structures. The teams were given two months to complete their work and present their recommendations to senior management. The Real Estate and Facilities Management components were linked and worked together as a single team. The plan-acquire-manage-service model was used to guide the overall organization design process (see Figure Pharmacia 1).

Following the approval of the design phase and proposed structures, Wave I implemented the merger integration plans across the enterprise. For the Corporate Services structure, most key positions were filled internally, but not necessarily from the former Facilities Management groups. A scientist who had been closely involved with facility planning as a key

Figure Pharmacia 1.

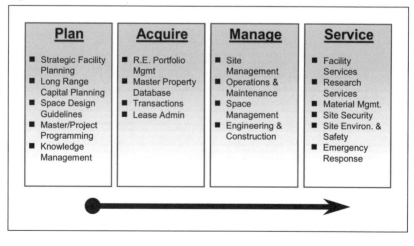

R&D customer, for example, filled the lead Strategic Facilities Planning position. An individual from the manufacturing organization who had strong operational, cost management, and people management skills filled the lead U.S. Facilities Management position. An outside candidate with experience from the consulting industry and strong systems, analytical expertise filled the key position in Operations Analysis. The resulting organization structure for the newly formed Corporate Services organization is illustrated in Figure Pharmacia 2.

Their Story

Creating the New Pharmacia Culture

The new Pharmacia is actually comprised of five legacy entities between 75 and 150 years old. This rich heritage has many advantages for the new enterprise, but also provides some challenges. The chairman is focused on building a new culture that draws on the best of the past while keeping a keen eye on customers and the path ahead. To that end, he has developed a set of behavioral guidelines termed *Best Managed Behaviors* and an overall strategy for the enterprise that provides direction for individual units and functions to strive toward. The 5 Best Managed Behaviors are:

Figure Pharmacia 2.

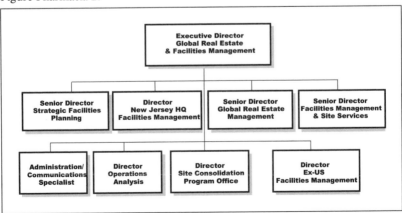

1. Shared Accountability & Transparency
2. Participative Management
3. Competitive Benchmarking & Continuous Improvement
4. Ongoing Listening & Learning
5. Coaching & Developing Other Colleagues

Developing a Vision and Strategy for the New Organization

Two of the steps in bringing the new organization together were to develop a business plan defining the strategy for the organization as a whole and to craft a vision statement that would inspire individuals working in that organization. The 7 points of the Corporate Services strategy are to:

1. Enhance the productivity of our customers by providing superbly managed sites and services.
2. Provide safe and secure work environments for our people, facilities, and information.
3. Facilitate ease of access to our services through proactive communication and Web-based technologies and other innovations.
4. Encourage continuous improvement through benchmarking best practices and measuring performance within a balanced context.
5. Provide best-in-class global portfolio management.
6. Optimize the corporate infrastructure.
7. Unlock the potential of our people by providing comprehensive, well-managed development plans and organizational effectiveness.

The vision statement is, "Corporate Services is valued as an indispensable provider of 'best managed' work environments and services."

Executing the New Vision and Strategy Through Performance Management

Wave II of the integration process focused on key processes, systems, methods, and drive synergies; best practices through benchmarking; and performance measurement. Corporate Services responded to this challenge with a thoroughly developed performance management program designed to deliver improvements across a balance of 5 perspectives:

1. Cost

2. Internal

3. Products & Services

4. Learning & Growth

5. Customer

The Corporate Services performance management model is graphically represented in Figure Pharmacia 3.

Figure Pharmacia 3.

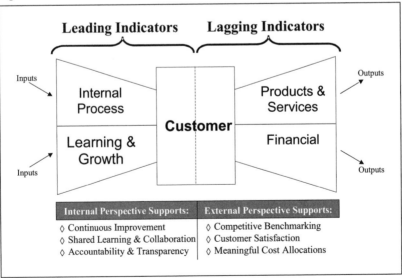

New Operating Model Supports Execution

For all of Corporate Services, an operating model was developed that segments the overall effort into 4 areas:

1. Global Functions

2. Sites & Networks

3. Business Office

4. Customer Relationship

Figure Pharmacia 4 depicts the new operating model.

A critical ingredient of the new operating model was the formation of Functional Networks linking all of the major sites through teams of individuals accountable for functional areas at each site but matrixed into functional networks. These networks include Space Management, Operations/Maintenance and Engineering/Construction, Research Services, Materials Management, Environmental Health & Safety, and Security. Figure Pharmacia 5 further describes the objectives of the Functional Networks.

The Global Functions are enterprise-wide teams that provide a key service to the enterprise. This area includes:

Figure Pharmacia 4.

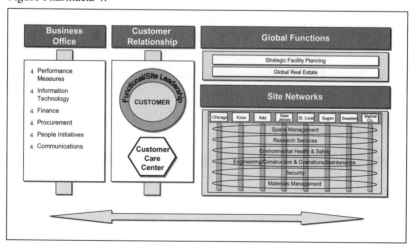

Figure Pharmacia 5.

Network Component   **Objectives**

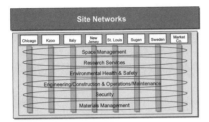

➢ Eliminate "silos" within Corporate Services
➢ Facilitate common business processes
➢ Encourage cross-site collaboration and knowledge sharing
➢ Enable identification of internal best practices through benchmarking

❐ Global Real Estate
❐ Strategic Facility Planning

The objectives of the Global Functions are articulated in Figure Pharmacia 6.

The Business Office component of the new model provides valuable analytical information to decision makers and drives the execution of the Corporate Services vision and strategy. The objectives of the Business Office are illustrated in Figure Pharmacia 7.

Figure Pharmacia 6.

Global Function Component   **Objectives**

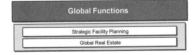

➢ Drive the delivery of optimized services across the global enterprise
➢ Use global leverage and common processes to ensure high quality, cost-effective, flexible, timely, and "frictionless" services

Figure Pharmacia 7.

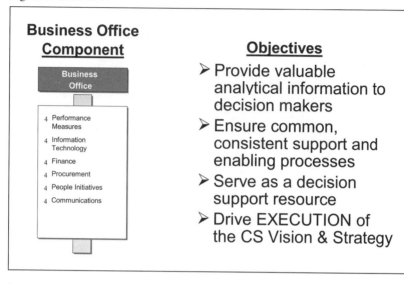

The Customer Relationship component ensures one common "face" to the customer by providing a single point of contact for requesting services. Figure Pharmacia 8 lists additional objectives of the Customer Relationship component.

Just as the new Pharmacia created awareness and brand-

Figure Pharmacia 8.

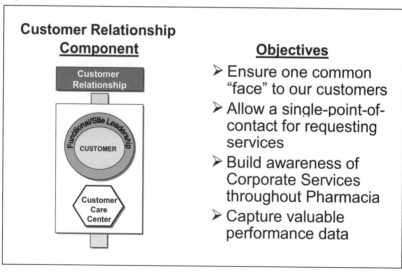

ing through its corporate identity initiatives, Corporate Services addressed its own identity via an internal design competition for a new logo and tag line. The winning logo and tag line were launched, along with an overall marketing and communications plan to ensure that all internal customers understood and could access available services.

The Importance of Information Technology

As expected, the various legacy entities used different systems and technology to support the Real Estate and Facilities Management functions. An overall information technology (IT) strategy complementing and integrating with the new operating model was crafted to ensure a well-planned approach to merging these systems. This strategy provided a balance across the three systems components: (1) Analytical, (2) User Interface, and (3) Transactional. Figure Pharmacia 9 illustrates the various components of the IT strategy within the context of the new operating model.

Figure Pharmacia 9.

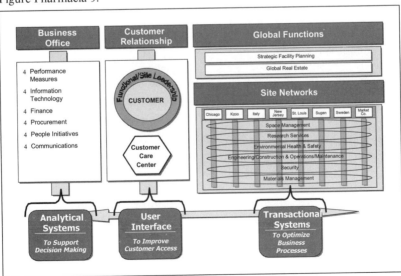

With an exceptional and talented staff, Pharmacia is on track to deliver on their business plan, performance management program, people initiatives, marketing and communications plan, and IT strategy. They are well on their way toward making Corporate Services a best-managed function within the new company.

Learning Points

❏ Merger integration of FM functions achieved through process action team

❏ Creation of new corporate culture key to integration strategy

❏ New vision and strategy tied to performance management

❏ Integrated organization model for major sites structured around linked and matrixed functional teams

❏ IT strategy maximizes technology tools to deliver business plan and track performance

---

About the Author

Mert Livingstone is executive director, Global Real Estate and Facilities Management for Pharmacia. In this capacity, Mert leads a team of 400 associates, managing the facilities' assets supporting Pharmacia's R&D, commercial, and headquarters operations, including the planning, acquiring, design, construction, operations and maintenance, and delivering a broad range of site services such as materials management, security, business, and research support services. Mert joined G.D. Searle in 1983 (Searle/Monsanto merged with Pharmacia & Upjohn to form Pharmacia in 2000), and during his career has been responsible for strategic facility planning, real estate, and facilities management for sites around the world.

Endnotes

1. Turid H. Horgen, Michael L. Jaroff, William L. Porter, and Donald A. Schon, *Excellence by Design: Transforming Workplace and Work Practice* (New York: John Wiley & Sons, 1999), pp. 8–11.
2. Ibid., p. 9.
3. Concepts are taken from reports written by The Friday Group for various clients.
4. Jonathan Katz, "Study Reveals Pressures Behind Mergers, Acquisitions," *IndustryWeek.com*, July 20, 2000, http://www.industryweek.com / DailyPage / newswiresfull.asp?month = 7& day = 20&year = 2000 (May 15, 2002).
5. Excerpts are taken from materials developed by The Friday Group for presentations on the impact of culture on FM.
6. Stephen H. Rhinesmith, *A Manager's Guide to Globalization: Six Keys to Success in a Changing World* (Burr Ridge, IL: Irwin Professional Publishing, 1993), p. 45.
7. David A. Garvin, "Building a Learning Organization" in *Harvard Business Review on Knowledge Management* (Boston: Harvard Business School Press, 1998), pp. 47–80.

BIBLIOGRAPHY

Argyris, Chris. *Personality and Organization.* New York: Harper & Row, 1957.

Ashby, Franklin C. *Revitalize Your Corporate Culture: Powerful Ways to Transform Your Company Into a High-Performance Organization.* Houston: Cashman Dudley, 1999.

Banner, David K., and T. Elaine Gagné. *Designing Effective Organizations: Traditional and Transformational Views.* Thousand Oaks, CA: Sage Publications, 1995.

Burley-Allen, Madelyn. *Managing Assertively: How to Improve Your People Skills.* New York: John Wiley & Sons, 1983.

Byrne, John A. "Jack: A Close-up Look at How America's #1 Manager Runs GE." *Business Week,* June 8, 1998, pp. 92–111.

Capozzoli, Thomas K. "Creating a Motivating Environment for Employees," *Supervision,* April 1997, p. 16.

Career Performance Strategies. *Stages of Group Development.* Crystal Lake, IL: Career Performance Strategies, 2002.

Catalyst Consulting Team. *Accelerating Team Development: The Tuckman's Model.* Capitola, CA: Catalyst Consulting Team, 2002.

Clark, Wendy. "Groups and Group Dynamics." http://www.onepine .demon.co.uk/mgrp.htm (July 12, 2002).

Cotts, David G. *The Facility Management Handbook, 2nd Edition.* New York: AMACOM, 1999.

Crandall, N. F. and M. J. Wallace, Jr. "Alternative Rewards in a Time-Competitive Organization," in *Compensation Guide,* edited by W. A. Caldwell. Boston: Warren Gorham & Lamont, 1994, Chapter 31.

Deal, Terrence E., and Allan A. Kennedy. *Corporate Cultures.* Cambridge, MA: Perseus Publishing, 1982.

————. *Corporate Cultures: The Rites and Rituals of Corporate Life.* Cambridge, MA: Perseus Publishing, 2000.

Designing the Facility Management Organization. Houston: IFMA Foundation, 2001.

Duffy, Daintry. "Cultural Evolution." January 15, 1999. http://www.cio.com/archive/enterprise/011599_rah_content.html?printversion=yes (April 26, 2002).

Facility Management Practices: Research Report #16. Houston: International Facility Management Association, 1996.

Facility Management Profiles 1989: Research Report #5. Houston: International Facility Management Association, 1989.

Feder, Barnaby J. "Frederick Herzberg: Challenged Thinking on Work and Motivation." *New York Times,* February 1, 2001, p. 8.

French, Wendell L., Cecil H. Bell, Jr., and Robert A. Zawacki. *Organization Development and Transformation: Managing Effective Change,* 5th edition. Boston: Irwin McGraw-Hill, 2000.

Friday, Stormy and David Cotts. *Quality Facility Management: A Marketing and Customer Service Approach.* New York: John Wiley & Sons, 1994.

Frost, Robert. *Mountain Interval.* New York: Henry Holt & Company, 1920.

Gagne, T. Elaine. *Designing Effective Organizations.* Thousand Oaks, CA: Sage Publications, 1995.

Galbraith, Jay, Diane Downey, and Amy Kates. *Designing Dynamic Organizations: A Hands-on Guide for Leaders at All Levels.* New York: AMACOM, 2002.

Garvin, David A. "Building a Learning Organization," in *Harvard Business Review on Knowledge Management.* Boston: Harvard Business School Press, 1998, Chapter 3.

Gellerman, Saul W. *Management by Motivation.* New York: American Management Association, 1968.

The George Mason University Center for Service and Leadership. "Leadership Tips: 5 Stages of Group Development." http://www.gmu.edu/student/csl/5stages.html (July 12, 2002).

Ghorpade, Jai, and Jerry T. Edge. *Understanding Skill-Based Pay: An Approach to Designing and Implementing an Effective Program.* Scottsdale, AZ: WorldatWork, 1997.

Goold, Michael, and Andrew Campbell. *Designing Effective Orga-*

nizations: How to Create Structured Networks. San Francisco: Jossey-Bass, 2002.

Gordon, Judith R. *Organizational Behavior: A Diagnostic Approach,* 5th edition. Upper Saddle River, NJ: Prentice Hall, 1996.

————. *Organizational Behavior: A Diagnostic Approach,* 6th edition. Upper Saddle River, NJ: Prentice Hall, 1999.

Gordon, Mark. "Corporate Cultural Manifesto: Athene Software Went by the Book to Create an Engineer-friendly Culture." March 15, 2001. http://www.cio.com/archive/031501/hs_culture_content.html (April 26, 2002).

Harvard Business Review on Knowledge Management. Boston: Harvard Business School Press, 1998.

Harvard Business Review on Leadership. Boston: Harvard Business School Press, 1998.

Harvard Business Review on Managing People. Boston: Harvard Business School Press, 1999.

HayGroup. *What Makes Great Leaders: Rethinking the Route to Effective Leadership—Findings From the Fortune Magazine/Hay Group 1999 Executive Survey of Leadership Effectiveness.* Philadelphia: HayGroup, 2000. (Available at: http://ei.haygroup.com/downloads/pdf/Leadership%20White%20Paper.pdf.)

HayGroup, Richard Hackman, and Ruth Wageman. *Top Teams: Why Some Work and Some Do Not: Five Things the Best CEOs Do to Create Outstanding Executive Teams.* Philadelphia: HayGroup, 2001. (Available at: http://www.haygroup.com/mediafiles/downloads/Top%20Teams%20Working%20Paper.pdf.)

Hay Insight, Dawn Sherman, William Alper, and Alan Wolfson. *The Retention Dilemma: Why Productive Workers Leave—Seven Suggestions for Keeping Them.* Philadelphia: HayGroup, 2001. (Available at: http://www.mediafiles/downloads/Retention%20Dilemma%20Working%20Paper.pdf.)

Hersey, Paul, and Kenneth H. Blanchard. *Management of Organizational Behavior: Utilizing Human Resources,* 2nd edition. Englewood Cliffs, NJ: Prentice Hall, 1972.

————. *Management of Organizational Behavior: Utilizing Human Resources,* 3rd edition. Englewood Cliffs, NJ: Prentice Hall, 1977.

————. *Management of Organizational Behavior: Utilizing Human Resources.* 5th edition. Englewood Cliffs, NJ: Prentice Hall, 1988.

Herzberg, Frederick. *The Managerial Choice: To Be Efficient and To Be Human.* Homewood, IL: Dow Jones-Irwin, 1976.

Hewitt Associates. "Hewitt Shows What Separates Fortune's 100 Best Companies From the Rest." January 7, 2000. http://www.was.hewitt.com/hewitt/resource/newsroom/pressrel/2000/01–07–00.htm (November 29, 2001).

————. "Summer Vacation Highlights Global Differences in Paid Time Off." June 6, 2001. http://was.hewitt.com/hewitt/resource/newsroom/pressrel/2001/06–06–01.htm (October 26, 2001).

Hicks, Robert F., and Diane Bone. *Self-Managing Teams: Creating and Maintaining Self-Managed Work Groups.* Los Altos, CA: Crisp Publications, 1990.

Horgen, Turid H., Michael L. Jarroff, William L. Porter, and David A. Schon. *Excellence by Design: Transforming Workplace and Work Practice.* New York: John Wiley & Sons, 1999.

Hudetz, Frank. "Self Actualization and Self Esteem are the Highest Order of Incentives." http://www.fed.org/resrclib/articles/hudetz.html (April 2002).

The IFMA Report #1. Houston: International Facility Management Association, 1984.

The IFMA Report #2: Demographics and Trends. Houston: International Facility Management Association, 1986.

Jusko, Jill. "Diversity Enhances Decision-Making: Benefits of Diversity in Employee Teams," *Industry Week*, April 2, 2001.

Katz, Jonathan. "Study Reveals Pressures Behind Mergers, Acquisitions." July 20, 2000. http://www.industryweek.com/DailyPage/newswiresfull.asp?month=7&day=20&year=2000 (May 15, 2002).

The Ken Blanchard Companies. "About Ken Blanchard." http://www.blanchardtraining.com/meetcomp/about.cfm (November 15, 2001).

Kennedy, Marilyn Moats. "What Makes People Work Hard?" *Across the Board,* May 1998, p. 25.

Kirsner, Scott. "Their 'Teamwork Agenda': Four Lessons on Teamwork From SEI Investments," *Fast Company*, issue 14, April 1998, p. 132.

Klammt, Fred. "What Does Your Gut Tell You? Let's Check the Scorecard." *The Outsource Report*, August 1998, p. 6.

Kohn, Alfie. "Rewards Produce Temporary Compliance." http://www.fed.org/resrclib/articles/kohn.html (March 2001).

Kolbe, Kathy. *Pure Instinct: Business's Untapped Resource*. New York: Times Books, 1993.

Kotter, John P. "What Leaders Really Do," in *Harvard Business Review on Leadership*. Boston: Harvard Business School Press, 1998, Chapter 2, pp. 37–60.

Kotter, John P., and James L. Heskett. *Corporate Culture and Performance*. New York: The Free Press, 1992.

Kushel, Gerald. *Reaching the Peak Performance Zone: How to Motivate Yourself and Others to Excel*. New York: AMACOM, 1994.

Lenhart, Maria. "Winner All." *Meetings and Conventions*, April 1998, p. 79.

Levering, Robert, and Milton Moskowitz. "100 Best Companies to Work For." January 8, 2001. http://www.fortune.com/indexw.jhtml?channel=artcol.jhtml&doc_id=00003095 (November 29, 2001).

———. "100 Best Companies to Work For: America's Top Employers." January 8, 2001. http://www.fortune.com/indext.jhtml?channel=print_article.jhtml&doc_id=q00003095 (January 2002).

———. "100 Best Companies to Work For: The Best in the Worst of Times." February 4, 2002. http://www.fortune.com/indext.jhtml?channel=print_article.jhtml&doc_id=q206026 (March 2002).

Levering, Robert, Milton Moskowitz, Feliciano Garcia, and Karen Vella-Zarb. "The 100 Best Companies to Work For." January 10, 2000. http://www.fortune.com/indext.jhtml?channel=print_article.jhtml&doc_id=q00001598 (January 2002).

Levine, David. *Reinventing the Workplace: How Business and Employees Can Both Win*. Washington, D.C.: The Brookings Institute, 1995.

March, James G., and Herbert A. Simon, *Organizations*. New York: John Wiley & Sons, 1958.

Maruca, Regina Fazio. "What Makes Teams Work?" *Fast Company*, issue 40, November 2000, p. 109.

McGregor, Douglas. *The Human Side of Enterprise*. New York: McGraw-Hill Book Company, 1960.

Mintzberg, Henry. *The Nature of Managerial Work*. New York: Harper & Row, 1973.

Murray, David C. "Rewarding the Right Stuff." *Security Management,* May 1998, p. 25.

Musante, Louis A. "Better Living Through Culture." November 2001. http://www.optimizemag.com/issue/001/culture2.htm (July 19, 2002).

Myers, John R. "What It Takes to Make a Team." *Purchasing,* September 2, 1999.

National Crime Prevention Council. *Becoming a Better Supervisor: A Resource Guide for Community Service Supervisors*. Washington, D.C.: National Crime Prevention Council, 1996.

Nelson, Bob. "Low-Cost Ways to Energize Employees." *HR Magazine,* December 1997, p. 45.

———. *1001 Ways to Reward Employees*. New York: Workman Publishing, 1994.

———. "Safety Incentives Can Be Fun." *Manage,* February 1998, p. 8.

Neuhauser, Peg C. "Strategies for Changing Your Corporate Culture." http://www.culturedotcom.com/article_4.htm (April 26, 2002).

"The Outsource Report." *Facilities Design & Management,* March 2001, pp. 1–14.

Perle, Ann. "What Makes Companies Well-Loved," *Workforce,* April 1998, p. 125.

Phegan, Barry. *Developing Your Company Culture: The Joy of Leadership—A Handbook for Leaders and Managers*. Berkeley, CA: Context Press, 1996.

Profiles '94 Salary Report: Research Report #12. Houston: International Facility Management Association, 1994.

Profiles '98 Salary Report: Research Report #19. Houston: International Facility Management Association, 1998.

Random House Webster's College Dictionary. New York: Random House, 1991.

Rasmusson, Erika. "Spurring Performance All Year." *Sales & Marketing Management,* January 1998, p. 78.

Rebori, Marlene, Steven R. Lewis, Elwood Miller, and Carl R. Dahlen. "Team Building—Stages of Group Development."

http://www/unce.unr.edu / publications / EB%20Pubs/EB-01–03%20CLG/teambuildin g2.ht m (July 12, 2002).

Research Report #13: Benchmarks II. Houston: International Facility Management Association, 1994.

Research Report #18: Benchmarks III. Houston: International Facility Management Association, 1997.

Rhinesmith, Stephen H. *A Manager's Guide to Globalization*. Burr Ridge, IL: Irwin Professional Publishing, 1993.

Richards, Dick, and Susan Smyth. *Assessing Your Team*. New York: John Wiley & Sons, 1994.

"The Road Not Taken." March 31, 2002. http://www.frost.free hosting.net/poems_road.htm#topb (March 26, 2002).

Rockefeller, John D., as quoted in Bergen, Garrett L., and William V. Haney. *Organizational Relations and Management Action*. New York: McGraw-Hill, 1966.

Saul Gellerman and Associates. "Saul Gellerman." http://www .saulgellerman.com (November 29, 2001).

Schneider, William E. "Why Good Management Ideas Fail—The Neglected Power of Organizational Culture." http://www .refresher.com/!neglected (April 26, 2002).

Sheley, Elizabeth. "Flexible Work Options: Beyond 9 to 5," *HR Magazine* February 1996, pp. 53–58.

Spiegel, Jerry, and Cresencio Torres. *Manager's Official Guide to Team Working*. New York: John Wiley & Sons, 1994.

Stevens, Michael J. "Staffing Work Teams: Development and Validation of a Selection Test for Teamwork Settings." *Journal of Management*, March-April 1999.

Stone, Florence M. *The AMA Handbook of Supervisory Management*. New York: AMACOM, 1996.

Strozniak, Peter. "Teams at Work: Team Culture at Small Manufacturers." *Industry Week*, September 18, 2000.

Stum, David L. "Re-inventing Employee Commitment." December 12, 2000. http://www.nehra.com/article.php?cat=6&id=110 (January 2001).

Taylor, F. W. *The Principles of Scientific Management*. New York: Harper & Brothers, 1911.

"Team Building at Its Best." *Info-Line: Practical Guidelines for Training and Development Professionals*, January 1987, pp. 1–16.

Terry, George R. *Supervisory Management*. Homewood, IL: Richard D. Irwin, 1974.

"The Top 25 Managers of the Year." *Business Week,* January 13, 2002, pp. 52–72.

Tuckman, B. W. "Developmental Sequence in Small Groups." *Psychological Bulletin*, vol. 63, no. 6, 1965, pp. 384–399.

"The 2000 100 Best Companies to Work For in America." *Fortune,* January 10, 2000, pp. 70–78.

The University of Western Ontario Business Library. "Frederick Herzberg—Biography." December 19, 2001. http://www.lib.uwo.ca/business/herzberg.html (November 16, 2001).

Views From the Top . . . Executives Evaluate the Facility Management Function: Research Report #17. Houston: International Facility Management Association, 1997.

Ward, Matt. "Creating an Ownership Culture." http://www.fed.org/resrclib/articles/create-ownership-culture.html (June 2002).

Workplaceissues.com. "Management Tips: Tips to Rejuvenate Tired Teams." http://www.workplaceissues.com/mgttired.htm (April 25, 2002).

WorldatWork and The Segal Company. "1999 Survey of Performance-Based Work/Life Programs." http://www.worldatwork.org/research/generic/html/worklife-survey-home.html (October 26, 2001).

Yandrick, Rudy M. "A Team Effort." *HR Magazine,* June 2001.

INDEX

304